Oxford. Church of S. Mary the Virgin—The Porch.

Highways and Byways

IN

Oxford and the Cotswolds

BY HERBERT A. EVANS
WITH · ILLUSTRATIONS · BY
FREDERICK L. GRIGGS

London
MACMILLAN AND CO., Limited
NEW YORK: THE MACMILLAN COMPANY
1905.

PREFACE

THIS is not "another book about Oxford"—of the making of which, as a recent reviewer reminds us, there is no end; it is only a summer excursion into the hill-country that lies to the north and west towards the broad vale of the Severn and Avon. But of Oxford and its Colleges our wayfarer is again and again reminded in the course of his wanderings; Oxford is at once his starting point and the goal of his returning footsteps. Accordingly in the opening chapter he takes a preliminary tour through the city.

The district explored is that which lies between the Cherwell on the east, and the fringe of the Cotswold on the west—in other words, the northern half of the basin of the upper Thames. This is a large area, and one which the present volume does not attempt to exhaust. What is here set down is the outcome of individual tastes and individual impressions, and as such it is offered to the reader. I have written of those places and those passages in their history which interested me; if they also interest him, my purpose will have been fulfilled.

I have used the old County Histories, and the Proceedings

of the local Archaeological Associations, as well as other works mentioned in the text. Some information I also owe to the kindness of my correspondents—Mr. C. R. Ashbee, Mr. O. V. Aplin, Mr. Cornell Price, Mr. Percy Manning, the Rev. G. B. Sharpe of Guiting Power, and in particular Mr. P. C. Rushen, who lent me his own copy of his now very scarce *History of Chipping Campden*. And lastly I must thank my old friend, Mr. Warde Fowler, for volunteering to read through the proofs.

H. A. EVANS.

October, 1905.

CONTENTS

CHAPTER I

PAGE

OXFORD I

CHAPTER II

YARNTON—WOODSTOCK—DEDDINGTON—ADDERBURY 34

CHAPTER III

BANBURY—BLOXHAM—MILCOMBE—SOUTH NEWINGTON—WIGGIN-
TON—SWERFORD—BROUGHTON 62

CHAPTER IV

SWALCLIFFE—SHUTFORD—SHENNINGTON—ALKERTON—WROXTON
—HORLEY—HANWELL—CROPREDY 80

CHAPTER V

CHIPPING WARDEN—EDGECOTE—CHARWELTON—WARMINGTON—
EDGEHILL 99

CHAPTER VI

EPWELL — COMPTON WYNYATES — BRAILES — LITTLE WOLFORD —
ROLLRIGHT—CHASTLETON . . . .

CHAPTER VII

ODDINGTON—STOW-ON-THE-WOLD—UPPER AND LOWER SWELL—
HINCHWICK—UPPER AND LOWER SLAUGHTER—BOURTON-ON-
THE-WATER—WESTCOT—BLEDINGTON—ICOMB . . . . .

CHAPTER VIII

THE UPPER WINDRUSH—NAUNTON—GUITING POWER—TEMPLE
GUITING—CHIPPING CAMPDEN . . . . :

CHAPTER IX

EBRINGTON — ILMINGTON—QUINTON — MICKLETON — ASTON SUB-
EDGE—WESTON SUBEDGE—SAINTBURY — BROADWAY — BUCK-
LAND — STANTON — STANWAY—FARMCOTE—HAYLES—WINCH-
COMBE . . . .

CHAPTER X

SUDELEY — CHARLTON ABBOTTS — BROCKHAMPTON — SEVENHAMP-
TON — ANDOVERSFORD — SEVEN SPRINGS — COBERLEY—REND-
COMBE—NORTH CERNEY—DAGLINGWORTH—DUNTESBOURNE—
ELKSTONE—BRIMPSFIELD—MISERDEN . . . .

CHAPTER XI

FOSS BRIDGE—CHEDWORTH—CASSEY COMPTON—STOWELL—NORTH-
LEACH—FARMINGTON—SHERBORNE—BARRINGTON—TAYNTON

CHAPTER XII

PAG

THE COLN VALLEY—BIBURY—QUENINGTON—FAIRFORD—BARNSLEY 30

, CHAPTER XIII

BIRDLIP—PAINSWICK—SAPERTON—PINBURY . . . . 31.

CHAPTER XIV

CIRENCESTER 33

CHAPTER XV

ALDSWORTH—BURFORD—SWINBROOK—MINSTER LOVEL . . . . 35.

CHAPTER XVI

WYCHWOOD—CHIPPING NORTON—GREAT TEW—ENSTONE . . . 37

INDEX   40

LIST OF ILLUSTRATIONS

                                                   PAGE

OXFORD. CHURCH OF S. MARY THE VIRGIN—THE PORCH

Frontispiece

QUEEN'S COLLEGE, FRONT QUADRANGLE I

THE OLD ASHMOLEAN, OXFORD 7

FISHER ROW, OXFORD 11

THE THAMES AT PARADISE, OXFORD 13

THE "GOLDEN CROSS" INN-YARD, OXFORD 32

WOODSTOCK MANOR-HOUSE IN 1723 43

ON THE BANBURY-OXFORD ROAD. 55

THE "REINDEER INN," BANBURY 63

HOUSE IN MARKET PLACE, BANBURY 65

SOUTH NEWINGTON 72

BROUGHTON CASTLE 75

A YARD AT WROXTON 85

SILVER STREET, WROXTON 88

HANWELL CASTLE 90

FENNY COMPTON 113

WARMINGTON 115

COMPTON WYNYATES FROM THE MOAT 126

COMPTON WYNYATES. THE ENTRANCE FRONT. 129

BRAILES CHURCH 133

LITTLE WOLFORD MANOR 135

THE FOUR-SHIRE STONE, MORETON-IN-THE-MARSH 136

DOVECOT AT CHASTLETON 143

	PAGE
BARN AT BROADWELL, NEAR STOW-ON-THE-WOLD	146
MORETON-IN-MARSH. CURFEW TOWER	152
AT BROADWELL, NEAR STOW	155
HOUSE IN MARKET SQUARE, STOW-ON-THE-WOLD	157
UPPER SWELL MANOR	160
MANOR HOUSE, UPPER SLAUGHTER	166
ICOMB CHURCH	170
NORMAN DOORWAY AT GUITING POWER	172
GREVEL'S HOUSE, CHIPPING CAMPDEN	183
A COURTYARD AT CHIPPING CAMPDEN	189
NORMAN DOORWAY AT BROAD CAMPDEN	191
CHURCH STREET, CHIPPING CAMPDEN	193
CHIPPING CAMPDEN CHURCH	195
MEON HILL	204
STANLEY PONTLARGE	207
EBRINGTON	209
THE VALE OF EVESHAM, FROM HIDCOTE BOYCE	213
COTTAGES AT WESTON SUBEDGE	219
SAINTBURY	221
WILLERSEY	223
BROADWAY, THE GRANGE	225
STANTON, WITH WARREN HOUSE	227
STANWAY	229
HAYLES ABBEY	234
BELL-TURRET, HAYLES CHURCH	236
POSTLIP. NORMAN CHAPEL	244
AT BROADWAY	246
GLOUCESTER STREET, WINCHCOMBE	247
SUDELEY CASTLE	250
NORTH CERNEY CHURCH	264
DOVECOT AT DAGLINGWORTH	266
DUNTESBOURNE ROUS CHURCH	269
CHEDWORTH CHURCH	276
CASSEY COMPTON	279
NORTHLEACH CHURCH	284
FAIRFORD CHURCH	308

PAGE

PAINSWICK CHURCHYARD 318

PAINSWICK. VICARAGE LANE 321

PAINSWICK BEACON AND KIMSBURY CAMP 323

PITCHCOMBE 326

SAPERTON 328

DANEWAY HOUSE 331

CALMSDEN. THE VILLAGE CROSS 333

ST. JOHN'S HOSPITAL, CIRENCESTER 335

CIRENCESTER CHURCH 342

SHIPTON COURT BEFORE THE RECENT RESTORATION 353

BURFORD CHURCH 361

ASTHALL 370

MINSTER LOVEL. DOVECOT 373

MAPS

OXFORD 393

SOUTH-EAST COTSWOLDS 395

NORTH COTSWOLDS 397

SOUTH-WEST COTSWOLDS 399

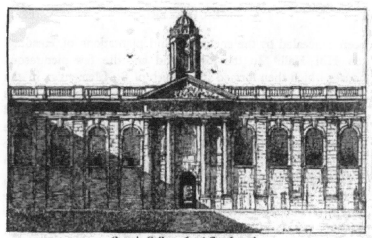

Queen's College, front Quadrangle.

HIGHWAYS AND BYWAYS

IN

OXFORD AND THE COTSWOLDS

CHAPTER I

Emp.   " Trust me, Plantagenet, these Oxford schools
       Are richly seated near the river-side :
       The mountains full of fat and fallow deer,
       The battling pastures lade with kine and flocks,
       The town gorgeous with high-built colleges,
       And scholars seemly in their grave attire,
       Learned in searching principles of art."
            —GREENE, *Friar Bacon and Friar Bungay.*

THE Oxford Almanack for the year 1808 displays a view by
Turner, in which the London coach is seen descending Headington Hill. Of all the approaches to Oxford this was the
most striking, but the prospect which Turner has sketched, and
on which the gaze of his outside passengers is fixed, has long

B

been concealed by the enclosures and plantations of Headington Hill Hall. In the foreground are the few picturesque
houses which then formed the suburb of St. Clement's; in the
middle distance are the groves of Magdalen, from the centre
of which rise the New Buildings, then some fifty years old, and
still the finest thing of its kind in Oxford; and on the left are
seen the glorious tower and the bridge. Further still to the
left rise the towers of Merton and of Christ Church, while on
the right predominant are the spires of All Saints' and St. Mary's,
and the great dome of the Radcliffe Library. In the background the scene is closed by the long line of the green-muffled
Cumnor hills and the dark wooded heights of Wytham.

Such would have been the picture spread before us had we
been journeying down the steep descent of Headington Hill in
1808, and we should have reached our comfortable quarters
at the Angel or the Mitre without encountering anything to
break the spell of first impressions. Nor were these impressions
the less enchanting from the fact that they had surpassed any
mental picture of the scene which we had been trying to form.
For this the long and leisurely journey from London had given
us ample time. As the coach crawled down the rugged slope
of the Chilterns, and as the coachman strove to make his eight
or nine miles an hour across the plain which divides the chalk
range from the heights of Shotover, there was nothing but the
sign-posts to indicate our approach to the enchanted city of
our imagination: anticipation had long to be nursed, curiosity
long held in suspense, until at a turn of the road, hardly more
than a mile away, the magic vision was suddenly revealed.

All this is altered now: you take your seat in the express
at Paddington, and have hardly scanned your newspaper
through, when you are gliding past reservoirs and gas works
into Oxford station. If the stranger is resolute enough to
close his eyes at Kennington Island and refuse to open them
till his cab deposits him at his hotel, he will be the happier
man. Then let him ascend the roof of the Radcliffe, or,

better still, walk to the top of Shotover, before he attempts to explore the city in detail.

But there are other distant views of Oxford besides that from Shotover. I have seen them all, and the best to my mind is the one (to be strictly accurate there is more than one, each with its special charm) from Stow Wood on the way to Beckley. If the day is a stormy one, and you are lucky enough to seize the moment when, from a rent in the black clouds which fill the valley and shroud the distant landscape, the sun breaks forth and lights up the towers and spires into bold relief, you will have seen a picture which you will never forget. From Stow Wood and Shotover your survey is from the north-east and west, but the famous view from the south must not be neglected, either from the meadow ground above the Hinkseys, or from the Abingdon Road, as you ascend to Boar's Hill; here, however, the suburbs assert their unblushing presence, and the foreground is more commonplace, but at any rate you see Oxford as it is from end to end, a city rising from the midst of a valley just at the point where the hills on either side, east and west, approach each other most nearly. It thus forms the gate through which all must pass who intend to accompany me into the land we are to explore in the present volume.

Oxford is so well known to the outside world as the seat of one of our two ancient Universities, that people are in danger of forgetting that it is also the capital of a flourishing county, and the cathedral city of an extensive diocese. Its latter dignity is of course a comparatively modern thing, but it was a town of considerable political and strategic importance for three hundred years at least before the University was heard of. When its name first appears in history, early in the tenth century, it was already a place of some note, and for a long period subsequent to this it constituted, with Wallingford and Windsor, one of the three great fortresses that guarded the line of the Thames above London. The proximity to the royal manor of

Woodstock, of which we shall have something to say in the next chapter, brought it into immediate relation with the Court, and the king had a palace just outside the city boundary, the name of which is still preserved in the street which passes over its site.[1] The early history of the University is the history of the struggle of a body of students, under royal and ecclesiastical patronage, to secure corporate independence and autonomy, as against the municipality—a struggle which by the opening of the sixteenth century had terminated in favour of the former. The wars of the Roses had but little effect on the fortunes either of the City or the University, but in no place in the kingdom were the changes brought about by the Reformation more extensive, or more profoundly felt. Two wealthy abbeys, one priory, four friaries, and four colleges belonging to monastic orders disappeared; the thirty years which followed the dissolution saw the foundation of four new colleges, and the priory church of St. Frideswide became the cathedral church of the new diocese of Oxford, carved out of the huge diocese of Lincoln, the original seat of which had been but ten miles away from Oxford at Dorchester-on-Thames. The municipal and academic repose of the century which succeeded the Reformation was broken by the religious persecutions and the Civil War. After the reaction of the Restoration and the passing cloud of the Revolution, Oxford settled down into the lettered (and unlettered) ease of the eighteenth and early nineteenth centuries. At last, in 1854, the trumpet sounded[2] which gave the signal for the passing away of the old order and the inauguration of the new era, in which the University, no longer a close corporation with aims and interests limited by those of the aristocracy and the church, has widened its sympathies, and extended its influence, till it has become in the truest sense a national institution. But the task of adjusting its machinery to the ever-increasing demands of the age has been long and laborious, and though the exactions thus made on the

---

[1] Beaumont Street.   [2] The first University Commission.

time and energies of a learned body are perhaps hardly consistent with the ideal of a University, there are at present no
signs of rest or relaxation.

It is of course impossible within the limits of a single chapter
to attempt to tell the story of Oxford, or to undertake a perambulation in any detail either of the City or the University.
The best advice I can give to those who can spare a few days
to spend in Oxford before starting with me northwards,
is to arm themselves with Mr. Wells's handy and useful
pocket-volume on Oxford and its Colleges—a complete *vade
mecum* which will not allow them to miss anything they ought
to see, or leave untold anything they ought to know on a first
general survey.

The great difference between Oxford in Term and Oxford
in Vacation cannot fail to strike the most hurried visitor.
Three times a year the streets leading from the railway station
to the academic quarters of the town are crowded with vehicles
bearing the undergraduate and his fortunes to pass a brief
eight weeks in the bosom of Alma Mater, and three times a
year the same vehicles may be seen bearing him away. In the
interval he reads, rows, runs, rides—and is examined. The
splendid palace, dedicated to the goddess of Examinations, richly
dight with sculptures, frescoes, marble mosaics, electric lights,
and electric clocks, occupies a commanding position in the
High Street, and will be one of the first wonders to be visited
by the stranger. As for the ceremonies here conducted, and
the previous course of probation required, these are high
matters on which he must seek for information elsewhere.
How the future examinee spends his days he may partly guess
from the gowned figures, each provided with its note-book,
which he will see flitting along the pavement from college to
college, or later on from the spectacle of the same figures, now
clad in the airy costume of the athlete, wending their way to
the river and the running grounds. If the crews are in training
for the boat-races, he will do wisely to make for the towing-path,

and he will there understand how the virtues of fortitude and endurance are still taught at Oxford.

It is not, however, only members of the University who are to be met thronging the streets on their way to lecture ; troops of the other sex, whom the magnanimity of Professors has admitted to the privilege of discipleship, will be seen hastening either on foot or on cycle to the same fountains of knowledge : like the men, you may know them by their note-books, the pages of which, I suspect, are less often desecrated by sketches and caricatures ; such follies they leave to their brothers, and I should not be surprised to hear that the lecturer often finds among them the most appreciative as well as the most critical part of his audience. The woman student hails from the great suburb known as North Oxford, which owes its existence to the great feminine invasion of the last thirty years. This invasion has been threefold : first, there are the families unconnected with the University who have settled here in Oxford, as a pleasant centre for concerts, lectures, libraries, museums, and tea-parties ; formerly they would have chosen Cheltenham or Leamington. Secondly, there is the married fellow, now a very numerous species, but in the old times a *rara avis* ; and lastly there are the colonies of women students. Hence, whereas the town used to come to an end just beyond St. Giles's Church, it now spreads over nearly the whole space between the canal and the Cherwell, and extends northwards for two miles till it includes the once rural hamlet of Summertown.

Should the visitor be less curious to see Oxford life than Oxford itself, and should he long to revel undisturbed in the silence that broods over College Quads and College Gardens, he will of course choose the Vacation. Then, indeed, like Elia, he " can play the gentleman and enact the student. In moods of humility he can be a Sizar, or a Servitor. When the peacock vein rises he can strut a gentleman commoner, in graver moments proceed Master of Arts, and in Christ Church reverend quadrangle be content to pass for nothing short of a

The Old Ashmolean, Oxford.

Seraphic Doctor." Should he mount the broad and easy staircase that leads to the reading room of the Bodleian, he will no
longer see any signs of vacation: to all appearances it is still
the height of full term; beneath the painted roof of Duke
Humphrey, and amidst the laden shelves of Sir Thomas, such
merely pædagogic distinctions of times and seasons are unknown. The librarians are at their posts, the clerks are hurry-
ing up and down with their armfuls of books, the readers are
hunting in the catalogue, or immersed in their researches at the
desks. And nowhere in the world can researches be prosecuted
with such readiness and comfort. Within easy reach of his
chair the student has all the books of reference he most
frequently wishes to consult, while by the simple process of
turning up an entry in the catalogue and writing the press-
mark, or title, on a slip, he may command the use of some
600,000 volumes of printed books, and 30,000 volumes of MSS.
Any guidance or information he may require is promptly and
courteously afforded him by the staff, and any complaints or
suggestions he may have to make he is invited to enter in a
book kept for the purpose, for the inspection and consideration
of the librarian.

But the charms of the Bodleian must not detain us now;
fascinated though we are, we must leave the happy scholars to
their books, and sally forth as in duty bound to explore the
" Highways and Byways in Oxford." The two principal
thoroughfares run from North to South, and from West to East.
The former enters the City at St. Giles's Church [1] and quits it
at Folly Bridge, while the latter enters by the station and leaves
by Magdalen Bridge. The two roads cross each other at Carfax
(the *quadrifurc*, or four-forked place), which marks the highest
point and centre of the City. The University quarter of the
town lies almost wholly to the east of the north and south
artery: only two Colleges are situated on its western side,

---

[1] The City boundary extends much further to the north, but for our
purposes the suburbs may be neglected.

Worcester, on the site of the pre-Reformation and Benedictine Gloucester College, and Pembroke, the successor of the older Broadgates Hall. It is the eastern side therefore which has most interest, and with which the guide-books are most concerned. For this very reason we shall begin our perambulations on the western side, for it is not the purpose of these scanty pages to weary the reader with what he will find better done elsewhere.

But first of all, in order to get some idea of the compass of mediæval Oxford, it may be well to make a brief circuit of the site of the City walls. Like the Castle, they early became ruinous and defective, and in the time of the Civil War the defences consisted practically of the two rivers, which were connected on the north by a line of entrenchments, starting from Holywell mill on the Cherwell, and carried round where the Museum and Keble College now stand, behind St. Giles's Church, and so down to the Thames, in the neighbourhood of Worcester College. If we start from Carfax and proceed down St. Aldate's, past the front of Christ Church, we shall find the first traces of the wall on the right at the corner of Brewers' Street. From this point, for some distance westwards its remains are incorporated with the south side of Pembroke College, but at the end of the street, where Little Gate once stood, we lose it again, and can only follow it in imagination to the south of St. Ebbe's Church, and across Church Street to the Castle, where it terminated in West Gate and the moat. For some distance northwards the Castle and its moat now carried on the line of fortification; but the wall started again from the moat somewhere near the present termination of the canal, and crossing Bulwarks (formerly Bullock's) Lane followed the line of St. Michael Street to North Gate, traces of which are visible on the tower of St. Michael's, and which, together with East Gate, was removed in consequence of the Oxford Improvements Act of 1771. From this gate it continued along the back of the houses on the south side of Broad Street, where a fragment still remains,

to Smith Gate at the end of Cat Street. Here you may enter
St. Helen's passage, and you will find a bastion still remaining
before New College Tower is reached. From this point it forms
the wall of the slipe and of two sides of the College garden.
The corner of the garden is its north-eastern angle, and hence
it ran southward to East Gate in the High Street, the site
of which is now marked by the new Eastgate Hotel. From
this gate it continues (a small fragment marks its course) at the
back of the houses on the east side of King Street, till it
appears again as the wall of Merton garden, the corner of which
forms its south-eastern angle. Between Merton and South Gate
it was destroyed as long ago as Edward the First's time by the
Priory of St. Frideswide, who, says Wood, "did damnify that
part of the wall . . . for they pulled downe the 'quarnelli,' or
the battlements with the uppermost part of the wall, to build
on." At South Gate we are again at the corner of Brewers'
Street, and have thus completed our circuit. The outside of
the walls northwards and eastwards from the Castle to St.
Frideswide's was surrounded by a ditch full of water, and from
St. Frideswide's back to the Castle its place appears to have
been taken by the Trill mill stream a few yards further south.
It will be seen that the space included within the walls was
rather more than half a mile from west to east, and rather more
than a quarter from north to south. With the exception of
the two principal thoroughfares the streets must have been
very narrow and the houses much crowded together.

To come now to the district west of Carfax, we shall not
easily find a quarter of any ancient city in which the vestiges
of the past have been more effectually swept away. It is now
mostly given up to cheap streets, slums, coal-yards, cattle
markets, railway stations, gaols, breweries, and gas-works. In
Fisher Row, and the Castle tower, Mr. Griggs has managed to
discover some remnants of the picturesque; I do not think he
could have found many more. The visitor's curiosity may for
instance lead him to the Clarendon Press. He will, of course,

Fisher Row, Oxford.

be amply rewarded for his trouble, but his way thither lies through Walton Street, one of the most depressing thoroughfares in Europe. It was once a country road leading through the fields to Aristotle's well, so called, says Wood, " because that it was then (as now 'tis) frequented in the summer season by our Peripateticks." Now by way of contrast let us see what this district formerly contained : the abbeys of Osney and Rewley, the Castle, Beaumont Palace, afterwards the house of the White Friars, and the houses of the Grey Friars, Black Friars, and Penitentiary Friars. Of all these there remains only the Castle mound and tower, and a few stones of the two abbeys—and first for the Castle.

Of the Castle as it once existed there is little left but the mound and the lofty square tower which forms so conspicuous an object from the railway as you enter Oxford from the south. To picture the fortress as it was, you must imagine an enclosure, roughly circular, and surrounded by a moat. Through this enclosure, in 1766, was cut the new road which now skirts the mound on the north-west, and, in the next century the modern prison and the assize courts were built within the circuit of the remaining precincts. We shall get the most impressive view of the tower if we quit the New Road at Pacey's bridge and walk up Fisher Row : the tower will face us all the way, we shall pass Quaking bridge on the left, and so a few yards farther arrive at New bridge, which is the central point of Mr. Griggs's sketch. The tower batters from the base, and at the top, above the lead roof, which is invisible from below, are traces of six round-headed doorways, now built up. These gave access to the " hourdes," a movable wooden gallery covered by raw hides, which could be thrown out in time of danger for the purpose of discharging missiles upon the assailants underneath. When not in use the timbers of this gallery would be stored in a room at the top of the tower. No greater monument of strength and durability than this tower exists in Oxford, though, owing to the greater attractions of the

The Thames at Paradise, Oxford.

University buildings, it is apt to be neglected by the casual visitor. It was built in 1071, by Robert d'Oilly, a comrade-in-arms of the Conqueror, and the grantee of many manors in this part of the country. The tower of St. Michael's Church, at North Gate, was probably built about the same time, and was also used for purposes of defence. The pre-Norman fortress was the mound to the north of d'Oilly's tower, which was probably crowned by a wooden palisade. Later it supported a ten-sided keep, represented in Agas's map (1578), and in other old drawings. It also defended the water supply of the garrison, for in its centre is a very deep well-chamber with groined roof. This is now empty, the water having been drained away by the construction of modern sewers.

Strong as Oxford Castle was, it does not seem to have been put to the test of an assault, and its history is well nigh a blank. The most famous event connected with it took place during the struggle between Stephen and his cousin, the Empress Maud. In the autumn of 1142, the Empress was driven to take refuge here, and was closely besieged by the king for three months. Winter came on, and provisions began to run short: the question of surrender could not be long deferred, when a happy device set the imprisoned lady at liberty. The winter was a hard one: the ground was covered with snow, and the streams thickly coated with ice. The bridges of course were strictly guarded, but on a dark night, with only three attendants clad from head to foot like herself in white garments, the intrepid Maud issued from a postern, or was let down from a window, and, crossing the frozen branches of the Thames on the ice, skirted round the south of the town over the snow-clad fields, and made her way safely to Wallingford, a dozen miles distant.

To the west of the castle were situated the abbeys of Osney and Rewley. The former was one of the largest and wealthiest in England, but both have disappeared as completely as the abbeys of Winchcombe and Cirencester, and the neighbouring abbey of Eynsham. If the visitor's enthusiasm sends him on a pilgrimage to explore the ground on which they stood, he will hardly be rewarded : instead of cloisters and convents he will find railways and railway stations. At Osney, near the cemetery which now covers the site of the abbey church, may be seen a fifteenth-century archway, and a small fragment of a range of buildings adjoining; at Rewley, amid allotment gardens and osier beds, a line of wall containing a pointed gateway, now blocked up, with a square label terminating in heads, and quatre-foils in the spandrils. Thomas Warton relates that when he visited these remnants with Johnson in 1754—and the place must have been less unlovely then—the latter's remark after half an hour's silence was, " I viewed them with indignation."

Osney was founded by Robert d'Oilly, the nephew of the builder of the castle. The story connected with its foundation has been often told, but nowhere better than by Wood, who himself derived it from Leland. It is worth telling once more, and would lack half its charm if I did not give it in Wood's own words :

" The place though low, where it had its situation, was yet very pleasant both in respect of the chinking rivuletts running about it, as also for the shady groves and walks ; and soe enticing a place was it for pleasure that it often gave occasion to a noble lady of this city called Editha Forne, wife of Robert de Oilley, (a woman given to noe lesse superstition then credulity,) to recreat and solace herself therin when she lived at the Castle. Who more particularly, as upon an evening she with her attendance walked by the river's side, saw a great company of pyes gathered togeather on a tree, making a hideous noise with their chattering. Which shee beholding, did with slight notice passe it by for that time ; but the next evening walking that way againe with her maidens, (as she did afterwards the third time) found againe the pyes on the same tree, and making the like noise as before, seeming as 'twere to direct their chatterings to her. With which being much perplexed, wondred what the meaning might be ; and returning home againe, sent for her confessor who was one Radulphus, a canon of St. Frideswyde's : and relating all the perticulars that had severall times hapned to her in this place, demanded of him what the reason of their chattering might be. He told her he could not directly resolve her at that time; but if she would walke there againe the next day, he would wait upon her and veiw the matter himselfe and then give her an exact account. That time being come, they all walked the same way; where they found the pyes againe as before and making the like noise. Radulphus, the wiliest pye of all, seing all this, seemed at the present to be amazed; but after mature deliberation told her (upon her often demands for resolution) 'O Madam these are noe pyes, but soe many poore soules in purgatory that doe begge and make all this complaint for succour and releif; and they (knowing you to be pittyfull and one that will have regard of their condition) doe direct their clamours to you, hoping that by your charity you would bestow something both worthy of their releif as also for the welfare of your's and your posteritye's soules as your husband's uncle did in founding the College and Church of St. Georg.' These words being finisht, she replied: 'And is it soe indeed? now, de pardieux, if old Robin my husband will conceede to my request, I shall doe my best endeavour to be a means to bring these wretched soules to rest.' And therupon relating the whole matter to her husband, did soe much (by her continuall and frequent importunityes to him) bring the business about, that he a little while after (with the consent of Theobaldus, archbishop of Canterbury, and Alexander, bishop of Lincolne, in whose diocess this place then was) founded this monastery neare or upon the place where these pyes chattered, anno Domini 1129, dedicating it to St. Mary, allotting it to be a receptacle of Canon Regulars of St. Augustine, and made Radulphus, before mentioned, the first priour thereof."

The contrast of the "chinking rivuletts" and "shady groves and walks" with the present dreary aspect of the place is touching, and many a man besides Doctor Johnson must have viewed it with indignation. The abbey church was rebuilt on a magnificent scale in the thirteenth century by Abbot Leech, and was "not only the envy of other religious houses in England, but also beyond the seas; not only the admiration of our neighbouring inhabitants but also of forreigners that occasionally came to the University." With its two stately towers, its splendid proportions, and lavish decoration it must have been by far the grandest church that Oxford has ever seen. At the Dissolution it was spared for the moment to serve as the cathedral of the new diocese, but a few years later the episcopal seat was removed to Christ Church, and the work

of destruction systematically begun. A few extracts from
the Christ Church accounts, still preserved, will illustrate the
business-like manner in which the work was done:

"Imprimis, to Popingjaye the joyner for taking downe the stalls and
sides of the quire and high altar and other things in the church, 5*s*. 4*d*.

"Item, to the said Popingjaye for himselfe 3 dayes at taking downe the
roof of the church, 18*d*.

"Item, paid to Mr. Raynolds for melting the lead of the church and
casting it into sowes, 16£ 18*s*. 8*d*.

"paid to William plummer for taking downe the lead of the cloyster and
casting it into sowes, 4£ 4*s*. 2*d*.

"Item, paid to John Wesburne, cheife carpenter, taking downe the bells,
for 6 dayes, 4*s*.

"Item, paid to Willouby of Einsham for carriage of the great bell to
Frydeswide's, 26 Sept., 20*s*."

The work of destruction, however, proved too laborious or
too expensive for completion; at any rate, enough of the
church was left for the celebration of Mass in Mary's reign, and
considerable ruins seem to have survived for another century.
As for the seven bells, on their arrival at Christ Church they
were hung in the tower of St. Frideswide's, and there, with one
exception, they remained till twenty-five years ago, when they
were removed to Mr. Bodley's new tower over the hall. The
exception, of course, is Great Tom, which was recast in 1680,
and removed to the campanile then added to Wolsey's
imposing gateway. Since that time its sullen roar has re-
verberated nightly through the city to indicate the closing of
the College gates throughout the University.

Less than half a mile to the north of Osney was the
Cistercian abbey of Rewley founded in 1281 by Edmund,
Earl of Cornwall, the donor of the Holy Blood to his father's
foundation of Hayles.[1] Though never so wealthy or so
important a foundation as its neighbour, it was a flourishing
society and at the Dissolution contained twenty-one monks
besides the abbot, a number typified by twenty-one elm trees
which stood in two rows between the inner and outer gate of

[1] See p. 235.

C

the abbey, with one standing alone for the abbot. Among its estates was Yarnton, the first village we shall visit on leaving Oxford. Little or nothing is known about its church, but Wood supposes that it was bought at its dissolution by the organist of Magdalen College, "one that inriched himselfe by the spoyle of religious places," for he sold much of the stone and timber for the building of the Lady Chapel at the church of St. Mary Magdalen. The site of Rewley must be sought for between the London and North-Western station and the canal. Considerable remains were still standing in the early part of the eighteenth century, but scarcely a stone will now be found except the wall and gateway already mentioned.

The presence of these two powerful ecclesiastical corporations together with the smaller one of St. Frideswide, and all that their existence implies, must have profoundly affected the everyday life and the everyday aspect both of the town and the University. Of the relations between the monks and the scholars we know next to nothing ; no Wood or Hearne arose to chronicle the tittle-tattle of pre-Reformation Oxford, and the severe outlines of the picture can only be filled in by the imagination. One thing that we do know is that the greater religious orders recognised the value of a university training, and that colleges under their special superintendence were founded to which the most promising among their novices were sent. Thus the Benedictines of the western monasteries had Gloucester College on the site of Worcester ; those of the north, Durham College, some of the buildings of which form a part of Trinity ; and those of the south-east, Canterbury College, the name of which still survives in Canterbury quad at Christ Church. The college buildings were divided into separate *mansiones*, or as we should now call them "staircases" appropriated to the individual monasteries, and some of these, including the one belonging to Winchcombe Abbey, you may still see on the south side of the quadrangle at Worcester.[1] In

[1] See p. 241.

these the students dwelt apart, while they all attended the chapel and hall in common. For the Cistercians, Archbishop Chichele in 1437 founded St. Bernard's College, a part of which is included in the present buildings of St. John's, while the Austin Canons had St. Mary's College, where Erasmus resided when he visited Oxford. It stood near the present site of St. Peter-le-Bailey in New Inn Hall Street.

As far as concerns these three great Orders, then, we may conclude that they adapted themselves amicably to the ordinary curriculum of the University. With the Friars who descended upon Oxford in the thirteenth century the case was different. Faithful to their mission, they at once assumed the *rôle* of proselytisers and teachers, and it seemed that if unchecked they would gradually secure for themselves a monopoly of all the serious studies of the place. The position and influence of the secular clergy—and all professed students, graduate and under-graduate, were included in their ranks—were seriously threatened, when a champion appeared in the person of Walter de Merton, and the first college founded in Oxford arose to be for them a symbol of unity and a tower of strength.

To Merton College we must return immediately, but a few words must first be said of the earliest in time, though but third in rank, of the three great Oxford religious houses—the Priory of St. Frideswide. The legend of St. Frideswide has taken various shapes : the extant versions have been examined by Mr. James Parker, and in his *Early History of Oxford* he has stated his conclusions as to the amount of truth which they contain. The outline of the story is as follows :—Frideswide, a royal maiden of the eighth century, as she grew to womanhood developed a strong inclination towards a religious life. She persuaded her father to build her a church within the precincts of the city of Oxford, which he made over to his daughter for the exercise of her devotions. In connection with this church she founded a nunnery, and herself became the first governess or abbess. But some time afterwards, being persecuted by the

C 2

addresses of a young and sprightly prince called Algar,
she fled from Oxford and took refuge at Binsey, between Oxford
and Godstow, where she built an oratory, and where the
well which burst forth in answer to her prayers may be seen
to this day. The remainder of her life she spent, sometimes at
Binsey, sometimes at Oxford, in great peace and comfort, full
of good deeds and adored by all. At last she died in the odour
of sanctity and was buried in the church of the nunnery.

After her death the nuns were removed and the monastery
became a house of canons, sometimes secular, sometimes regular. At last in the reign of Henry the First it settled down into
what it remained till the Dissolution, a society of Augustinian
regular canons. That the church of St. Frideswide did not
share the fate of its neighbours at Osney and Rewley is due to
the patriotism and munificence of the Cardinal Archbishop of
York. Some fifteen years before the general dissolution of the
monasteries, Wolsey, ambitious of founding a great seat of
learning in Oxford which should be a worthy monument of
his name, "procured" the dissolution of the Priory, and began
to build the present college of Christ Church on its site. He
so far interfered with the church as to pull down the three
westernmost bays of the nave in order to make room for the
east side of his great quadrangle : here he stopped, and one
would gladly believe that he never intended to carry the
work of destruction further, but the fact remains, that he did
not in any case intend to use the priory church as his
college chapel ; for he had planned the construction on the
north side of the quadrangle of a great chapel which was to
rival that of King's College in Cambridge. But of this he had
got no further than the foundations, when his disgrace put an
end to all his projects. Yet his labour had not been wasted :
his college, it is true, was dissolved, but only to be founded
afresh ; and though completed by other hands, the princely
buildings he had raised remained ; and in the hall, the great
gateway, and the proportions at any rate of the great quadrangle

he has left a monument which will last as long as Oxford itself.

Besides the church, since 1546 the cathedral church of the diocese, very little is left of the priory itself. If you pass from Tom quad into the' lofty portico which contains the staircase ascending to the hall, and after pausing to wonder at the slender central shaft spreading out above into the elaborate fan tracery of the vaulting—a combination of dignity and delicate beauty unparalleled in Oxford—step out into the small cloister garth, you will come in the eastern walk to the chapter-house of the prior and canons, and rising above the roof of the southern walk you will see the tall windows of their refectory. For the rest, if your purpose is to explore the history of the days before the college and before the cathedral, you must confine yourself to the church. And here I would fain leave the reader to the safe protection of his hand-books, with the proviso that if he seek further details he should lose no time in procuring the *History of Christ Church* by the late vicar of St. Mary's; but, remembering how often I shall have to put his patience to the test in reference to many a lesser church, it would be unbecoming to pass by the only cathedral in absolute silence. Let us at any rate attend a Sunday service, and then, if it is term time, we shall find the separation between the church and the world still in force. Monks and canons, we know, worshipped in the centre of their churches, while citizens and strangers worshipped in the aisles : so at Christ Church the nave and choir are *par excellence* the college chapel. The dean and canons are in their stalls, and beyond them are the students [1] and the other graduate members not on the foundation : in the nave are the choristers, clerks, and chaplains, together with the bulk of the undergraduate members of the house, distinguished by wearing the surplice open in front, while right and left of the entrance a few students who hold college offices are seated. The aisles

[1] At Christ Church the students answer to the fellows at other colleges.

and transepts are filled with the rest of the congregation.   At the conclusion of the service, as the dean and canons pass out beneath the organ-loft, each, according to an ancient custom never dropped even in the most puritanic age, turns and bows reverently towards the altar.

The church is in the main of twelfth-century date, with later alterations and additions, which do not however detract from the Romanesque effect of the whole.   The eastern wall of the choir is a reconstruction by Sir Gilbert Scott of what he imagined to be its original form : to do this he had to remove a large and handsome window of the Decorated period.   Historical fact was thus sacrificed to conjecture ; and, strong and effective as the modern work is, there must always be two opinions as to its justification.   North of the northern choir aisle are two other aisles known as the Lady Chapel and the Latin Chapel.   Under the south-eastern arch of the former the fragments of the thirteenth-century shrine of St. Frideswide (for she was canonised not long after her death) have been pieced together with great judgment on a stone and wooden framework : they are interesting as a very early instance of natural, as opposed to conventional foliage.   Opposite is the curious carved wooden watching-chamber, from which the priest in charge could keep guard over the valuable ornaments of the shrine and the offerings made there by the worshippers. It is unnecessary for me to linger over the architecture or the monuments, which the visitor will find fully described in his books.   What the choir was like before the alterations of the 'seventies may be seen in a plate in Winkles's *Cathedrals.* The large window already mentioned completely fills the space now occupied by the three modern windows, and the stalls are enclosed by a tall panelled Jacobean wainscoting, the square projections of which have the appearance of a series of pulpits. All this was removed and replaced by the present stalls, backed by a fence of wrought iron.   At the same time the easternmost of the three western bays destroyed by Wolsey was rebuilt, and a west entrance opened out through the college buildings into Tom quad.

If the visitor should leave the cathedral by this entrance, and, turning to the right, pass under the archway that bears the ominous name of Kill-Canon, he will find himself in Peck-water quad, built by Dean Aldrich, and in summer term gay with long lines of many-coloured window-boxes. Here in the time of Henry the Third lived Ralph Peckwater, citizen and bailiff of Oxford. From him the house, long known as Peckwater's Inn, passed to John Gifford, baron of Brimpsfield in the Cotswold, "who," writes Wood, "for the great esteeme he had for learning and the benefit of the com-monweale, constituted and converted it into an house for stu-dents in the Civil Law. Which soe continued till the utter decay thereof in King Henry viii's raigne." On the south side of this quad is the great library built in the eighteenth century, and further to the east is Canterbury quad occupying the site of Canterbury College already mentioned. Beneath its pon-derous portal you may issue forth into the street, and, holding a straight course between Oriel and Corpus, you will soon reach the foot of the noble tower of Merton. The praises of this tower, with the good leave of any Magdalen man who may do me the honour to glance through these pages, I must allow the latest historian of the college to tell in his own eloquent words :

"None who have lived for however brief a time under its protecting shadow; who have looked up to its pinnacles soaring up over the little quadrangle nestling beneath into the dark blue cloudless sky on some mid-summer morning, or seen it cut clear against the purple on a night of full moon, strong as some great rock in the Tuscan sea; who have known it at dawn first clothe itself slowly with the delicate rose of the morning, and then flash back the gold of the sun; none after such visions of delight may fear the challenge of its rival and imitator Tower in the East. Their pride is unshaken; their confidence not to be assailed."

In its tower Merton has a visible token worthy of the pre-cedence which it may justly claim among its sister colleges.

Though the society had existed for nearly two centuries when it was built, it put the fitting crown upon the work of the founder, and one which we may feel sure he would have wished to see. As the oldest of the Oxford colleges, Merton must always have an especial claim upon the stranger, and if he hails from a distant land, in which the college system is unknown—and even in these islands he will find it nowhere but in Oxford and Cambridge—he may care to dwell for a few moments on its meaning and significance.

Before the coming of Walter de Merton the Oxford students had lived in private houses—whether called halls, inns, or hotels, it makes little difference. The discipline and supervision to which they were liable were merely such as could be supplied by the rather remote agency of the university officers. Under these conditions there was little beyond the uncertain and precarious influence of some prominent teacher to form a centre round which any company of scholars could rally. A field for competition was thus opened, and, as we have already seen, the Friars were not slow to enter it. Nor can we blame them if the interests of their Order were their first consideration, and the widening of its sphere of influence their ultimate aim. This however was something quite distinct from the true aims and the true ideals of a university; these might best be served in quite another fashion, and to Walter de Merton is due the credit of devising an expedient which solved the question. It was he who saw the gain which would result from the formation of a society bound together by the domestic bond of a common habitation and a common discipline—a society the whole aim and purpose of which should be the advancement of learning and the training of citizens qualified to serve God in church and state. To this end order and discipline were the first essentials for seniors and juniors alike, and in 1264 he drew up the code of statutes to which Merton College owes its inception.

We have seen that it was for the benefit of the secular clergy that his foundation was designed. Not that he had any quarrel with the regulars, but he saw that their position was sufficiently secure, while the ground they were gaining in Oxford was actually being won at the expense of the seculars. He therefore provided that membership of any religious order whatever should be a disqualification for enrolment in his new society. The very buildings which he designed for its use proclaimed its non-monastic character. Like the religious houses they included a common church and a common refectory, but they were plainly marked off from them by the absence of that distinctive feature of the convent, the cloister. It was in the cloister that the chief part of the indoor labours of the monk were performed : here he pursued his studies, copied his manuscripts, or composed the chronicle of his house. The members of a college, on the other hand, had their private chambers, and the cloister became superfluous. It is true that in the next century the magnificent founder of New College so far reverted to the ancient plan, but the cloister which he attached to his splendid foundation was designed for no monastic use. It might serve as a place of exercise and meditation for the living, and as a place of sepulture for the dead, but essentially it was a survival, and I imagine that the paramount idea in the mind of the founder was, that like the tower the cloister was an appanage indispensable to the completion of the great ecclesiastical structure which he had reared. In this as in other respects he was followed eighty years afterwards by the founder of Magdalen.

To return to Merton : little remains of the buildings actually erected by Walter de Merton except the walls of the hall, but the arrangement of the front quadrangle is his. There is a certain irregularity about this which distinguishes it from the symmetrical quadrangles of a later date. At New College, All Souls, and Magdalen the hall is attached to the east end of the chapel, and the whole forms one side of the principal quad : at St. John's again and at Wadham the arrangement is similar, but in the one case the hall is joined to the west end of the chapel, and in the other to the south transept. At Merton, on the other hand, the chapel stands apart, at right angles to the hall, and its eastern extremity with its grand geometrical window of seven lights is the most striking feature of the quad. This chapel, built in the last decade of the thirteenth century some twenty years after the death of the founder, was completed in the fifteenth century by the addition of the transepts and tower. As the visitor will see from the indications in the west wall, it was evidently the intention of the college at this time to finish the whole church by the building of a nave, but perhaps owing to the example set by New College, the design was abandoned, and the chapel retains its T-shape plan, which is characteristic of the greater chapels such as those of New College, All Souls, Magdalen, and Wadham. From the time of its foundation up to 1891 Merton Chapel was also used as a parish church, but the parish of St. John the Baptist has now been united with that of St. Peter in the East, and the parochial service at Merton has been dropped.

Among the many monuments contained in the chapel, we must not fail to mention that to Merton's diligent antiquary, Anthony Wood (1695), in the north transept, and the two famous brasses to Warden Bloxham (1387) and Warden Sever (1471) in the choir. The choir was once divided from the transepts by a seemly screen, but in an evil hour it was destroyed and its place taken by a piece of uncompromising masonry. The organ in its present position beneath the great west window can only be described as a painful sight. Were it rebuilt upon a suitable choir screen, such as that at New College, there would be nothing to mar the finest college chapel in Oxford.

The buildings adjoining the chapel have a unique interest. To the south is the most ancient quad in Oxford, dignified, no one knows why, by the name of Mob Quad. In the north-eastern corner is the singular building called the

Treasury, remarkable for its high-pitched roof of solid stone flags. So steep is the slope from the roof-tree, and such is the weight of the flags, that as a piece of constructive masonry it has excited the wonder of every generation; it has stood as it now stands for six centuries, and yet no Merton scholar has ever felt it "tremble o'er his head." To the fourteenth century also belong the four sides of the quad; nor do they show any signs of decay. They are in fact for the most part built, not of the perishable Headington sand-stone, but of the hard and durable oolite from the quarries of Taynton, a pretty village on the Oxfordshire flanks of the Cotswold, which will lie in our way another day. The same stone was used for the facing of the tower, and here and there elsewhere in Oxford. The far-sighted architects were not to be deterred by the twenty miles or more of haulage—a serious consideration in those days—and posterity has had good reason to be grateful to them. The upper story of the west and south sides of the quad is occupied by the college library, and the chained books which it still contains are a fitting token of its antiquity. As the statutes of Walter de Merton served as a model for subsequent foundations, so the arrangement of the Merton library was followed by the other college libraries as they one by one came into existence. Its pride is a first edition of the Caxton Chaucer (re-coated, *horresco referens*, by Lewis, who tricked out so many of the Althorp incunabula), of which only eight other copies are known.

To pass from the solemn seclusion of Mob Quad into the spacious ease of the Fellows' Quadrangle is to pass in a moment from the rigour of mediævalism into the amenities of modern life. Built at a time when, in another Midland town less than forty miles away, *Cymbeline*, *The Tempest*, and *A Winter's Tale* were being written, the Fellows' Quad at Merton is, like those immortal dramas, redolent of romance. It may rank with the beautiful buildings of Wad-ham, the unrivalled garden front of St. John's, and the glorious staircase of Christ Church as the last expression of the romantic feeling in Oxford architecture before the advancing wave of Puritanism swept all such sentiments away. Did it not form part of a college it might easily be mistaken for the courtyard of a Jacobean mansion of the first rank. It is the most delightful habitation in Oxford, and we cannot wonder that the queens " of either Charles's days " chose it as their abode. It was in this quad that in 1661 the first Common Room in Oxford was opened, and here it still remains. Access from the hall is easy, and on a winter's night, when the mist lies thick on Christ Church meadow, or the storm comes driving across the valley from the Cumnor hills, when the dark-panelled walls are glowing in the firelight, and the candles in their silver sconces are reflected in the vistaed depths of the polished table, when the fellows and their guests are assembled, and the college port goes round, it would be hard to find a pleasanter fireside in Oxford.

The privileged person may pass through the gateway of the Four Orders on the south side of the quad into the college garden, and from the raised terrace that is carried along the inside of the city wall he will survey a scene in which every prospect still pleases : on his left are Magdalen tower and the Botanic garden, before him the Meadow and the Broad Walk, and on his right the cathedral and its precincts. He will not see that great blot on the picture when viewed from the Broad Walk, the new building of Merton. This was one of the first of the atrocities perpetrated in Oxford in the dark age of its architectural history, the latter half of the nineteenth century. If the stranger desires to see the other triumphs of this period, he must inspect certain portions of Christ Church, Balliol, and New College, which it will be as well to leave to his own discovery and censure.

Even the present cursory survey of the Highways and Byways of Oxford must not be silent on the *rus in urbe*, or the country airing which may be taken without quitting the precincts

of the University.   There are, of course, the College gardens.
The wealthy Societies of Merton and New College excepted,
the most considerable of these belong to those foundations
which arose after the middle of the fifteenth century outside the
circuit of the ancient walls.   Here land was less valuable, and
Magdalen, Trinity, St. John's, and Worcester secured without
difficulty, or even extended, the domains of those older
foundations which they replaced, while the liberality of Dorothy
Wadham enriched her college with grounds which stretch from
the Museum almost up to Holywell Street.   Magdalen indeed
with its deer park and its water walks combines the dignity of
a college with the magnificence of a country seat.

But we need not confine ourselves to the college gardens.
We may start from Merton garden gate in the sheltered alley
known as Deadman's Walk, and take our way across the
Broad Walk through Christ Church meadow to the Barges.
Each college has its barge or house-boat, which is to the river
what the pavilion is to the cricket field.   Cross the river in a
punt and stroll down the towing-path, and you will have a good
view of the practising eights and fours, as well as of sundry
smaller craft.   This will give you a good idea of Oxford
"form" in its various stages of efficiency, but if you want to see
it at its best, you must wait for the bumping races in February
and May.   The towing-path is then a less desirable point
of observation, for it is crowded by an excited multitude, tearing
along to keep pace with the competing boats, and cheering
their crews not merely vocally, but by all such sounds of
harmony as may be produced by rattles of large size, mega-
phones, and even pistol shots ; while if a *bump* be imminent,
the air is rent by shouts that may be heard half a mile away ;
" Now you're gaining ! " " Now put it on ! " " Now you've got
them ! " " Well rowed, stroke ! " " Keep it up, bow ! " and so on.
But I must not assume that the reader is initiated into the
mysteries of Oxford boating, and he may very naturally wonder
what a *bump* may be.   I hasten therefore to explain that

the river is not wide enough for more than two boats to start abreast, and that arrangements have to be made for at least a score. Each College has its own boat, and in the "Torpids" some colleges have two.   Under these circumstances the problem is solved as follows: the several boats are posted in a long line at equal distances apart, the tail boat being close to Iffley Lock.[1] On the first day of the races, which last a week, the order of precedence is that of the final order resulting from the races of the previous year.   At a given signal the boats start simultaneously, and it is the object of each to foul with its bows the stern of the one immediately ahead of it.   This manœuvre is the *bump*, and the next day the bumping boat takes precedence of the bumped.   The February races are those of the junior crews or "Torpids"; the May races those of the senior crews or "Eights."   The Eights are recruited from the Torpids, and the University Eight from the College Eights.

The May races are the great Oxford carnival: mothers, sisters, cousins, aunts come flocking in their hundreds; picnics, promenades, teas, dinners are the order of the day; even dances—long supposed the peculiar privilege of Commemoration week—have been heard of, and both entertainers and entertained may boast with Lord Foppington that life is an eternal round O of delights.   But Eights' week or not Eights' week, summer term is the time for "the Joys of Oxford Living," the time for Panama hats and loose attire, the time for lounging in punts, or flirting in "Canaders."   It may be that presently when we turn out of Mesopotamia into the Parks and saunter along the willowed margin of the "Cher," we may chance to spy Youth on the prow, and Pleasure at the helm gliding softly up towards distant Islip, babbling "of many things," but not unmindful of luncheon and of a descent upon the ripening meadow hay of some long suffering Marston farmer.   Or it may be, we shall see made fast beneath the

---

[1] For our purposes the modern practice of starting in divisions may be neglected.

shadow of some overhanging poplar the cushioned punt, where

> " Some on earnest business bent
>   Their murmuring labours ply
> 'Gainst graver hours, that bring constraint
>   To sweeten liberty,"

for even in summer term the victim of " Exams." cannot for ever play regardless of his doom.   Even in summer term the paths of Oxford lead but to the Schools.

But I am anticipating.   Before we reach the Parks we have still some way to go : from the barges the Meadow walk takes us to the Botanic Garden, where we can sit for a while almost under the shadow of Magdalen Tower—and the view of the Tower from this spot is one to linger in the memory—before crossing Magdalen bridge and threading our way through the purlieus of St. Clement's to the entrance of Mesopotamia.   Now Mesopotamia is an avenue of pollard willows, winding between two branches of the Cherwell to the lasher at Parsons' Pleasure, well known to all bird-lovers as a favourite haunt of Oxford birds.   Here in May you may chance to hear the notes of the nightingale, or in winter to catch sight either of a kingfisher darting upon his prey, or of that most agile and graceful bird of the north as he runs swiftly hither and hither in search of tiny crustaceans—the grey wagtail.   For in Oxford gardens and meadows the birds are religiously protected, and encouraged to nest undisturbed.   Warblers, finches, and titmice build in the willows or the sedges ; the hollow trees are well known to starlings, jackdaws, and sparrows, and in the Botanic Garden even so wary a bird as the lesser woodpecker has made its home.

The Parks are a broad expanse of grass planted with shrubberies and laid out with gravel walks and borders of flowers, dividing North Oxford from the region of Holywell.   They are the property of the University, but are thrown open impartially to the public, and their bracing atmosphere and pleasant promenades are appreciated alike by the nursery-maid and the

The "Golden Cross" Inn-yard, Oxford.

professor. With the circuit of the parks we must bring our perambulation to a conclusion, and for the rest of his stay I must leave the reader in other hands. The passing glimpse of one impatient to set forth upon his proper pilgrimage is all that I can offer him, and for such a passing glimpse the fact that this pilgrimage begins and ends with Oxford is my excuse. To try to do more, to try to tell the story of Oxford as it must be told, would require a volume to itself, and how this may be done Mr. Cecil Headlam has lately shown us in his handsome quarto. To the enjoyment of this in the privacy of his inn I now commend my reader ; for my own part I am content to wait his pleasure, and when he can find it in his heart to tear himself away from Oxford and all its manifold delights he will find me ready to accompany him in the next chapter.

CHAPTER II

STRETCHING away north and north-west from Oxford—from the Cherwell to the western fringe of Cotswold—lies the upland region towards which we are shaping our journey this morning. It is a region unfrequented by the majority of those whose pleasure it is to roam abroad. To the wearied brain scenes wilder and more majestic than those which we are now about to survey will always make the first appeal, but the curious traveller who has leisure at his call, and is content to tempt the peaceful charms of an old-world English countryside, may spend many a long summer's day, and spend it well, in exploring the breezy downs and the secluded vales of North Oxfordshire and the Cotswold.

The method of locomotion will vary with the inclination of the individual traveller. For ourselves the bicycle is the conveyance we have chosen, and for the firm smooth main roads of our district no easier mode of travelling can be devised. It is true there will be many a stiff hill to climb, for whereas in a highland country the roads will descend the larger valleys parallel with the course of the river, here they are for the most part carried along the ridges of the hills, often following the line of the ancient trackways, and crossing the valleys by the shortest and most convenient route, without respect to the villages which mostly lie sequestered in the sheltered nooks formed by the windings of the stream. To reach these villages we

must quit the main road, and commit ourselves to the
cross road : nor are these cross roads all of one sort, or
all paths of pleasantness to the cyclist ; at times indeed they
affect the dignity of the highway, and need then cause him no
concern, but oftener they are little more than cart tracks leading
him from gate to gate across the fields in a fine open fashion ;
and sometimes they are deep, well worn hollow ways, full
of stones and ruts, plunging headlong down the steep sides
of the valley in their haste to pass the old grey bridge and
climb the opposite ascent. But on highroad and byroad, the
cyclist in the Cotswold will find to his cost that ever and
anon he will have to dismount, and wheel his machine it may
be a mile or more. Again while the main roads are now
constructed of hard dark blue Leicestershire grit, the
byways are still repaired with the soft local oolite, and
though they may be crisp and "scrimpy" enough when the sun
is shining, after a few hours' rain they become hopelessly sticky
and impassable.

But by this time we have left Oxford three or four miles
behind and have reached Peyman's Gate, the famous turnpike
where Mr. Verdant Green and his friends on their return from
Chipping Norton Steeplechase were confronted by the proctor.
The gate has long been cleared away, and Peyman's is now the
Grapes Inn ; but those who are familiar with Cuthbert Bede's
illustration of the scene will not fail to recognise its leading
features, and to testify to the faithfulness of the artist. Here it
is worth while to make a detour of half a mile in order to pay
a visit to the little village of Yarnton, well known to the
traveller by railway for its fine combination of church tower and
gabled manor house. It is a well worn truth that even the
obscurest village has a story worth the telling, for those who will
be at the pains to ask for it, and Yarnton is so notable an
example of this, that I must perforce detain the reader here for
a while. The pre-historic associations of the place I must pass
over : the visitor to the Museum at Oxford will find ample

evidence of them, and no doubt much more might still be
discovered by further excavations.   In historic times it is as the
property of the church that Yarnton is first heard of.   Early in
the eleventh century it was given to the Abbey of Eynsham, then
newly founded, but property in those days was a precarious
thing, and down to the end of the thirteenth small respect was
shown for the rights of the monastery by the reigning sovereign
and his barons.   At last, in the time of Edward I., Edmund,
second earl of Cornwall, who among the other estates of his
father Richard—brother of Henry III. and founder of the Abbey
of Hayles, which we shall visit later on—inherited Yarnton,
gave it to his own Cistercian foundation of Rewley.   Now or
never was the time for the monks of Eynsham to make one more
effort to assert their claims, and after prolonged litigation a
compromise was effected, by which, though the manor remained
in the possession of Rewley, Eynsham retained the rectory, and
the right of presentation to the vicarage.   Interesting traces of
this connection with religious houses remain : in the churchyard you will find a cross of a design more than ordinarily
elaborate ; on the base are sculptured four knights kneeling on
one knee, and canopied figures of ecclesiastics on the shaft ;
another cross, almost identical in design, stands in the village
square at Eynsham on the north side of the church, and between
the two were other crosses, long since destroyed, though the
base of one of them may even now be discovered by the antiquary
dishonoured and cast aside in the purlieus of a farm.   These
crosses marked the halting places of religious processions, and
the names of Paternoster farm, and Alleluiah or Vocat Alleluiah,
which still exist, or in the latter case once existed, in Yarnton,
may well be relics of the same rite.

At the dissolution the manor of course fell into lay hands,
and in Elizabeth's time it came into the possession of a branch
of the great Northamptonshire house of Spencer.   Four generations of this family reigned here, Sir William the First, Sir
Thomas the First, Sir William the Second, and Sir Thomas the

Second. It was the first Sir Thomas who built the beautiful manor-house, now, after a century and a half of neglect and dishonour, so admirably restored, the present tower of the church, and the chapel on the south side of the chancel known as the Spencer aisle. Of this tower and chapel both the architect and the builder may well have been proud : had we not proof documentary to the contrary we should without hesitation have ascribed them to the reign of Richard II. rather than to the reign of James I. The tower bears the date 1611, and is faultless both in design and execution, while the windows of the chapel resemble those of the hall and chapel of Wadham College, which was built about the same time. It is indeed quite possible that the same architect was employed both by the founder of Wadham and the munificent benefactor of Yarnton. The good people of Yarnton, however (if, that is, we may judge from the exterior appearance of their church), are somewhat remiss in showing that respect for founders and benefactors which is characteristic of an Oxford College. The visitor with a sympathetic feeling for the conscientious handicraft of a vanished age finds to his dismay that the masonry of the lower part of the tower, and of the whole of the body of the church, is rendered invisible by a sturdy and impenetrable covering of ivy. On the rough-cast exterior of the older part of the building this deadly and insidious creeper might perhaps be tolerated—in moderation, but that it should be suffered to spread its monotonous pall over the perfect ashlar work of his tower and chapel—shade of good Sir Thomas !

The interior of the church prepossesses one at once, for it has been gently dealt with by the restorer. No neat expanse of varnished deal, no glaring tiles of chequered red and blue, no scraped nakedness of arch and wall have blotted out the traces of the past; and it is still possible for the men of Yarnton to realise that the church in which they worship is the same church as that in which their fathers worshipped. There are indeed no ancient brasses, but

on the altar tomb of Alderman Fletcher, of Oxford, who died in
1827, we shall find one of the earliest attempts to revive a forgotten art.   The alderman was a notable collector of antiquities and particularly of old stained glass, some of which may be
seen in the great window of the picture gallery at the Bodleian.
Almost all the coloured quarries in the windows of this church
are his gift, for he loved Yarnton, his "childhood's home," as
he calls it in the inscription on his tomb.   Much of this glass
appears to be of foreign origin, but there is in the windows of
the north wall of the nave a curious set of birds with English
mottoes, each one depicted on a small quarry of its own; for
instance, a hen, in a fashionable head-dress of the fifteenth
century with a gauze veil hanging down her neck, and the
motto "greete richlyng greete" (*i.e.*, weep, lament); a kind of
tit girt with belt and key like a cellarer, and holding a flat dish
in its claw, motto "Who blamyth this ale?" and an owl ringing a bell with the legend "Ye schal praye for the Fox."   Among
the carved work, which was collected from various sources by a
former vicar to fill the upper part of the arch opening into the
tower, are the arms of Charles I. with the date 1634.   If these
arms were originally put up in the church at this date, it is remarkable that they should have survived the iconoclastic rage
of the Protectorate; but there is no proof of this, and they may
have been brought here from the manor house hard by or from
elsewhere.   In the Spencer aisle are the handsome monuments
of the first Sir William, who died in 1609, and the second Sir
Thomas, who died in 1684; the latter has been attributed to
Rysbrach owing to the pyramidical grouping of the figures, an
arrangement which is found on the famous monument of the
great Duke of Marlborough by this artist at Blenheim; but as
the Spencer family became extinct at Yarnton with the death
of the widow of Sir Thomas in 1712, and Rysbrach was then
only a youth of eighteen—this ascription is, to say the least,
extremely doubtful.   Of this good lady, Dame Jane Spencer,
tradition used to relate that she continued to reside at the

manor house after her husband's death, keeping up the kindly interest of a great lady of the old *régime* in her tenantry : and old inhabitants of the village loved to tell how she would be carried in her Sedan-chair to the great elm trees on the green to watch the rustic dances and amusements which took place there. We must not leave the church without seeing a notable piece of carving of the earlier half of the fifteenth century, another gift of Alderman Fletcher : this is an alabaster reredos representing scenes from the Passion of our Lord. It was discovered under the floor of a house near St. Edmund Hall, in Oxford, and when presented to the church had six compartments, but two of them have since disappeared, how or where no one seems to know.

Although no events of national import have given Yarnton a place in the pages of history, the night of June 3rd, 1644, must have been long remembered by the villagers. It was on this night that the king at the head of 3,000 horse and 2,500 foot made his memorable dash from Oxford between the two armies destined by the Parliament to complete the circumvallation of the city—the army of Essex on his right, and that of Waller on his left. The former had passed the Cherwell and had already pushed as far westwards as Woodstock and Kidlington, while the latter lay on the left bank of the Thames round about Stanton Harcourt and Eynsham. A few more hours and the two commanders would have joined hands, Oxford would have been completely surrounded, and a single fortnight have sufficed to compel it to surrender. This catastrophe was only prevented by the spirited resolution and prompt action of the King ; the enterprise was a hazardous one, and he could not hope to succeed in it without the utmost caution and secrecy. His object was to secure the passage of the Evenlode at Handborough bridge, a point about midway between the hostile armies, before either of their generals had any suspicion that he had quitted Oxford. It was therefore an imperative necessity to keep out of sight and hearing of the enemy, and this he could not do if he took the

ordinary high road to the bridge across the open plain of
Campsfield : here, in spite of the darkness, his advance would
inevitably be detected by Essex's scouts, and a flank attack
would force on an engagement, which would bring up Waller
from the other side, and the two armies would crush the
Royalists between them. Charles therefore chose the lower road,
where the rising ground on his right would conceal his move-
ments, and by means of which under the cover of night he
might hope to reach the bridge unperceived. It was this lower road
which brought him through Yarnton.   The changes in the water
level brought about by the Thames Navigation Act have since
then rendered it impracticable, but in those days it was the
shortest way from Oxford to Yarnton and Handborough, and
was the one commonly used by the market people of both
villages.   From Oxford it led across Portmeadow to Lower
Wolvercot, and thence across the meadows quaintly called Pixey
and Oxey, where as each summer comes round the Yarnton
farmers still draw lots for the several portions of mowing-grass,
past the manor house and church till it reached the mouth of a
wide green lane, which then ran through an unenclosed country
in a straight line to the Evenlode bridge.   About a mile of this
green track, now known as Frogwelldown lane, still remains to
remind the traveller of the dawn of the June morning two
centuries and a half ago when King Charles and his troopers
passed along it.   By this skilful manœuvre the great scheme of
the Parliament was frustrated, and for the rest of the year, as far
as the south of England was concerned, the tide of success was
turned in favour of the Royalists.   The King had crossed the
Evenlode and halted his army on Northleigh heath before any
intelligence of his successful sortie reached either Waller or
Essex, and he had made good his way as far as Burford before
any of their cavalry came up with him.   A month later we shall
meet him again at Cropredy.

   But it is time we were on our way over " Campsfield's tempting plains," well known to Oxford horsemen before the days of

enclosures, to Woodstock. Of Woodstock and Blenheim, or
Blenheim and Woodstock, as the railway has it, whether in the
order of euphony or of importance—the size of this volume
will not allow me to say as much as some readers may
expect. Woodstock is not a country town which at any
period in its history has been left to languish in obscurity.
During more than six centuries a residence of kings, for
the last two hundred years it has basked in the sunshine of
ducal patronage. As to the artistic merits of the palace of the
Dukes of Marlborough opinions will differ: I will only say that
in the magnificent strength of its solid proportions, and in the
imposing severity of its classic design, it is a fitting
monument both of its age and of the military hero in whose
honour it was erected.

Let us leave our cycles at the Bear and proceed to
the park on foot. On the right we pass what is known
as Chaucer's house, in spite of the fact that the poet never
owned it or lived in it: there is, however, some justification
for the appellation, inasmuch as it formed part of the estates
of the wife of his son Thomas; it was then called Hanwell
House, but the present name occurs as early as 1570. We
enter the park beneath the Triumphal Arch: "then," says
Dr. Mavor in his *New Description of Blenheim* written in 1810,
"one of the most enchanting prospects in nature discloses
itself to our view"; he adds in a foot-note, "When George III.,
with his Queen and the three elder Princesses, first entered this
gate he was so struck with the magnificence of the view, as to
exclaim, 'We have nothing equal to this': and he spoke
correctly." Without going so far as the doctor or his late
Majesty, it must be admitted that the lake and the spacious arch
of the great bridge, with the wooded slopes of the park in the
background, form a picture which might well arouse their
enthusiasm. The curious thing about the bridge is that it was
there before the lake; when it was first built the valley was
watered only by the tiny stream of the Glyme, a circumstance

which gave rise to the following epigram on the penurious tendencies of the first Duke :

> " The lofty arch his high ambition shows,
> The stream an emblem of his bounty flows."

It was Capability Brown who dammed up the Glyme and formed the present lake ("the Thames," he boasted, "would never forgive him for what he had done at Blenheim"); and enabled Boswell, when he visited Blenheim with Dr. Johnson in 1776, to remark, "They have drowned the epigram."

Before the building of the new palace a causeway led across the marshy ground of the valley to the old palace, or manor-house as it was usually called, and of this causeway the small island on this side of the bridge, known as Queen Elizabeth's Island, formed a part. It is a melancholy fact that every vestige of this ancient manor-house, a favourite residence of our monarchs from Ethelred II. to Charles I. has been ruthlessly destroyed. We may see the place where it stood across the lake a little to the right of the bridge ; the site is now overgrown with nettles and coarse grass, and planted with horse-chestnuts, while behind it towers the heaven-directed column of Victory with its colossal figure of the great duke attired in the garb of antique Rome. Indeed, so completely has the fame of the old palace been eclipsed by the modern glories of Blenheim, that it is not without some effort of the imagination that we realise that even before Agamemnon there lived brave men. Certainly it is only in imagination that we can reconstruct the ancient edifice : much of it was pulled down in the years that followed the Civil Wars, but the gate-house was still capable of being used as a residence in the time of Charles II., and it was not till 1723 that all that remained was taken down and the ground levelled. Two sycamores, now fine umbrageous trees, were then planted to mark the spot. Sir John Vanbrugh, the Blenheim architect, was anxious to preserve these " Remains of distant Times," but the all-powerful Duchess had quarrelled with him, and the uncompromising order went forth for their

destruction : besides, had not no less a personage than Lord
Treasurer Godolphin himself complained to her "that a pile of
ruins in front of the Palace was an unsightly object"?

We may stroll down to the bridge and contemplate more nearly
the scene of so many notable events in our past history.   Here
Elizabeth, suspected by her sister of knowing too much of Sir
Thomas Wyatt's rebellion, was detained a close prisoner for a
twelvemonth, and here, according to Holinshed, she "wrote

Woodstock Manor-house in 1723 (from a copy by S. Ireland, after J. Wood).

these verses with a diamond in a glasse window verie legible, as
followeth :

> " 'Much suspected, of me
> Nothing proved can be,
> Quoth Elizabeth, Prisoner.' "

Holinshed also records with a brave confusion of pronouns
that "she hearing upon a time out of hir garden at Wood-
stocke a certaine milkmaid singing pleasantlie, wished herselfe
to be a milkemaid as she was, saieing that hir case was better,
and life more merier than was hirs in that state as she was."

Another effort of her muse at this time, a ten-line stanza, too often reprinted to necessitate its reproduction here, and originally written with charcoal on a shutter, has been preserved by a German traveller who visited Woodstock before the end of the sixteenth century. But the lady Elizabeth was not the only fair captive of Woodstock whose troubled wit Fortune's "restlesse wavering state" had "fraught with cares." The story of fair Rosamund, the silken clue, the dagger, and the poisoned bowl, is known to us all from nursery days, with how much of fable twined round the central stem of fact we leave to the historian to decide. A few yards behind us as we stand upon the bridge, facing the site of the old palace, is a spring which has been known for generations as Rosamund's Well. In Aubrey's day it was surrounded by the remains of buildings, of which that painstaking antiquary sent his friend Anthony Wood a sketch, confidently headed "Description of Rosamond's Bower at Woodstock park." This has been reproduced in Mr. Clark's edition of the *Life of Wood*, and the well will be seen clearly indicated. Fair Rosamund died about the year 1175 and was buried in the church of Godstow nunnery, of which her father, Walter, Lord Clifford, was a benefactor, but her bones were not long permitted to rest in peace. Anthony Wood, following the account of the chronicler, Roger of Hoveden, writes that "Hugh, bishop of Lyncoln, afterwards called St. Hughe, being in visiting his diocess anno 1191, came to this place of Godstowe and going to the altar to do his devotions, observed an hearse, covered with silke, with tapers burning about it, which the nunns at that time had in great veneration. He therupon enquired of the standers by, 'whose it was'; and they answering 'it was faire Rosamund's whom King Henry so dearly loved and for whose sake he had been a munificent benefactor to their poorhouse by giving larg revenewes for the maintenance of those lights,' he replied :—' Take her hence . . . for the king's affections to her were unlawfull and adulterous ; and bury her out of the church with other common people, to the end that religion be not vilified and that other women might be terrified from such adulterous practices.' Wherupon, as some say, they removed her into the churchyard, but I rather suppose they laid her with her ston-coffin in the chapter-house, where she continued severall yeares. At length her flesh being quite perished these chast sisters put all her bones in a perfumed leather bagge, which bagg they enclosed in lead and layd them againe (with her stone coffin) in the church under a larg grave stone." Three centuries and a half later her grave was again disturbed, and Leland's record of this was evidently Wood's authority for the latter part of his story : " Rosamunde's tumbe at Godestowe Nunnery was taken up a late ; it is a stone with the inscription TUMBA ROSAMUNDAE. Her bones were closid in lede, and withyn that bones were closid in letter [leather] ; when it was openid there was a very swete smell came owt of it."

The mention of St. Hugh of Lincoln reminds us of the pathetic story of one of his predecessors in that See, who died while on a visit to Henry's grandfather at Woodstock : " It fell out on a Wednesday," says the Chronicle, " being the fourth before the Ides of January, that the King rode in his deer park, and Roger, bishop of Salisbury, was on one side of him, and Robert Bloet, bishop of Lincoln, on the other ; and they rode there talking. Then the bishop of Lincoln sank down, and said to the King, ' My lord King, I am dying' ; and the King alighted from his horse, and took him between his arms, and bade them bear him to his inn, and he soon lay there dead."

The last of the Royal owners of the manor to visit Woodstock was William III. In November, 1695, he passed the night here, after a day's hunting in the forest on his way from Burford to Oxford. By this time the old manorhouse, or what remained of it, seems to have been in too dilapidated a condition to afford suitable quarters for royalty. The King therefore "lay at Mr. Cary's, an old gentleman's of near a hundred years of age, who had been servant to James I.,

Charles I., Oliver Cromwell, Charles II., James II., and was then servant to King William. . . . The King being informed of a humour of his in showing his pictures, desired to see them, and pretending not to know whom they were drawn for, asked of the first in order, 'Who that was?' 'That,' replied Cary, 'was my good old master, King James I.; I served him several years.' 'Who is the next?' says his Majesty. 'That,' replied Cary, 'is my good master, Charles I.; he was a good master to me, let them say what they will of him'—'Pray who is the next?' the King said. 'Why truly sir,' replied Cary, 'that is my master Oliver Cromwell, he too was my very good master; and so was the next there, King Charles II.; and the next, King James II.; and so now is your Majesty, whose picture there is still room for.' Whether the King gave him his portrait does not appear, but he was pleased at the old gentleman's simplicity in his way of setting out his pictures, which, it seems, had all been given him."[1]

But all this time, although on our way to the park we passed the church, where the Rev. Nehemiah Holdenough in his blue Geneva cloak was ousted from his own pulpit by that righteous champion of the Independent cause, Trusty Tomkins, I have said nothing of that episode in the history of the manor-house which will be best known to the majority of my readers. Everybody who has turned from the romantic pages of *Woodstock* to those of sober history is aware that Sir Walter found it convenient to transplant his loyal and venerable knight from the days of Elizabeth to those of Cromwell. Like his prototype, the worthy knight of the novel held the office of ranger of Woodstock Park, like him he was renowned for his loyalty to his sovereign and his military prowess, but in other respects his character is the creation of the author. The real Sir Henry Lee, voluntary champion of Queen Elizabeth and Knight of the Garter, although at Court his ways were the ways of orthodoxy, when he came down to his estates showed himself to be a country gentleman of the new school. He was one of those

[1] Tindal's *Continuation of Rapin*.

"shepe maisters, decayers of husbandrye," against whom Sir
Thomas More in his *Utopia* had testified earlier in the century.
Like many another large landowner he saw that there was
more money to be made out of sheep-farming on a large scale,
than by letting his land in strips to small tenants under the old
system. We are not surprised therefore, to find that he made
himself very unpopular with the Oxfordshire farmers, many of
whom had no doubt been evicted from their holdings to make
room for his extensive enclosures. Yet he found to his cost
that the new industry had its drawbacks; in the great storm of
1570, he lost as many as 3,000 sheep, besides a large number
of cattle; and Sir Thomas More takes care to inform us that
"after so much grounde was inclosed for pasture, an infinite
multitude of shepe dyed of the rotte, suche vengeaunce God
toke of their inordinate and unsociable covetousnes, sendinge
amonge the shepe that pestiferous morrein, whiche much more
justely shoulde have fallen on the shepe-masters owne heades."
But as ranger or comptroller of Woodstock park he would
have to give his attention to venison as well as to wool; to this
office he was appointed about 1570, through the interest of the
Earl of Leicester, and he held it to his death in 1611. Besides
the several lodges which he occupied officially in the park, he
owned the neighbouring estate of Ditchley, where he also had
a residence. Ditchley he bequeathed to his second cousin, Sir
Henry Lee, baronet, whose grandson, another Sir Henry, was
the actual head of the family at the period in which the scene
of the novel of *Woodstock* is laid. Although, as a matter of
fact, neither the old knight of Ditchley nor any of his successors
ever resided at the Royal manor-house, there is excellent
contemporary authority for the mysterious events which Sir
Walter describes as taking place there with his connivance.
The curious thing is that these events remain a mystery to the
present day. Of course, an explanation, matter of fact enough,
is set down in the story, and readers of the Introduction to the
novel will remember that the part played by Roger Wildrake

is said to have been really played by one " Joseph Collins, commonly called Funny Joe," who hired himself as servant to the Commissioners under the feigned name of Giles Sharp. Ever since the publication of *Woodstock*, all the guide-books have accepted the said Joseph as a historical personage : it was clear, however, that Sir Walter did not feel quite comfortable about him, and on attempting to run him to ground, I found that both the " memorable " wag himself and the whole history of his contrivances are the invention of an ingenious magazine article concocted a hundred years after the events it purports to explain took place.[1]

In the days of Sir Henry Lee (I am still speaking of the ranger), the parks of Woodstock and Ditchley and the forest of Wychwood formed an unbroken stretch of wild country, and many an exciting chase must have been followed by the great Queen and her successor, who were fond of visiting the knight at one or other of his houses. The hall of the old house at Ditchley—" a low ancient timber-house, with a pretty bowling greene," when Evelyn visited it in 1664, and was regaled with " an extraordinary dinner " by " my Lady "—was adorned with stags' horns under some of which were brass plates recording the death of the game [2]: Hearne, the Oxford antiquary who saw them in 1718, copied six of these inscriptions, two of which will serve as samples :—

" 1608, August 26, Munday.
" King James made me to run for Life from Dead man' Riding,
I ran to Gorcil [Gorril ?] Gate, where Death for me was biding.
" 1610, August 25, Saturzday.
" From Foxehole driven, what could I doe ; being lame, I fell,
Before the King & Prince, neere Rozamond, her well."

The present handsome house at Ditchley, designed by James Gibbs, the architect of the Radcliffe, replaced the old one a few years after Hearne's visit; and forty years later was

[1] I may refer the reader who wishes for a further account of this silly hoax to an article of mine in *Notes and Queries*, Series IX., 280 (May 9, 1903).

[2] These plates are still preserved in the present house.

the scene of an event which will have its interest for Oxford men ; for here " in a state-room accommodated for the solemnity " on October 5, 1762, George Henry Lee, third Earl of Lichfield, was installed as Chancellor of the University, the Vice-Chancellor, the Heads of Houses, Proctors, and representative Masters of Arts having come over from Oxford for the occasion. " The Vice-Chancellor," says the only account I have seen,[1] " having opened the Convocation. . . . some of the senior Doctors introduced his Lordship, and placed him at the right hand of the Vice-Chancellor, who then addressed his Lordship in a Latin oration, gave him the proper oaths, invested him with the insignia of his office (the keys, the seal, and book of statutes) and resigned the chair ; making a suitable observation, and a genteel compliment to his Lordship on each part of the ceremony.   His Lordship then addressed the Convocation in a Latin speech, expressing his sense of the honour conferred upon him, and assuring them of his utmost diligence and fidelity in the discharge of the trust reposed in him : after which, Mr. Thomas Nowell, the University orator, congratulated his Lordship in a Latin harangue adapted to the occasion.   The solemnity of the installation being thus concluded, his Lordship entertained his constituents with a splendid dinner ; and with that ended the business of the day, the whole having been conducted with the utmost propriety and elegance."   After this we are quite prepared to learn from another source that his Lordship filled the office " with graceful dignity and polite condescension."

I will not spoil the pleasure of those discreet readers who enjoy a surprise by conducting them to Ditchley.   I will leave them to discover this secluded paradise for themselves.   Far away from the public road and defended by a ravine deep and thickly wooded, its very existence is unsuspected by the ordinary cyclist, and we will leave him to " scorch " along to Chipping Norton or Stratford in blissful ignorance.   But for those who

[1] Collins's *Peerage*.

E

have once seen it there is a homeliness and dignity about the sober old Georgian mansion and its surroundings which will leave a lasting impression on the memory. I may add that with a liberality which the cyclist will know how to appreciate, the present distinguished representative of the Lees allows him to ride through the park and woods.

I remarked just now the continuity of the parks of Blenheim and Ditchley with the forest of Wychwood; in fact the whole of this part of Oxfordshire was once an open forest, and Woodstock was probably one of the earliest settlements in it, being *stockaded* out of the wood; while a neighbouring village was a later settlement, and distinguished as wood *town* (Wootton). Then when Woodstock became a royal residence, it was the natural consequence that a further portion of the forest should be enclosed to form a park, in which beasts of the chase could be confined. The oldest part of the present park is that which lies to the south of the site of the manor-house, and is easily distinguished from the rest by the magnificent oaks which it contains, some of which must be at least 700 years old.[1] Henry I. surrounded the park with a wall of stone, of which there was an abundant supply on the spot; what was the extent of this wall is not known, but it was no doubt much less than that of the present wall, which is some eight miles in circumference, and commends itself even to the unprofessional eye as an excellent example of drystone masonry. On the highest ground in the park, flanked by a wide expanse of primæval forest, stands the High Lodge. Some time since the middle of the eighteenth century it put on its present pretentious battlemented exterior of sham Gothic; before then, as may be seen in an old print of 1752, it was a comfortable, substantial-looking building with a high-pitched roof and dormer windows. It was the official residence of the ranger, and thus came to be tenanted by John Wilmot, second Earl of Rochester, who had been

[1] Such, at least, was the opinion of the Duke of Marlborough's former forester.

appointed to the office by Charles II. The career of this
bright star of the restoration firmament belongs to a page of
court history too well known to detain us here. It may be less
generally known that it was here at the High Lodge that he
repented and died : Dr. Gilbert Burnet, afterwards Bishop of
Salisbury, who visited the penitent on his death-bed, was
convinced of the sincerity of his conversion, and has recorded
his experiences in a pamphlet often reprinted. A tattered
bedstead and a rusty sword are still preserved here, and these
poor relics are all the visible tokens that remain to link the
name of Rochester with Woodstock. From the roof of
the lodge, the eye may travel down to Oxford's towers,
and far beyond them to the Berkshire moors. The view
is a more distant one than that from Cumnor Hurst and
is perhaps the most distant view of Oxford that can be
found : this, however, is a delicate point that I have been
unable to decide ; the view from Bletchingdon, whence on the
June morning already spoken of Essex, looking towards Oxford,
"saw our colours standing, as they did, and thence believed
that we were still in his power," must be a formidable rival. In
any case it is our last sight of Oxford, for we must now leave
Woodstock and set our faces northwards.

As we ride through the little town we may stop to
purchase a pair of the excellent gloves for which it has
been famous since the end of the sixteenth century. At
the right season you may see the hedges and clothes
lines covered with sheep skins and goat skins bleaching
in the sun, while at the cottage doors both here and
in the neighbouring villages the women are hard at work with
their needles, for the hand-sewn article ranks above the glove
wholly turned out by machinery. Doubtless the waters of the
Glyme have the same efficacy as those of the Cherwell, its near
neighbour on the east, for the Cherwell, says Anthony Wood,
"hath soe great vertue therein that all the skins of a more
delicate kind (as it hath bin generally observed) are soe well

seasoned with it for the making of white leather that none whiter softer or better is hardly found." He further tells us that the river is "cleare and well stored with fish": for the sake of the patient angler, a familiar spectacle to the wanderer along its banks, it is to be hoped that the store is still plentiful. One well-known native of these Oxfordshire streams at any rate has for generations afforded sport—of a kind—to the villagers. This is the crayfish, hereabouts called *crawfish*, a delicacy which the local connoisseur pronounces superior to lobster, and for the true enjoyment of which, I am advised that considerable industry is required: a certain amount of privacy may also be recommended on grounds similar to those which induced two considerate old ladies of whom I have "heard tell" to admonish their butler, whenever poultry or game appeared upon the table, with the words, "Thomas, you may retire." Others will prefer catching the animal to eating it; the sport begins at nightfall, and the method is as follows: certain nets with stiff rims of saucer or basket shape, are baited with liver (if a little gamy so much the better) or herring, and let down into the stream where the fish "run" in the course of the afternoon. When it begins to get dark the fisherman visits the nets armed with a long hooked pole; with this he lifts and examines the nets one by one, and puts the fish into a wallet, taking care to catch hold of it in such a way that it cannot seize his fingers with its nippers. There is considerable uncertainty as to the amount of the bags, —the crayfish, by the way, are always reckoned by the score— sometimes you may have to wait a couple of hours before the fish are "on the run," and then suddenly you may catch them as fast as you can lift the nets and pick them out; a friend tells me he has taken a score out of a single basket. As soon as the evening's sport is over, the bag is carried home and the contents emptied into boiling water with salt in it; next morning you may begin your feast.

For this sport one of the best rivers is the Glyme: our road to Banbury runs along the summit of the ridge which divides this little stream from the Cherwell.   We enter the high road at an inn called Sturdy's Castle, though why "castle" you may ask in vain.   The rustic can only tell you that "it always *have* been Sturdy's Castle," nor are you much enlightened by the recollection that in a neighbouring village exists the "Killingworth Castle," while "Pomfret's Castle" is the name of a farm high up upon the Banbury and Chipping Norton road : perhaps the height either of the building itself, or of its situation, may have had something to do with it ; I am told that in a small village not many miles from Banbury, when a small proprietor took it into his head to raise his house by the addition of a third story, the place was henceforth known among his neighbours as "George's Castle."   At Sturdy's castle the road is crossed by Akeman Street, the Roman road leading from St. Albans to Bath, and still well marked during the greater part of its course.   We are now well up in the stonebrash country, an elevated tract of treeless stony hills which stretches from Woodstock to Deddington and Great Roll-right, while north of this lies the rich red-land country round Banbury, the most fertile in the county.   Here on either side of the road the land is almost entirely under the plough, but it is a fine open stretch of country, and the air is always fresh and exhilarating : on the left, the Column of Victory towering above the trees of Blenheim is still visible, while deep down on the right lies the broad green valley of the Cherwell, and on the hills on its further side are the well wooded parks of Aynho, Kirtlington and Bletchingdon.   At Hopcroft's Holt, readers of Pope may turn aside to see the gigantic monument of the judge pilloried by the poet in his Imitations of Horace :

> " Slander or poison dread from Delia's rage,
> Hard words or hanging if your judge be Page."

It was erected by the judge in his lifetime to perpetuate the memory of himself and his wife, on the north side of the chancel of the church of Steeple Aston, and it says much for the complacence of the rector and churchwardens of the day that he was allowed to destroy existing monuments to make room for it. The artist he employed was Peter Scheemakers, better known as the author of the cenotaph of Shakespeare in Westminster Abbey. Page was the son of the vicar of the neighbouring parish of Bloxham, and his success at the bar, coupled with his vigorous support of the Whig interest, enabled him to realise a fortune, with which he purchased an estate at Steeple Aston, where he lived the life of a country squire. Events proved that he was wise in erecting his monument, for on the death of his bachelor nephew and heir, the estate passed into other hands and the judge's mansion was destroyed. But if the hanging judge and his effigy in marble are not enough to draw the reader to this village, he may find a greater attraction in an embroidered cope of the fourteenth century, which, by some strange and rare good fortune, has escaped destruction and still exists to be the proud possession of the parish. In the days when, to quote a popular historian, "the halls of country-houses were hung with altar-cloths ; tables and beds were quilted with copes"; "when the knights and squires drank their claret out of chalices, and watered their horses in marble coffins," it went hard with the sacred vestments ; a generation or two of domestic wear and tear, and what was left of them? Among country parishes, I know only of one other that can boast a relic of this kind.

Before we get to Banbury two or three tributaries of the Cherwell have to be crossed. Climbing the steep hill on the further side of the first of these we are at Deddington, which, like so many other ancient settlements in this district, is a "decayed market town." Needless to say the market has long ago disappeared, but of markets and marketing we have no time to think ; all unawares we seem suddenly to have passed into a land of gold, and for the moment we are conscious of nothing but the magic fascination of the scene. But the secret is soon out ; it is the rich golden brown of the stone

On the Banbury-Oxford Road.

of which the walls and houses on every side of us are built that
has cast this spell upon us, and how admirably it harmonises
with the mellow thatch or old lichened tiling of the high-
pitched roofs! Time was when Deddington must have been a
paradise for a painter, but times have changed; we turn into
the spacious market-place to find that even Deddington has
had to mix the useful with the charming; the "simple Early
Gothic" of yesterday and the inevitable red brick and blue
slate of the usual economical and elegant design have thrust
themselves into every corner. Nevertheless, if the artist will
confine himself to the less fashionable quarters he will find
compensation, and, may moreover console himself with the
reflection that this feast of colour will be with him till he
passes from the skirts of the Edgehills into the Cotswold. But
we have not yet done with Deddington. In the first place there
is the castle, or, lest I should be accused of enticing any reader
there on false pretences, I should rather say the mound where
once the castle stood : for even in Leland's time every vestige
of the building had disappeared. As at Swerford, as at
Chipping Norton and at Brimpsfield, banks and ditches
are all that remain. If the town has a history, the castle
has none : no one knows either when it was built or when
demolished. It has been surmised that within its walls
Piers Gaveston, the Gascon favourite of the second Edward,
was a prisoner when he was seized by the Earl of Warwick and
hurried to his death at Blacklow Hill, but the chronicler who
records his seizure at Deddington merely says, "where no
natural hiding place, nor any castle or stronghold made by art
could conceal him." As to the existence of a castle at this time
of course these words are not decisive; the bare facts are that
Gaveston, having surrendered to the barons at Scarborough, was
on his way to Wallingford in the custody of the Earl of Pembroke when he was pounced upon by Warwick at Deddington.
The church is remarkable for the width of the nave and aisles,
while the chancel is singularly narrow, but the general impres-

sion as one enters is that of light and space: there are but
few stained windows, an excess of which in a country church
always has a depressing effect. I like to see the branches
of the trees waving against the sky through the crystal-
white or very pale green glass that filled the windows half a
century ago, before the fashion for coloured glass, or what is
worse, the vulgar opaque stuff called "cathedral glass" became
so despotic. The meaning of the steps in the jambs
of two windows, one in the north and the other in the
south aisle, may, at first sight, be a puzzle to the visitor;
they led to the galleries of rood-screens which formerly
enclosed chapels at the east end of either aisle. Here, for the
first time, in the mutilated tomb of William Bylling, we
light upon the commemoration of a merchant of the staple of
Calais; in the wool-growing country, which we shall reach in
due time, we shall meet with them again and again. The
circular dome-shaped roof of the north porch is curious; its
presence there is perhaps to be attributed to the damage done
to the original roof by the fall of the tower which happened in
1635. Eight years later it was still a ruin, and the bells being
useless were sent to the royal magazine at New College to be
transformed—such was the irony of fate—into engines of war.
Next year after the fighting at Cropredy and before starting for
the west in pursuit of Essex the King was here himself. He
slept at the Parsonage, probably the gaunt old balustraded
building which you may see standing on the north of the
churchyard.

Old customs lingered long in Oxfordshire after they had died
out in other counties. Dr. Robert Plot, who in 1677 published
a queer rambling treatise on the natural curiosities of the
county, saw the sport of riding at the quintain practised at
Deddington: the game was then, he writes, "only in request
at marriages, and set up in the way for young men to ride at
as they carry home the bride, he that breaks the board being
counted the best man." Indeed, a century before this time

thé quintain had ceased to be a military exercise and had
become simply a rustic pastime.

Now, in spite of the deep warm hues of the native stone,
whose praises I have already sung ; in spite furthermore of
" the goodness of its malt liquors," for which a century ago,
and still for all I know, it was " particularly famous," it is to
be feared that in the stranger's memory the record of Deddington will be as of a town not merely "decayed," but
positively bleak and forlorn. Like Cassius it certainly does
wear a lean and hungry look, and therein forms a striking
contrast to the village where our next halt is made. As soon
as ever the traveller begins to descend the hill out of
Deddington he is conscious of a difference. The green slopes
of the hills portioned out into small enclosures, and the
patches of wood dotted about the valley of the Swere, are
enough to certify that he has now left far behind the long
furrows of the stonebrash country. Instead of a deserted
market-place he finds at Adderbury a trim village green shaded
by giant elms and surrounded by cosy-looking cottages thickly
festooned with creepers. The whole village has a comfortable
well-to-do air, suggestive of centuries of peace and prosperity.
On the east side of the green is Adderbury House, once the
abode of the Earl of Rochester, whom we have already had to
speak of in connection with Woodstock, and afterwards of
Pope's Duke of Argyll,

> " Argyll the state's whole thunder born to wield,
> And shake alike the senate and the field."

If we may believe some verses which appeared in a magazine
of the day, and have been reprinted in the collected works of
the poet, he visited the Duke here in 1739 and pressed " the
bed where Wilmot lay." He probably came over to Adderbury
from his friend General Dormer's house at Rousham, down in
the Cherwell valley about a mile from Steeple Aston : at any
rate he was at Rousham in the summer of that year, and

wrote thence to his friend Judge Fortescue, a letter which contains an allusion to another judge already mentioned : " I am within a mile of your brother Page, who threatens to come hither; and it is very probable I may see him at dinner to-morrow.   If we were well enough acquainted, I might be tempted to go the circuit with you as far as Southampton. I fancy no coaches are so easy as the judges', and no journeys more gradual : then ;I might be sure of reposing some days between whiles, and keeping sober and sad company." Of the manuscript treasures of Rousham, one of the very few estates in Oxfordshire which have remained in the same family for more than two centuries, this is not the place to speak ; the reader will find them fully described in the report of the Historical MSS. Commission.

The church of Adderbury is one of the finest in the county, and its spire rivals those of the neighbouring churches of King's Sutton and Bloxham.   The interior has been treated with better taste than at Bloxham, but in both cases the walls have been denuded of their plaster : this was a favourite practice with restorers some years ago, but to speak of it as restoration is a misnomer.   The very fact that large portions of the surface, especially the west side of the chancel arch, were covered with frescoes is enough to prove its existence in pre-Reformation times, and a Flemish divine of the twelfth century in a sermon on the dedication of a church which has come down to us, says that the white plaster of the interior signifies the cleanness of the heart, of the exterior the cleanness of the body.   Its removal gives to the whole of the interior of the church a very cold and bare appearance ; the result at Adderbury and Bloxham is bad enough, but the most lament-able instance which I have seen is the present scraped interior of the magnificent church of Brailes, which we shall come to later on.   Yet in spite of this drawback, Adderbury is admir-able both in design and in detail.   Among its most interesting features are the graceful pillars which divide the transepts from the aisles of the nave, and the vestry on the north side of the chancel. The latter is not a modern excrescence tacked on to the ancient fabric without regard to dignity or proportion, but an integral part of the original building with a beautiful oriel window, and an upper chamber formerly the repository of the parish records. The chancel was built by William of Wykeham, whose family had estates in these parts ; and the heads in which the hood-mouldings of the windows terminate are those of the founder and of his master Edward III. The vicarage was presented by him to New College, which also owns the fine rectory-house and the tithe barn on the north of the church : similar barns, also the property of New College, exist at Heyford Warren and at Swalcliffe. The college has always presented one of its fellows to the living : a tablet erected to the memory of one of its vicars, Dr. William Oldys, records the fact that he was murdered by the rebels during the Civil War. The story as told by the Rev. John Walker in his *Sufferings of the Clergy* (1714) is worth quoting : " Having by his great Loyalty and Affection to the Royal Cause render'd himself very obnoxious to the Rebels, it was not any longer Safe for him to stay at home ; and therefore he was forced to betake himself to the Neighbouring Town of Banbury, which was at that time a Garrison for the King ; and some time after he had fled thither, intending his Son for Winchester-School, or as Others say for the University of Oxford, he sent word to his Wife, that on such a Day (which he named) he would go part of the Way with them. A Neighbour of his happening to know of this, sent word of it to some of the Parliament Soldiers ; who accordingly waited at a Place where he was to pass by, for his Coming. He perceiving that there were Soldiers there, and finding himself in Danger, sent his Wife and Son before, telling his Wife, that if they were of the King's Party, she should Hold up her Hand, and he would come on ; if not, she should pass on without any further Notice. She going on, without Holding up her Hand, he knew they were Parlia-

mentarians, and therefore Rid back as fast as he could : They
perceiving this followed him as fast as they could. He being
to pass by his own House in his Way to Banbury; when his
Horse came to his House, he could not by all the means he
could use, get his Horse forward; which gave them time
to Overtake him; which as soon as they had done, one of
them discharged a Pistol at him, and Shot him dead. Some
of the Parish have since affirmed, that the Person who had
given notice to the Party of the Doctor's Journey, fell down
dead upon that very Spot of Ground where the Doctor fell
when he was shot. I have heard that he scattered his Money
along the Highway, and by that Artifice delayed all of them
but one, who thirsted more for Blood than Plunder. And 'tis
said the Villain had been Supported formerly by the Doctor's
Charity ; and that his very Comrades abhorred the Baseness
of this Action."

CHAPTER III

I suspect that to most of my readers the name Banbury is
suggestive of little else than cakes and the performances of a
certain famous equestrian lady at the cross; perhaps they may
remember the squabble which led one of Sir John Falstaff's
hangers-on to apostrophise Master Abraham Slender as "you
Banbury cheese," and if they have ever dipped into their Ben
Jonson, they may have a bowing acquaintance with Zeal-of-
the-Land Busy and the Banbury elders,—and here an end.
But we cannot ourselves pass the place so lightly by; it is, if
nothing else, the second town in the county and deserves a
more respectful treatment.   It cannot indeed pretend to have
any out-of-the-way attractions for the stranger, but it is a typical
example of a well-to-do Midland country town, and having no
other place of importance nearer than Oxford, Leamington, or
Northampton, it forms the centre of a large agricultural district.
Moreover, it will make a very convenient starting point, from
which to explore the villages we are about to visit, and we shall
do well to make it our headquarters for a time.

I shall not accompany the reader in the stroll through the
town, which he is sure to take sooner or later: and for the
ancient houses, the old inn gateways and the Globe room at the
"Reindeer" with its elaborate stucco ceiling, I shall refer him to
the guide-book which he carries in his pocket.   The excellent
local history, by the late Alfred Beesley, is too bulky for carrying
about, but if he finds it at his inn he may profitably be-

The " *Reindeer Inn*," *Banbury.*

guile his evenings by turning over its pages. Here he will find an engraving of the "original" cake-shop in Parson's Street, and as we have arrived by road and have therefore escaped the assiduous purveyors of these delicacies at the station, we will look in here, and form our own opinion on the merits of the genuine article as it comes fresh from the oven. The recipe is no modern one: Banbury Cakes were famous in the days of Camden and Ben Jonson, and the secret is traditional. The shop, which has wisely refused to sacrifice its decent window-panes for modern plate glass, has been in the hands of the same family for some generations. Title deeds in their possession prove that the premises date at least from 1616, and the present proprietor will show you with a legitimate pride the bakehouse, now converted into a parlour, in which the cakes of those days were made. As for the cakes of to-day, I am told that you do not get quite so much for your money as you did when my informant was a boy, but this, of course, is a perennial grievance; old Betty White, who made and sold her cakes at this very shop when George III. was King, was well used to complaints of this kind; "Only think," she would say, "there's currans, they be double the price th' used to be, and then there's butter an' sugar, why they be double the price th' was formerly," or else it would be, "God help y', I 'oonder how much butter and sugar y' could buy for a ha'penny."

It is not far from the cake-shop to the market-place, where on market day temporary booths are still erected in the good old style, and hard by is the site of the Castle, for the building itself, which had been a royalist stronghold, was demolished by the victorious party at the end of the Civil War. In the autumn of 1644 it was gallantly defended for thirteen weeks against the Roundheads by Sir William Compton, a younger son of that Earl of Northampton who had fallen at Hopton Heath, till at last the King dispatched to its relief three of his best regiments of horse from Newbury field. In the spring of 1646 Sir William had to stand a still longer siege conducted by Colonel Whalley,

House in Market Place, Banbury.

F

one of Fairfax's most capable lieutenants, who afterwards had the unenviable notoriety of figuring as one of the fifty-two judges of the King. But the Royal cause was now at its last ebb, and Sir William, recognising that further resistance was useless, capitulated upon honourable terms. Two years later, on "the humble Petition of divers of the Well-affected of the county o1 Oxford, principally of the inhabitants in and about Banbury," the Commons resolved "that Banbury Castle be forthwith demolished." It is not difficult to imagine that the worthy citizens of Banbury, as well as the farmers of the surrounding district, with the fear of the requisitions of a hungry garrison before their eyes, were anxious enough to secure themselves against a repetition of such delicate attentions for the future , and although under the influence of the powerful house of Fiennes of Broughton, and of the Puritan ministers for whom their neighbourhood was so famous, they had generally thrown in their lot with the Parliament, yet they seem to have been treated pretty impartially by both sides. "The country men," says a news-sheet of the day, "have a pretty observation, which is this : They say, they pay contribution on both sides : when Banbury men come to gather their money, they observe a time when their enemies of Northampton are at home, then come they in, and with a loud cry, say, where are these Roundheads ? wee'll kill them all for raysing mony of you, you shall pay to none but us : when Banbury men are gone, then comes the other party, where are the Cavaliers ? wee'll kill them all, you shall pay to none but us, we will protect you ; but hardly in a year doth one interrupt the others collections."

But whatever may have been the sentiments of the citizens of Banbury in those days, the loyalty of their descendants is un-impeachable. In 1858, having resolved to commemorate the marriage of the Princess Royal with the Crown Prince of Prussia, they decided that the famous Banbury Cross should no longer be merely the shadow of a name : for two centuries and a half nothing but the nursery rhyme, which has made Banbury a household word wherever the English language is spoken, had kept its memory alive, but now the town was to have its Cross once more. Nor was Sir William Compton and his gallant defence of the Castle forgotten; his arms together with those of other local worthies may be seen emblazoned on the panels of the far from imposing monument then erected. There was of course no pretence that the new Cross in any way resembled the old one: what that was like no one knows; but the fact is ascertained that at the end of Elizabeth's reign it fell a victim to the Puritanic zeal for which Banbury was then so notorious. It is likely enough that the learned Camden had this act of vandalism in his mind when he added this virtue to the other famous products of the place. The story goes that when the English translation of his *Britannia* was passing through the press, he found that to his original remark in his Latin version that Banbury was famous for "cheese," the translator had added on his own authority "cakes and ale," and that he forthwith substituted the word "zeal" for "ale": hence it is that in all the English editions of the *Britannia* we read that the town is famous for "cheese, cakes, and zeal."

But the destruction of the Cross is not the worst act of vandalism that has been perpetrated by the citizens of Banbury. The stranger who inquires his way to the church will find to his amazement "a hideous square mass of stone, without form or proportion"; if he enters, he will not care to linger, for he will soon have seen enough to convince him "that he has at last reached the nadir of ecclesiastical architecture." That the monstrosity he is contemplating is the product of the last quarter of the eighteenth or the first quarter of the nineteenth century, he will of course feel certain[1]; and he will naturally conjecture that the previously existing church perished either by earthquake or by fire. If he has seen the engravings of it in Skelton's beautiful folio, he will remember that it was

[1] It may be contrasted with the fine church of All Saints at Northampton, rebuilt in the classical style about 1676.

one of the largest and most magnificent churches in Oxford-shire, with its long and lofty nave, its gabled transepts, and its massive central tower, "appearing," says one who saw it in its glory, "rather like a Cathedral than a common parochial church." Surely nothing short of some terrible catastrophe can have swept it away! Yet incredible as it may seem, this splendid edifice was deliberately demolished in 1790 in order to save the expense of a few necessary repairs, and to put money into the pockets of interested persons. The whole of the sordid story may be read at length in Beesley, and may be commended to the historian of local institutions. The destruction of the tower, which rested upon great square Norman pillars, was a formidable undertaking, but the Philistines were not to be baulked: " timber and wedges were applied beneath it, to give it temporary support; and then the pillars were partially knocked away; fire was applied, for twenty-four hours, to consume the timbers which had been substituted, and at the expiration of that time the noble pile fell down, burying the parts beneath it amid its ruins."

After this we shall not be loth to get away from Banbury for a while in search of metal more attractive. Taking the Chipping Norton road we soon reach the wide-spreading village of Bloxham. Here the church which crowns the hill on the further side of the little brook at once challenges compari-son with Adderbury. Undoubtedly in its size and in the splendour of its tower and spire it surpasses its rival, but the interior is less pleasing; not only has modernisation had freer scope, but there is less delicacy of detail, and the general impression is harder and less restful. The vestiges of its history are not difficult to follow: to the original Norman church, which stood on the ground covered by the present chancel, was added an Early English nave and aisles; when these aisles were enlarged and the chancel rebuilt in the Decorated period, the Norman mouldings were worked up in the present chancel windows. Of the Early English work only the arcades of the nave (afterwards raised by a clerestory) remain, but a fine doorway, doubtless removed from the church during the fourteenth century alterations, remains at the "Joiners' Arms" in the village. In many a village the inhabitants no doubt utilised the discarded doorways and windows of their church : and though most of them have disappeared, the observant eye may still find traces of them here and there. In the village of Sherborne, between Burford and Northleach, we shall find a perfect Norman doorway, the sole relic of a vanished Norman church, serving as the entrance to one of the humblest cottages.[1]

The Bloxham people are naturally proud of their lofty crocketed spire; round the octagonal base from which it springs is a broad band of elaborately carved stone-work, which they call the "allis"; when viewed from a distance this band has all the effect of a wreath loosely encircling the spire. The south transept with its huge perpendicular windows is the latest part of the church; this is known as the Milcombe chapel, from its having been the burial place of the Thorney-crofts of the dependent hamlet so-called. Milcombe knows the Thorneycrofts no more, but they were the leading family here in their day; Sir John Thorneycroft, Bart., who died in 1725, was "a person of Singular Piety, and Eldest son of John Thorneycroft, Esq., of Gray's Inn, and Dorothy, his wife," as you may read on his monument, where his marble effigy, attired in flowing wig and loose morning gown, is the very picture of graceful benignity. He lived at Milcombe Hall, one of those numerous mansions of the lesser gentry, which now linger on as farmhouses,—pleasant and homely places still, but amid their grass-grown alleys and mouldering terraces eloquent ever of a vanished splendour. In former times the manor-house was the pride and ornament of the country village. The former owner, the small squire of a thousand a year or less in land, had no

[1] See p. 291.

temptation to sacrifice elegance to utility; he kept his dwelling in repair and his pleasure grounds in order, he was a good neighbour, and village life was the poorer for his disappearance. With the advent of his successor the prestige of the old house necessarily departed; the tenant farmer had neither the leisure nor the inclination to keep up the refinements of the place; if the house was too large for his needs, one wing of it was destroyed; the bowling-green became a chicken run, and the pleasaunce a potato-ground; his working-day was a long one, and when he had done his work, he had done his duty, and might enjoy his pipe by his fireside with a clear conscience. In these days of agricultural depression if he can pay his rent, keep a roof over his head, and bring up his family, he has done all that can be expected of him, and therefore, though we may deplore the uses of adversity which have brought the old house down to its present state, we must accept it as one of the inevitable consequences of that concentration of land in the hands of the wealthy minority, which has been the standing grievance of the political philosopher from the times of the *latifundia* to the present day.

Here at Milcombe Hall, which we may visit on our road to the valley of the Swere, is one of those substantial dove-cotes or pigeon-houses, which are a sure sign of a residence of manorial rank. For the pigeon, wild or domestic, ever had the reputation of a bird most injurious to the farmer's crops, and it was a recognised necessity that a limit should be placed upon its numbers; hence the privilege of erecting a dove-cot was reserved for the lord of the manor, and no tenant might possess one without the lord's license. In many parts of the country these ancient dove-cots have quite disappeared, but in our district, being built of stone and not of wood, many of them have survived; the modern pigeon-fancier will be astonished at their size, but the fancy pigeon is of comparatively recent origin, and in the days when these cots were built, the bird was regarded merely from the point of view of the table ; in fact, as old domestic records show, it formed a far more important item in the bill of fare than it does to-day ; nor need we wonder at this, when we remember that in the days when the artificial-feeding of stock was an unknown art, fresh meat of any kind during the winter months was a rare delicacy, and the cheap and convenient pigeon would be the more appreciated. Most of these dove-cots are circular in shape, like the beacon towers, one of which still remains on the Edgehills ; but this one at Milcombe is octangular, and has a corresponding octangular slab or table on the floor of the cote, for the purpose of feeding the birds ; the care which was taken that every detail should be thoroughly finished is evidenced by the bevelled edge raised round the table to prevent the food being wasted. Nesting-holes to the number of 999 line the whole of the interior of the building, and in the sloping roof are dormer windows, closed by lattices, which admit light and air : the birds enter through the lantern at the top, which may be closed with a shutter when required. Access to the nesting-holes here is obtained by climbing up the walls, the holes themselves affording the necessary hold for hand and foot, but at Rousham and at Daglingworth, in the Cotswold, there is a curious contrivance, consisting of a ladder revolving upon a central shaft, which may be applied to any part of the interior as required.[1] Milcombe Hall was bought by New College at a time when land was still a profitable investment, and is now tenanted by a courteous old lady and her two sons, known to their neighbours and workpeople in the good old country style as " Master Ernest " and " Master George."

We regain the Chipping Norton road, and drop down into the Swere valley at the primitive village of South Newington. South Newington with its neighbours, Wigginton and Swerford, higher up the stream, may be taken as the type of the poorer Oxfordshire village, a type which presents a marked

[1] See p. 2c6.

contrast to the well-to-do and populous Adderbury or Bloxham. Swerford, it is true, has its park and great house, and as before mentioned the mounds of its castle, but Wigginton and Newington consist chiefly of rows of humble cottages, which have suffered little change for generations. As you wander down the village street you are made to feel that times are bad, that the flower of the rising generation has taken this to heart and has departed to seek its fortune elsewhere. But

South Newington.

there is another side to the picture; if South Newington is poor, it has at any rate lacked the means of self-destruction, for its church is still unrestored and must not be left without a visit. A good attempt at "beautifying" was indeed made in the so-called churchwarden epoch, which may, I suppose, be taken roughly to lie between the years 1650 and 1850: the lead was stripped off the roofs of the nave and chancel, and replaced by slates, while the interior was reseated with squalid deal pews. In addition to this a vulgar varnished ceiling has been put up in the chancel, but otherwise the church has escaped mutilation.

Nor has the destroyer been suffered to ramp unchecked at Wigginton, to which village a short ride up the homely green valley will bring us. Here in the modest and unpretentious church we shall find one of the most beautiful, and (save for the added perpendicular clerestory) one of the most unaltered examples of the Early English style in this part of the country. I am one of those who find a peculiar charm in the clustered columns, deep mouldings, and high-pitched roofs of this particular style, and the scene that meets the eye as you enter through the porch, curiously placed at the north-west angle of the building, is wholly delightful. In a country church, where you can generally take everything in at a glance, the first impression on entering counts for much; you are at once either cheered or depressed, and at Wigginton there is no question which; there is nothing, except perhaps some excessive wall-scraping, to offend. If he enters the chancel the curious in such matters will see on either hand what is known to ecclesiologists as a "low-side window"; the remarkable thing here is that there should be two of them; one is common enough, and may be noticed over and over again in the churches of our district. Here, as at Upper Swell, in the Cotswold, they are formed under a transom in the lower part of one of the lights of an ordinary window. They were formerly unglazed and closed by a shutter, the traces of which may still be seen. Obviously their use was to communicate with the churchyard outside, but what the nature of this communication was can only be a matter of conjecture. Probably they served more purposes than one; for instance, in the absence of a sanctus bell-cot the bell might be rung through them by an acolyte, or they may have been utilised in connection with the funeral service; the idea that they were used to administer the sacrament to lepers requires confirmation.

We may now, if we please, push up to Swerford, near the head of the valley, from which a short but stiff ascent will land us again in the Chipping Norton road near the turning to Great Tew. Now " Tewland," as it is sometimes called, is a neighbourhood with immortal associations which I hope to approach with all proper respect at a later period. At present I mean to set my face northward, from Wiggington, and ride up hill and down dale till I reach Tadmarton Heath, a spot well known to the Oxfordshire botanist, where the Stow and Banbury road is carried right through the centre of the ancient camp at an altitude of about 650 feet. This camp is one of the many memorials of a distant age which crown the scattered hill-tops in this part of the county. Just this side of the fosse, on my left hand, a pleasant bridle-road leads over the fields to Tadmarton village, but I must now keep to the main road which takes me down the hill, and past Broughton Castle on my way back to Banbury. Three miles away Bloxham spire rises out of the valley on the right, and after crossing the brook at the foot of the hill the ground ascends again, till it reaches a point from which I can survey the valley watered by the little stream called the Sor Brook, in which the village of Broughton lies. The term village is, however, rather apt to be misleading, for it gives you no idea of the size of the aggregate of buildings intended ; it covers populous places like Bloxham or Adderbury where the houses may be reckoned by the score, as well as tiny settlements such as Broughton, where besides the Castle and the Rectory there are only some half-dozen scattered houses to be seen. Indeed, from the spot where I am now standing the venerable walls of the Castle, with the church spire rising up close behind them are alone visible. Solemn and imposing in its solitary grandeur, and shut off from busy Banbury by a vast intervening hill, Broughton Castle is indeed a haunt of ancient peace. I am not fond of stock phrases ; they are apt to become mechanical and meaningless, but I can find no other which so adequately expresses the impression which a first sight of Broughton makes upon the stranger. From this side the effect is almost gaunt owing to the great height of the building, and the severity of the outline, but if we descend the hill, and turning to our left by the church, climb the slope of the park, we shall have a view of the north and west sides, where the rigour of the original structure has been softened by Tudor additions. The house and grounds are completely surrounded by a rectangular moat, and the only access is by a single bridge on the north defended by an ancient battlemented

Broughton Castle.

gatehouse. The house adjoins the eastern side of the moat, and the rest of the enclosure is laid out in gardens, in which the present tenants have wrought wonders. There is also a walk right round the outside of the moat, the bank of which has been formed into a kind of wild garden. To complete the picture I may add that the Castle lies at the junction of two valleys, and that the hills rise above it on every side to the height of some sixty feet.

Broughton came into the family of its present possessor in the middle of the fifteenth century, when William Fiennes, second Baron Saye and Sele, married the great-great-grand-daughter of the sister of the founder of New College: he fell fighting on the winning side at the Battle of Barnet, in 1471. His father, the first baron, was the unpopular Lord Saye of Shakespeare's *Henry VI.*, who was beheaded by Jack Cade; a large historical painting in which he is represented as pleading with the rebel for his life hangs in the Castle. To the Wykehams the Manor had passed from the De Broughton family, who built the Castle at the beginning of the fourteenth century. In the church is the effigy of a knight in chain armour, now daubed over with crude colouring, said to represent Sir Thomas de Broughton, a Latin inscription to whose memory, long disappeared, is preserved by Anthony Wood. From the time of the Wars of the Roses to the Civil War, the Fiennes are not conspicuous, but when the differences between King Charles and his several Parliaments began to develop they at once assumed a leading position on the popular side. William Fiennes, eighth baron and first Viscount Saye and Sele, had joined Hampden in his stand against the illegal exaction of ship-money, and he remained one of the most active members of the Westminster House of Lords till the end of the Civil Wars. After the trial and execution of the King, in which he took no part, he retired into private life till the Restoration, when he became Lord Privy Seal and Chamberlain of the Household. He died at Broughton at a ripe old age in 1662; his altar tomb of alabaster, covered with a black marble slab, stands beside that of his wife in the church. Staunch Royalists, such as Clarendon and Wood, draw an unfavourable picture of him, and he does not appear to have been wholly undeserving of his nickname "Old Subtlety," but unfortunately we have no character of him from a writer on his own side, to enable us to restore the balance. In his own neighbourhood his influence was supreme: a Puritan news-sheet recorded that he " sparkled many glimpses into the consciences of all that were near him, and enlightened more places besides Banbury." When the war broke out he raised a regiment of infantry

among his tenants, known from the colour of their uniforms as
"Lord Saye's Blue-coats," and in the top story of the Castle,
running the whole length of the house, is a long gallery, now
partitioned off into separate rooms, but still known as the
"Barracks," in which the soldiers slept. The Blue-coats did
good service at Edgehill, but Broughton surrendered quietly to
the King a few days after the battle, and from that time to the
end of the war it shared the fortunes of the neighbouring and
more important Castle of Banbury.

In the troublous times that preceded the outbreak of hostilities, Broughton was one of those retired country-houses where
the leaders of the Parliamentary party were wont to meet together
for consultation. A small room at the top of the house with
three outer walls is still called the "Council Chamber," and
here the Lord Saye is said to have assembled such men
as Pym, Hampden, Vane, Lord Brooke, and the Earls of
Warwick, Bedford and Essex. "The truth is," writes Anthony
Wood of Lord Saye, "he being ill-natur'd, choleric, severe and
rigid, and withal highly conceited of his own worth, did expect
great matters at Court ; but they failing, he sided therefore with
the discontented party, the Puritan, and took all occasions cun-
ningly to promote a rebellion. For so it was, that several years
before the Civil War began, he being looked upon at that time
the godfather of that party, had meetings of them in his house at
Broughton, where was a room and a passage thereunto, which
his servants were prohibited to come near ; and when they
were of a compleat number, there would be great noises and
talkings heard among them, to the admiration of those that
lived in the house, yet could they never discern their lord's
companions." There is an air of the stage conspiracy about
the story, but this would be no disadvantage in the eyes of the
worthy antiquary, who had no doubt picked up his account
from local gossip. He goes on to relate that similar meetings
were held at Fawsley, the home of the Knightleys, less than a
score of miles distant, and not far from the head waters of the

Cherwell, to which we shall soon have to make our pilgrimage. The son and heir of the house at this time was Sir Richard Knightley, who had married Hampden's eldest daughter, and was one of the chief local supporters of the popular party : like his friend Lord Saye, however, he held aloof from its final excesses and took part in the restoration of the monarchy. We cannot doubt that he was often one of the mysterious visitors to Broughton, and we can picture him riding over the hills from Fawsley, lost in anxious thought and awaking from his reverie at his journey's end to stable his horse in the ancient range of buildings by the moat.

It is with regret that we turn our backs upon the fine old mansion and church of Broughton, but since the days of the Civil War we have no record either of the history of the family, or of any events connected with the place. Would that one of the Fiennes, like Sir Ralph Verney, whose accumulations have furnished the materials for the delightful *Memoirs of the Verney Family*, had religiously preserved his correspondence and domestic papers ! The family story of Broughton might then have vied in interest with that of Claydon.

On reaching the top of the hill, before descending into Banbury, we pass an eminence on the right crowned with a clump of trees. This is Crouch Hill, the "May-morn Hill" as a local bard of the later eighteenth century calls it, from the fact that it was formerly visited on May morning by the young people of the neighbourhood. The view to be obtained from it extends for many miles over the surrounding country, and is duly lauded by the bard in question ; his poetic powers I will merely indicate here by quoting his comforting assurance that

" No craggy precipices here affright,
But gently rising hills and vales delight."

The top of the hill is evidently artificial, and was no doubt raised in order to communicate with the neighbouring camps. Thus the whole has a clearly defined conical appearance when

seen from a distance, and has of course been attributed to dia
bolical agency. The story, as quoted by the Banbury historian
is, that the three churches of Bloxham, Adderbury, and King'
Sutton were built by three masons, who were brothers; tha
the devil served them all as a labourer, and that one day h
fell down with a load of mortar and so made Crouch Hill.

CHAPTER IV

A BROKEN undulating region, full of ups and downs, is this
North Oxfordshire country. With the exception of the Stour,
which rises in Wigginton Heath, and the little brook which
waters the village of Long Compton, the many rills the
traveller has to cross all make their way southward to swell the
volume of the Thames. Towards one of these, the Swale, I am
taking my journey this morning, for it gives its name to a
village which may boast one of the most interesting churches
in the county. The church of Swalcliffe, like its neighbour at
Tadmarton, has been respected by the restorer. You have no
need to peer here and there with anxious eye to discover that
you have not entered a spick-and-span erection of yesterday.
The carved oak pews of the seventeenth century, the venerable
arcades, the fine, open, timber roof, and the perpendicular
chancel screen, which still retains traces of its original colouring,
strike you at once, and the charm of the whole is enhanced by
the warm tints of the native stone, and the flood of light which
in the absence of objectionable glass the windows are still able to
admit. Only in the chancel do we find scraped walls, and
other traces of the enemy. The pews and pulpit were the gift
of a branch of the Wykeham family, who long resided here ;
and the squire's house is still the property of their representative, while New College is the patron of the living. There
are two curious features in the church which we must notice ;
one, a doorway in the jamb of one of the windows of the south

aisle, approached by a staircase on the outside; it no doubt
led to a raised chapel; the other, two small windows over two
arches of the nave, one on either side. How they got there,
for they are evidently much older than the arches, is a puzzle.
It has been suggested they belonged to a pre-existing Saxon
church without aisles, and that when the arches were built, the
wall above containing these windows was shored up with props
to prevent the necessity of taking the roof off. Similar windows
are found at Witney and at Tysoe.

We may make our way northward from the village across the
fields by Madmarston camp to Shutford. To the south-east
of the camp, on some ground known as Blacklands, traces of
British and Roman settlements have been discovered. The
name of course refers to the colour of the soil, and occurs elsewhere in this district, where remains of ancient villages or
encampments have been found. The fact that the same site
had been occupied and built over by successive bands of
settlers would account for the darker colour of the earth. At
Shutford we shall stop to look at the tall, grey manor-house,
which quite dwarfs its near neighbour the church, but if we
express a desire to see the interior, we shall find that Highways
and Byways, and all such very unpractical matters, are by no
means to the taste of the occupier, and that we must confine
our curiosity to the outside. There is nothing else to detain
us at Shutford, so speculating on the carved mantel-pieces, long
galleries, and secret chambers which the forbidden mansion
doubtless contains, we take the Edgehill road, and turning off to
the right in a mile or two by a field-road we reach the twin
villages of Shenington and Alkerton, which crown the hill-tops
on either side of the Sor brook here running at the bottom
of a deep valley. Shenington is one of the villages in which
the custom of strewing the church with grass or rushes at
Whitsuntide is still kept up; certain lands were bound to
provide these materials, but the obligation is now commuted for a
fixed payment. The visitor, however, who is led to hope that a

G

church which preserves this old custom must have preserved
all else that should be preserved will be disappointed; it will be
enough to say that the fine Norman chancel arch has been
taken down, and actually put up again in the north wall of the
chancel! Accordingly we will lose no time in crossing the
valley to the still more picturesque village, and really unspoilt church of Alkerton. Round the outside of the church
is a cornice ornamented with figures in relief, as at Adderbury
and Hanwell: the figures on the south side have been taken
to represent the life of a man, and local tradition goes a step
further, and affirms that the man in question is the Black
Prince, even pointing to his triumphant entry into London on
his return from the French wars. Hard by the church is the
venerable Jacobean Rectory-house, built by Alkerton's most
celebrated rector, Thomas Lydyat. The son of the Lord of
the Manor of Alkerton, Scholar of Winchester, Fellow of New
College, and a writer of European reputation, in addition to
divinity, he devoted himself to the study of astronomy and
chronology. He recommended himself to Henry, Prince of
Wales, who appointed him his chronographer and cosmo-
grapher, and would have promoted him to higher honours had
he lived. But the Prince's early death in 1612 put an end
to his hopes, and he accepted the rectory of his native
village, of which his father was the patron. In this retired
spot he gave himself up to his studies, and published many
learned scientific treatises, of which the reader will find a
list in the *Dictionary of National Biography*. I do not, however, expect that he will be tempted to make the acquaintance
of the works themselves; he will be more interested in the
fortunes or misfortunes of the author, who after all his toil is
best known to-day by Johnson's famous lines in *The Vanity of
Human Wishes*:

> " There mark what ills the scholar's life assail,
> Toil, envy, want, the patron, and the gaol.
> See nations, slowly wise, and meanly just,

To buried merit raise the tardy bust.
If dreams yet flatter, once again attend,
Hear Lydyat's life, and Galileo's end."

In fact he had at one time generously pledged himself as
security for a brother's debts, and being unable to find the
money he was imprisoned, first in Bocardo at Oxford, and afterwards in the King's Bench, till the Warden of New College,
and other influential friends subscribed for his release. Nor
was this his only experience of duress; a staunch Royalist,
he suffered plunder and imprisonment at the hands of the
Roundheads, and returned to Alkerton so "infamously used"
by the soldiers, that his health was seriously affected. He died
at Alkerton in April, 1646, and was buried in the chancel of the
church.

A considerable portion of the county is owned by the
Colleges of Oxford: the traveller will notice how often his
inquiries as to the ownership of a farm are met by the answer
that it belongs to such and such a college. College property
it is true is scattered throughout the length and breadth of
England, but, it is naturally more frequent in the parts adjacent
to the University. Much of it came from founders and benefactors, but much was also bought by the colleges themselves
in the days when land was a profitable investment. Things
are otherwise now, but the farmer will still tell you that he would
rather hold under a college than under a private landowner;
the reason I fear often being that he manages to get more out
of the college in the way of improvements. It has been
said that the modern bursar is not such a good business
man as his predecessor, who himself often belonged to the
landed interest, but it is only natural that a corporation
should keep a less jealous eye on the margin of profit
than the individual landlord, whose rents are already too
reduced for him to exist upon. The Head of the House or
the Bursar still pays occasional visits to the farms, but much of
the inspection is now left in the hands of professional agents.

G 2

Formerly a college would make a solemn progress at stated periods through its estates: and in one of the Magdalen common-rooms still hang the horse-pistols and blunderbusses which it was prudent to carry on these occasions, while among the most interesting of the muniments of Merton are the accounts of the expenses incurred by the Warden and Fellows on a business journey down to Northumberland in the fourteenth century. At some colleges the annual rent dinner is still kept up; on these festive occasions the farmers gather together from a score or more of miles round the University town, and from early afternoon to late at eve the common-rooms steam with long churchwarden pipes and jorums of whisky punch. No wonder these hospitable societies make popular landlords!

But College tenants are not always farmers; Magdalen, for instance, has a considerable amount of valuable property in London, and I have been tempted into this digression because I am now approaching a kind of college property which I believe to be unique as such. At any rate I know of no other country mansion of the first rank belonging to an Oxford or Cambridge foundation; yet such is Wroxton. Wroxton Abbey, the home of the North family for seven generations, is the property of Trinity College, Oxford. I will explain how this came about directly; I first have to get there. From Alkerton to Wroxton is an easy ride of not more than three miles, and just before I enter the village I pass a venerable guide post, perhaps the oldest in the Midlands; it consists of a stone pillar with the names of the towns to which the divergent roads lead carved upon three of its sides, while on the fourth is an inscription recording the gift of this "handpost" by Mr. Fr. White in 1686. Turning to the right in the village I descend the hill, and reach the entrance to the Abbey. From the road you will see nothing of the house, but go a short distance up the drive and the fine gabled seventeenth century mansion stands facing you. Should you have permission to enter the house, the hall, the chapel, the library, the very remarkable collection of portraits and the

A Yard at Wroxton.

relics of the Stuarts and their times are enough to occupy you for many hours, and you may then wander through the grounds and look at the other side of the house across the long sweep of shaven lawn on the east. The Abbey the house is called, and has been so-called ever since it was built in 1618 by Sir William Pope, nephew of the founder of Trinity, and afterwards Earl of Downe; but in point of fact, the religious house which stood upon its site never ranked higher than a Priory. The distinction however, was generally forgotten after the Reformation, and Wroxton is by no means the only instance of the confusion.

Wroxton Priory was founded in the reign of John for a prior and regular Augustinian canons by one Michael Belet, whose family was connected with the neighbouring hamlet of Balscot. In 1534, the last prior surrendered to Henry VIII., and subscribed to the Royal supremacy. A few years later the site and demesnes of the Priory passed into the hands of Sir Thomas Pope, a native of Deddington, who rose to a position of great wealth and influence under Henry VIII. and his successors. He acquired vast estates in his native country as well as elsewhere, and Aubrey mentions that " he could have rode in his owne lands from Cogges (by Witney) to Banbury, about 18 miles." He is best known to posterity as the munificent founder of Trinity College, and the chief demesne with which he endowed his new foundation was the manor of Wroxton, subject however to a long lease, which was then (1555) held by his brother John Pope, and has been renewed by the College from time to time to John's descendants up to the present day. It was John's son William Pope, who, as already mentioned, built the existing mansion on the site of the Priory. William's grand-daughter, after the death of her brother, the last Earl of Downe, without issue, carried the lease into the family of the present lessees, by her marriage with Francis North, first Lord Guilford and Keeper of the Great Seal under Charles the Second. The Lord Keeper and his great-grandson, George the Third's Prime Minister, are the two most famous members of the North family; the former is perhaps best known to the general reader by his brother Roger's racy *Lives of the Norths.* The said Roger gives an amusing account of the way in which he and another brother, Dudley North, used to spend the summer time at Wroxton after the Lord Keeper's death. Under their brother's will they had been appointed trustees to his children, and they "thought it no disservice to our trust to reside upon the spot some time in summer; which we did and had therein our own convenience and charged ourselves in the accounts to the full value of ourselves and the diet for our horses." They turned an old building which had formerly served as mews for hawks (there must have been fine sport on the broad Oxfordshire uplands in old days) into a forge and carpenter's shop, and there they worked away till they were as black as tinkers. Indeed, the neighbours began to surmise that there was something uncanny about the whole proceeding: Dudley "coming out sometimes with a red short waistcoat, red cap, and black face, the country people began to talk as if we used some unlawful trades there, clipping at least; and it might be coining of money. Upon this we were forced to call in the blacksmith and some of the neighbours, that it might be known there was neither danger nor damage to the state by our operations." One of the toys they devised was a "way-wiser," which they fixed upon a chaise for the purpose of measuring the distances they travelled. It was a contrivance of wheels within wheels, and was fondly christened by its inventors "Sir Theophilus Gimcrack": then, as always, the rustic notions of distance were as vague as they are various, and the two brothers experienced "no small entertainment" in comparing their own measurements with "the unaccountable variety of vulgar estimates." Had the motor-car been invented in those days, we may be sure they would have delighted in it but they had to be contented with the "calash" and the "chaise." Since their time we

Silver Street, Wroxton.

hear no more of mechanical inventions at Wroxton. Just a
hundred years later, Francis North, third baron, and first earl
of Guilford,—the "noble Guilford" of the poet of Crouch
Hill,—seems to have been a country gentleman of the good
old style, and to have encouraged rural gatherings and festivities
in his grounds : my authority is the aforesaid local poet, and I
present the reader with a sample of his muse :—

> " Who knows not Wroxton's groves ? when spring revives,
>   To view the scenes where art with nature strives,
>   The nymphs and swains put on their best attire,
>   The season calls them, and their partners fire ;
>   Joyous they go ; they rove from sight to sight,
>   And shade to shade with wonder and delight ;
>   Till, Sol descending in the western skies,
>   They quit the prospect with unsated eyes ;
>   Then stop awhile at Drayton in the way,
>   Eat a plumb cake, or sip a cup of tea."

Drayton lay on the homeward road of those nymphs and
swains, who had come over from Banbury, but its "plumb cake"
and fragrant "tay" must be left untasted, for I do not pass
through it on my way to Hanwell, whither I am now bound. I
climb the hill to the picturesque village of Horley, whose grey
weather-beaten cottages cluster round its fine unrestored church.
As you enter the church by the south door you are confronted
by a large fresco of St. Christopher on the wall of the north
aisle. The saint, as usual, is represented as carrying the infant
Christ upon his shoulders, to whom he says :

> " What art thou, and art so yynge ?
>   Bar I never so hevy a thynge,"

and the answer is :

> " Yey, I be hevy, no wunther nys,
>   For I am the Kynge of blys."

These figures of St. Christopher were always large, and in
situations where they might be easily seen, for it was an ancient

Hanwell Castle.

belief, that whosoever had seen the figure would not die that day any sudden or accidental death.[1]

Hanwell lies across the valley to the west and a bend to the right after entering the village brings us face to face with a massive tower of brick with stone quoins, and large stone-mullioned windows, now blocked up. It reminds us of the almost contemporary work at Hampton Court, or of some of the college gate-houses at Cambridge. This tower is the sole surviving one of four which stood at each corner of the mansion, for three centuries the seat of the Cope family. It was built by William Cope, "cofferer of the household" to Henry the Seventh, who died in 1513, and was buried at Banbury: his tomb of black marble shared the fate of that church in 1790, and after lying there for 277 years his body was again exposed to the light, but immediately crumbled to dust. This was indeed an age in which the spirit of destruction ramped unchecked in this neighbourhood: some ten years previous to the demolition of the church of Banbury, Hanwell Castle was wantonly pulled down, and nothing left but this tower and part of the adjoining buildings. The remains are now used as a farm house. On the east side, sloping down to the valley are the once well-kept terraced gardens and fishponds; one of the latter alone is left, and the whole has a strangely pathetic, wistful air of desolation.[2] Yet here in Henry VIII.'s time lived Sir Anthony Cope, courtier, traveller, scholar, and writer: here his grandson, another Sir Anthony, kept "a hospitable house in the old English style," counting even Royalty among his guests; here the latter's son, Sir William, again entertained his sovereign, and here in the days of a third Sir Anthony were hatched some of the schemes which led to the happy Restoration of his late Majesty, King Charles the Second.

[1] See p. 303 for another example.

[2] "This was the state of affairs in August 1902: I am informed that the place has since been let on lease to a tenant who is judiciously restoring what remains."

From this it might be thought that the loyalty of the Hanwell family was unquestionable. Yet like the powerful neighbouring houses of Fiennes and Knightley, the Copes were noted far and wide for their Puritan tendencies, and from the middle of Elizabeth's reign to the opening of the Civil War, they were the patrons of some of the most celebrated Puritan divines of the day. When the war broke out the lord of Hanwell was a mere child, but his mother was a·Fane, a family which had espoused the cause of the Parliament, and the moral support of the Copes as long as their influence prevailed would be given to the same side. Nevertheless, as we shall see directly, the young Sir Anthony grew up to be an ardent royalist, and one of the most active promoters of the King's recall. But I am anticipating the march of events: two of the Puritan divines I have just alluded to were so closely associated with Hanwell that it would be a flagrant dereliction of duty on my part if I were to pass them by in silence. These were John Dod, Fellow of Jesus College, Cambridge, and Robert Harris, afterwards President of Trinity College, Oxford. The former held the living of Hanwell from 1580 to 1604, and according to the unimpeachable testimony of Fuller, was "by nature a witty, by industry a learned, by grace a godly divine." Time was when "the worthy sayings of old Mr. Dod" were the oracle of the country folk, and were long to be seen pasted upon the walls of their cottages : he is perhaps now chiefly remembered for his famous Malt sermon, which belongs to a time when he happened to be residing in a village near Cambridge. The story goes that he had become unpopular with the undergraduates by his denunciations of their excessive potations, and accordingly when a party of them in the course of a country ride descried " Father Dod " as they called him, coming towards them, they determined to have some sport with him, and compel him to preach them a sermon from the stump of a hollow tree, that was on the spot. Mr. Dod now came up, and they proceeded to ask him if the report of his having preached against drunkenness was true; on his admitting that it was, they said they had a favour to ask of him, that he would indulge them with a sermon on a text of their own choosing. It was in vain that the divine demurred to such an unreasonable request, they declared " that they were thoroughly persuaded he was master of elocution, never at a loss for matter upon any subject, that they could not bear the thoughts of a denial, and perhaps such a fair opportunity might never again present itself. Mr. Dod seeing himself beset replied, ' Well, gentlemen, as you are thus urgent for my compliance, pray what is the subject I am to handle ? ' They answered ' Sir the word is Malt, and for want of a better, here, sir, is your pulpit.' " Mr. Dod accordingly mounted the stump and began as follows : " Beloved, I am a little man, come at a short warning to deliver a brief discourse, upon a small subject, to a thin congregation, and from an unworthy pulpit. Beloved, my text is Malt, which cannot be divided into words, it being but one; nor into syllables, it being but one; therefore of necessity I must reduce it into letters, which I find to be these." He then made the letters, M, A, L, T do duty as initial letters for as many sentences as he required, the moral of the whole being the evil consequences of a misuse of malt liquor. The good old man, who lived to the age of ninety-five, spent the last twenty years of his life under the patronage of the Knightleys at Fawsley, where he died in 1645 ;

> " A grave divine ; precise, not turbulent ;
> And never guilty of the churches rent :
> Meek even to sinners ; most devout to God :
> This is but part of the due praise of Dod."

Robert Harris was a Gloucestershire man, and rector of Hanwell from 1614 to 1642. He was a scholar, a learned theologian, and a noted preacher. He gathered round him at Hanwell a select band of youthful students, and his sermons attracted hearers from all the country round. But the war brought his duties here to a close : one Sunday evening in

October, after he had finished his ministrations for the day, a man stained with blood and blackened with powder entered the village, with the news that a great battle had been fought that day at Edgehill, some half-dozen miles distant. The thunder of the artillery must have been clearly audible in the village, but so engrossed was the rector in the service of religion that, says his biographer, "hee heard not the least noise of it (which he took for a great mercy) till the publick work of the day was over." From Hanwell he removed to London, and afterwards to Oxford. He continued an energetic worker to the last, and died President of Trinity in 1658.

There is yet another divine, though of the opposite school, whose name will always be connected with Hanwell. Richard Allestree, student and afterwards Canon of Christ Church, and finally Provost of Eton, was an active adherent of the royal cause, and had fought both at Edgehill and at Worcester. He was one of those venturous spirits who secretly kept up the Church of England services in Oxford under Cromwell, and while thus engaged he attracted the attention of the young Sir Anthony Cope who, as mentioned above, had grown up an ardent royalist. He induced Allestree to come and reside with him at Hanwell, where in conjunction with others of the neighbouring gentry, he was busily engaged in fostering secret plans for the restoration of the king. Allestree, who besides being scholar, soldier, and divine, was also an accomplished courtier, threw himself heart and soul into their projects, and made several hazardous journeys between Hanwell and the exiled court, in the capacity of confidential agent. Unfortunately he has left us no journal of his adventures, or there would certainly have been ample material for another Stuart romance. Even as it is, we hear of an English lady who kept a lodging house at Dunkirk, and who seems to have become the wife of a brother of Sir Anthony's, much to the displeasure of the latter. After the Restoration Allestree became Canon of Christ Church, and Regius Professor of Divinity. His library, which still preserves his name, he bequeathed to the college for the use of his successors in the Professorship, who ever since have been its jealous custodians.

But I have lingered long enough in Hanwell. My road now leads me down through the village to the top of Bourton Hill overlooking the green valley of the Cherwell. From this vantage-ground on the morning of June 29, 1644, Sir William Waller watched the royal army marching northwards on the other side of the river. This manœuvre had been executed by the king, with the view of drawing the Parliamentary general from the strong position which he occupied on Crouch Hill south of Banbury, and so bringing him to an engagement. In this, as we shall see, he was successful. Sir William on his part was no less anxious to fight than the king. His troops were merely volunteers, composed of the London trained bands, and country levies, all heartily tired of soldiering, and eager to get back to their homes. They had not, like the men on the other side, taken up arms with any idea of entering the service as a profession, and the experience of this day convinced their general that nothing short of a radical reformation in this respect could ensure the ultimate success of the Parliamentary cause. Yet a decisive advantage might help to keep his men together for a time, and we may well believe that it was with an anxious heart that he surveyed the enemy separated from him only by the village of Cropredy, and the bridge over the Cherwell which was to give its name to that day's fight. At last he saw his opportunity. For some reason unknown to him, the van and centre of the royal columns had hurried forward above the bridge, leaving the rear in an isolated position below it.

How this had come to pass we shall see directly, but for a moment we will leave him, and descending the hill, pass through the village to the bridge, and survey the field of battle for ourselves. Two centuries and a half have rolled away since then, but the general features of the landscape have altered little. There is the venerable

church, itself more than three hundred years old on the day
when the battle was fought ; and there are the clustered roofs of
the cottages—brown thatch or grey tile—looking much as they
did then, for in these old world villages fashions change but
slowly.   There the little river comes bending round beneath
the church on its way from Edgcote, which Charles had quitted
nearly two years earlier in the grey dawn of an October
morning, passing over this very bridge on his march to Kineton
field, and there, half a mile down stream, is Slate Mill, and its
ancient ford—a passage to be contested to-day as hotly as the
bridge itself.   I say to-day, for in endeavouring to recall the
scenes of a vanished time, the fancy is prone to fall into the
present, but in sober earnest it is a bright summer's evening in
the twentieth century, and an aged countryman is leaning over
the wooden parapet of the bridge, in the contemplative mood,
that bespeaks the close of the labours of the day : yes, he has
heard tell of the fighting ; it was only nine or ten years ago
that his son was at work on the widening of the bridge, and
picked up bullets, and other "curiosities" in the bed of the
stream ; and hence he opines that here on the bridge "they
finished it up."   But he loves better to talk of things within
his own recollection ; of the coal which he used to cart to
Edgcote and other outlying villages, before the new railway
came, or of the great families of the neighbourhood, some of
whom, alas, were absentees and had "set" [i.e. let] their estates
at a mighty sum.   Of one of the most interesting relics he
does not tell me ; this is a small bugle-shaped whistle of silver
attached by two chains to a ring, which must have been lost in
the course of the struggle by some officer.   It was discovered
in grubbing up a hedge some fifty years since, and is now in
the possession of Mr. Loveday of Williamscot house, hard by
Slate Mill, whose ancestor, Captain Loveday, served in the
king's army, and it may be in this very battle.

    To that June morning we must now return.   Eastward from
the bridge the ground rises in the direction of the village of

Wardington, and on the summit, on this side of the Daventry road, there stands an ash tree, the successor of a famous tree known as the "Wardington ash," which perished of natural decay more than a century ago. Charles had reached this spot and was dining beneath the shade of this stately tree, when news was brought to him that a party of 300 horse was advancing from the north to join the forces of the enemy. He at once gave orders that the van and centre should push forward and cut them off, but in the hurry of the moment no notice was sent to the rearguard, which was at some little distance behind, together with the cavalry brigades of the Earl of Northampton and the Earl of Cleveland. This oversight, as we have seen, Waller's eye had not been slow to detect. Here was the chance he had been watching for, and he forthwith despatched a strong party of horse and foot to cross the bridge and take the royalist rearguard in front, while another body of horse was ordered to pass the river by the ford at Slate Mill, and fall upon them from behind. The former easily drove back from the bridge the dragoons, whom the king had posted there earlier in the day, and clattering across, were advancing to attack the leading division when they were brought up by a gallant charge of the Earl of Cleveland, and driven back by the way they had come. Before long, however, they rallied, and got themselves into order for a second advance; but by this time the king, alarmed by the noise of the *mêlée*, had halted, and realising the state of affairs, sent Lord Bernard Stuart in all haste to the assistance of the rear. Meanwhile, and before Stuart could reach him, Cleveland had formed his brigade on the hill round the Wardington Ash, but only to find the hedges within gunshot of him lined with the enemy both horse and foot. "This," says an eye-witness, "caused him suddenly to advance, the rebels doing the like; and having stoutly stood out their musket and carbine shot, he gave command to charge, and by his singular valour and resolution, seconded by the officers of his brigade, he routed all those horse and foot, and chased

H

them beyond their cannon; all which (being eleven pieces) were then taken, and two barricades of wood drawn with wheels, in each seven small brass and leathern guns, charged with case shot." Many of the enemy were slain and many prisoners taken; the rest were driven pell-mell over the bridge. This, however, the Earl was unable to carry, and was therefore compelled to fall back, having lost on his side two gallant gentlemen of Kent, Sir William Boteler and Sir William Clerk, "and," says my authority, "not above fourteen soldiers more." Meanwhile the Earl of Northampton had been equally success-ful against the party who had crossed by the ford: scarcely had they made their way across and begun to threaten his rear, when he faced about and "forced [them] to a speedy flight over the pass [*i. e.* the ford] but with little loss, they not being willing to abide a second charge." It was now three o'clock in the afternoon and the fighting was practically at an end. The advantage lay with the king, but he was unable to push it further. He secured the ford and the mill, but the enemy held grimly to the bridge, and all his efforts to dislodge them were in vain. Waller was worsted but far from annihilated, and for the rest of the day and the whole of the next, the armies lay facing each other on either side of the Cherwell, the king sleeping both nights at "a very poor man's house" at Williamscot. Early on Monday morning, intelligence having arrived that a large force under Major-General Browne was advancing to join Waller, Charles deemed it expedient to fall back upon Aynho and Deddington. At Deddington he lay at "the Parsonage house," probably the fine house already mentioned on the north side of the churchyard, and on the following day he set out for Evesham. But whatever hopes he may have built upon the discomfiture of Waller were soon to be dashed. As he was marching with colours flying through the pleasant Oxfordshire villages on that fatal second of July, another scene was being enacted in the north, and he was soon to be met by the disastrous tidings of the defeat of Marston Moor.

CHAPTER V

Less than a couple of miles above Cropredy the Cherwell makes its entrance into Oxfordshire, and the railway, which has been its constant follower all the way from Hampton Gay, some half-dozen miles to the north of Oxford city, here deserts it. Our business, however, is with the river rather than the rail, and I am therefore about to make a short excursion into Northamptonshire in order to trace the Cherwell to its source. This south-west corner of Northamptonshire was till quite modern times one of the most primitive and unfrequented districts in the Midlands. Readers of Thomas Mozley's rambling *Recollections* will remember the lively picture he draws of Moreton Pinkney, the Oriel living which he held in the 'thirties. In those days the farmer was content to spend the whole day in jogging to the local market at Towcester or at Daventry, and home again, but now that the railways have brought the more populous centres almost to his door, he will reach Northampton or Rugby in less than a quarter of the time, and the old markets are deserted or decayed. Not that the face of the country has been much changed; the Great Central, it is true, is a magnificent piece of engineering, and it sweeps through these rural solitudes with a royal disregard for impediments; but except at Woodford, where a new red-brick settlement has sprung up, the villages do not appear to have been much flustered by its arrival. On our route to-day we shall see little of it. The Daventry road passes under it

less than two miles from Banbury, and does not meet it again
till we get to Charwelton, where the line disappears into a tunnel
and we see the last of it. This Daventry road, by the way,
might not have been so pleasant to travel along in the earlier
days of George the Third as it is to-day. A few miles to my
right lies the village of Culworth, which was then the headquarters of a notorious confederacy of housebreakers and
highwaymen known as the Culworth Gang. Such a terror were
these miscreants to the whole country-side, and so inefficient
were the local Dogberries, that they managed to carry on their
depredations for nearly twenty years before they were brought
to justice. This was at last effected as follows: one evening
two men, known to be inhabitants of Culworth, arrived at a
public-house in Towcester, and signified their intention of
passing the night. They brought with them two bags which
as they said contained fighting-cocks. When they retired to
bed, the landlord, whose curiosity had been aroused, contrived
to open these bags, and found instead of the birds, smock-
frocks and masks. This was, to say the least, very suspicious,
particularly as several houses in the neighbourhood had recently
been broken into and robbed by persons thus disguised.
Nevertheless the landlord and the constable, whom he at once
took into his counsel, determined to say nothing for the present,
and watch events. They were not disappointed; in a day or
two another burglary of the same character was committed in
an adjacent village, and the two *soi-disant* cock-fighters were
arrested. Needless to say they belonged to the gang, and at
length, being uncertain how much information was in the hands
of the magistrates, and eager to shift the guilt off their own
shoulders, they turned upon their confederates, who were thus
brought to justice and the gang was at an end. Most of the
gang were ordinary agricultural labourers, but, sad to say, one of
them—a shoemaker by trade—filled the dignified office of parish
clerk at Sulgrave, and had taken advantage of his position to
conceal his share of the spoil in the church. This worthy was

also reported to have made a constant practice of carrying pistols in his pocket when performing his part in the church service.

But I have not got many miles on my journey when I am reminded that deeds of violence were not confined to the days of the Culworth Gang. As I wheel my machine up the steep hill leading to Wardington a monumental stone by the roadside attracts my attention. The inscription has become quite illegible, but the natives will tell you that the stone was put up to mark the scene of the murder of Kalabergo and that it is called Kalabergo's stone.[1] Kalabergo was an Italian watch-maker, who had left his native soil to escape the conscription of Napoleon and had been settled in Banbury for forty years. He was a familiar figure in the villages and farmhouses of the district, which he was in the habit of visiting periodically to mend the clocks, and sell his famous weather-glasses. At last in the autumn of 1851 a nephew arrived from Italy to assist him in his business, and it was understood that the old man looked upon him as his successor. Young Kalabergo, however, seems to have thought that waiting for dead men's shoes was tedious work, and one evening in the following winter as they were coming down this hill on their return from one of their rounds he drew a pistol and shot his uncle dead. He then hurried into Banbury with a story that they had been set upon by foot-pads, and that old Kalabergo had been killed. Suspicion however fastened upon the real culprit; the murder was clearly brought home to him, and he was hanged at Oxford Castle.

Wardington is soon reached, and at the further end of the village I turn off the high road to the right in quest of Danes-moor, a spot notable not merely as the traditional site of a conflict with the Danes, but for a more famous and more

[1] Since the above was written I am informed that this stone has been removed by some unknown mischievous persons. It has, however, been recovered, and is now in safe custody at the office of the Banbury District Council.

authentic struggle in the wars of the Roses. As for the Danes, they are known to have made a raid into this part of the country in the time of Edward the Elder, and John Morton, who was the first to write a history of Northampton-shire, records that in his day (the early eighteenth century) the country people used to repeat a "notable rhime," which they put into the mouth of the advancing host of Danes:

> " If we can Padwell overgoe, and Horestone we can see,
>   Then lords of England we shall be."

Padwell being "a noted flush spring in Edgcote grounds," and Horestone "a famous old stone on the borders of Warwick-shire in Wardlinton field." As we shall see later this distich is merely a variant of the better known one connected with the Rollright circle and as evidence of a battle with the Danes it will be safer to rely on the name Danesmoor itself. But one can well believe that these devastating hordes of heathen barbarians left many a legend behind them which in out of the way country places would be handed down from father to son for generations. To the later battle of 1469 we shall come directly. The Cherwell here flows through the secluded and beautifully wooded park of Edgcote, and through this park lies my road.

For a few short years Edgcote belonged to Thomas Cromwell, Henry VIII.'s Vicar-General, but in 1543 it became the property of the Chauncy family, from whom it passed to its present owners. The church, which is hard by the mansion, must be visited if only for its fine series of Chauncy monu-ments; it is still unrestored and has many features which will delight the antiquary. The present house is one of those spacious comfortable looking country homes it was the fashion to build 150 years ago; its solid substantial air indicates at a glance hospitality and good living, and suggests that here at any rate we have found a place where the orthodox old English Christmas of Bracebridge Hall might still be kept. It was in

the Tudor mansion which it replaced that Charles the First
and his sons were entertained the night before Edgehill fight by
the squire of that day.

Danesmoor I find marked on the ordnance map about a
mile to the south-east of the village—I should explain, by the
way, that I use the word village in a retrospective sense : such
village as there was, and there were less than a score of houses,
was pulled down when the new mansion was built, now
besides this and the rectory there are barely a dozen scattered
houses in the whole parish—and I therefore follow the road
that winds through the park in that direction to Trafford
bridge, where an ancient trackway, still called the Welsh Road
from the fact that it was used by Welsh drovers on their way
to southern fairs, crosses the Cherwell. Here I endeavour to
gather from some labourers in an adjacent field whether any
traditions of the battle still lingered on the spot, but all that is
to be elicited from them is that "over there" across the
brook *that* is Danesmoor. So over there I go, and after
surveying the field and making my own conjectures as to the
battlefield make my way back to the bridge. Here I meet
with a neat-looking woman on her way to an adjacent farm ;
perhaps she may have something to tell me : well, if she had
not actually heard of a battle, she had heard tell of something
of the kind. At any rate years ago her husband had taken her
up into the wood on the other side of the river near the great
house, and had shown her certain stone statues, "the bloody
something, they call them, I can't remember what." All this
sounds so promising that I determine to explore the said wood
at once, and inspect the awful figures myself. Further on, near
the house, I find an aged carpenter at work, from whom I learn
that they are familiarly known as the "Bloody Warriors," and
that in his opinion they once formed part of a large tomb in
the churchyard, and were removed to their present situation
about a hundred years ago. The latter part of this statement
is certainly rather discouraging, but then—"The Bloody

Warriors"! Here in the immediate vicinity of a York and Lancaster battlefield, can it be that some frail memorials of the struggle still survive? What if these "Warriors" should prove to be the verae effigies, clad in complete steel, of the Earl of Pembroke himself and his redoubtable brother? I am not to be deterred by the old man's hints of the difficulty of finding them, or of the danger to be apprehended from the squire; and I therefore lose no time in engaging the services of a youthful native, who leads me past the mill, and across the river to the outskirts of a thick wood. We then plunge through a tangled undergrowth of nettles and reach an unfrequented woodland road. Here my guide is for some time altogether at fault, but at last I hear his voice calling to me that he has found them, and I follow the sound till I emerge in an open place in the middle of a dark thicket overshadowed by funereal trees,— the place of all others for a rustic Dodona. Whether like the Whispering Knights, which we shall come to later, the Bloody Warriors have ever been used as the rustic oracle I cannot say, but here they stand—or rather here *it* stands, for all that I can see is a four-sided stone pillar, which occupies in solitary grandeur the centre of the arena. Four figures there certainly are cut in relief on the four sides, but as for the "Warriors"— they are and must remain the phantoms of the rustic brain: all that the profaner eye can see is the conventional presentment of the four ages of man ornamenting the four sides of what was evidently once the pillar of a sun-dial: the style of the whole, as well as the costumes of the figures, is sixteenth century, and the sun dial no doubt once ornamented the grounds of the former Tudor mansion-house, and was removed to its present position when that was pulled down, and the present eighteenth century mansion erected.

After this mild disappointment it is time we returned to the scene of the actual battle. In 1469 an insurrection, encouraged by the great Earl of Warwick, broke out in the North of England, and a host of disaffected Northerners marched southwards upon London. They were nominally under the command of a person of doubtful identity who took the name of "Robin of Redesdale," but the actual leader was Sir John Conyers, of Hornby in the County of York, an old soldier of influence and ability. King Edward was now at Nottingham waiting for reinforcements. The troops at his disposal consisted of 18,000 Welshmen under the command of William Herbert, Earl of Pembroke, and his brother Sir Richard Herbert of Coldbrook. These were advancing from Wales, and as they crossed the Cotswold they were joined by Lord Stafford of Southwick, newly created Earl of Devon, with 6,000 archers from the south-western counties. The combined forces now altered the direction of their march towards Northampton, for which town the rebels were reported to be making, and they had got as far as Daventry, or somewhere not far from that place, when they caught sight of the enemy's columns; Pembroke sent forward a party to attack them in the rear, but this attempt was a failure, and the royalists pressed on to Banbury. Here a quarrel as to quarters took place between the leaders, which resulted in the defection of the Earl of Devon and all his archers. "The erle of Pembroke," says the Chronicler, "putte the Lorde Stafforde out of an Inne, wherein he delighted muche to be, for the loue of a damosell that dwelled in the house. . . . After many great woordes and crakes, had betwene these twoo capitaines, the lord Stafford of Southwyke, in greate dispite departed with his whole compaignie and band of Archers, leauynge the erle of Pembroke almost desolate in the toune." Meanwhile the Welshmen had taken up a position on the hill to the west of Danesmore, where Edgcote Lodge now stands, while the rebels occupied the hill to the south near Thorpe Mandeville. Pembroke arrived in the camp on the 25th of July, the day after his quarrel with Devon. On the evening of this day "Sir Henry Neuell sonne to the Lorde Latimer, tooke with hym certaine light horssemen, and skirmished with the Welshemen . . . euen before their campe, where he did diuerse valiaunt feates of armes, but a litle to hardy, he went so farre forward that he was taken and yelded, and yet cruelly slain: which unmercifull acte, the Welshmen sore ruied the next daie." For the next morning the rebels, who had by this time heard of the departure of Devon and his archers, attacked the royalist position, and drove them down the slope to the low-lying meadow of Danesmoor, which is watered by a tiny brook, that joins the Cherwell at Trafford bridge. Here the day was hotly contested, and the Welshmen were beginning to get the best of it, when they were startled by a cry of " a Warwick, a Warwick!" and raising their eyes to the hillside on the east of the valley, they saw a body of men descending the slope, headed by the well known standard of that house, with its dreaded cognisance, the White Bear. Thinking that the terrible Earl was upon them, they turned and fled. The Northerners were not slow to pursue, and they took a terrible vengeance for the death of young Henry Neville; 5,000 Welshmen were slain, and among the prisoners were the Earl of Pembroke and his brother. The advantage had however only been gained by a ruse: "beholde the mutabilitie of fortune," exclaims the Chronicler, "when the Welshemen were at the very poynt to haue obteyned the victory (the Northernmen beyng in manner disco'fited) Iohn Clappam Esquier, seruante to the erle of Warwycke, mou'ted up the syde of ye east hyl, acco'panied onley with ccccc. men gathered of all the Rascal of the towne of Northampton and other villages about, hauying borne before them the standard of the Erle." Two days later Pembroke and his brother were beheaded,— according to the earliest and best authorities, at Northampton; but according to Hall, a sixteenth century chronicler, at Banbury. A tradition, adopted by Wordsworth in his *White Doe of Rylstone*, states that the church porch at Banbury was the scene of the execution, and that Clapham there beheaded the

Earl with his own hands. The reader may like to refresh his memory of Wordsworth's lines ; the poet is speaking of Bolton Priory :—

> " Pass, pass who will, yon chantry door ;
> And through the chink in the fractured floor
> Look down and see a griesly sight ;
> A vault where the bodies are buried upright
> There, face by face, and hand by hand,
> The Claphams and Mauleverers stand ;
> And, in his place, among son and sire,
> Is John de Clapham, that fierce Esquire,
> A valiant man, and a name of dread,
> In the ruthless wars of the White and Red ;
> Who dragged Earl Pembroke from Banbury Church,
> And smote off his head on the stones of the porch ! "

Soon after crossing the Cherwell the road through the park from Edgcote to Chipping Warden passes the earthworks of an ancient fortress, probably one of those numerous Norman " castles " which were so lightly thrown up in Stephen's reign and as lightly demolished. Except however for the view over the valley behind me there is nothing to tempt me to stop, and I pass through the lodge gates to find myself face to face with the church of Chipping Warden, and the tiers of steps which form the massive base that once supported its market-cross. We may praise the men of old time, who set up their crosses on these substantial foundations ; the expense and trouble which their removal would entail was more than the most zealous of Puritan iconoclasts cared to face. Let us ascend the steps and take a survey of the church, one of the most noteworthy and, like Edgcote, one of the most unspoilt that we have come upon so far. The spacious and harmonious proportions of the interior, the old oak pews, the fine original roofs, the curious chapel at the end of the north aisle, and the beautiful early English sedilia and piscina at the end of the south aisle, all demand a tribute of admiration. Opposite the church the sixteenth century manor-house of the Saltonstalls completes the picture. Here in William the Third's time resided a certain Colonel Montagu, a relative of Charles Montagu the "Junto" minister and poet, into whose family the property had passed by marriage. This gallant gentleman was of course one of the principal supporters of the Whig interest in the county, and by no means disposed to shut his eyes to the dangerous proclivities of his Tory neighbours. Of one of them at any rate he was determined to make an example. This was William Plowden, Esq., of Aston-le-walls and the builder of the present manor-house there, himself also a colonel, but a colonel of King James, and ancestor of the Plowdens of Plowden Hall in Shropshire. It does not appear that Colonel Montagu had any definite grounds for suspicion, but what could be expected but treason from a Romanist and a Jacobite? It conveniently happened that a somewhat severe Act of Parliament had been passed as a terror to the Nonjurors, and he resolved that the rival colonel should have a taste of its penalties. Accordingly one fine morning when the Squire of Aston-le-walls drove into Banbury according to his custom in his coach and six, his horses were seized and impounded in his Majesty's name. The story does not say how soon he succeeded in getting them out of pound or how he managed to get back to Aston manor, but so disgusted was he at the way in which he had been treated by his Whig neighbours that he left Aston altogether, and his descendants who still own the estate have never lived there since.

We can pursue our journey to Charwelton either along the high road through Byfield, or further to the right by the devious course of the Cherwell valley, where the modern hunting inn at Hinton Gorse can offer us rest and refreshment; the latter route is the more picturesque, but as I am anxious to reach what will be the "farthest north" of this volume as soon as possible, I shall take the former. I shall therefore leave unvisited both the Roman bath down close to the river at

Trafford bridge, and the extensive villa at Blackgrounds
nearer to the village, to which under the idea that the remains
were those of a whole town the fanciful name of Brinavis was
formerly given.

The high road commands an extensive view of the Edgehills
to the left, and at the foot of the steep rise about a mile from
Chipping Warden, is one of those " leaping-blocks " that were
so commonly to be seen at inn doors in former days. This one
bears an inscription partially defaced, but you can still make
out that "Thomas Hight . . . . of Warden set up this . . . .
July 30 1659." The road now passes through a deep cutting
in the hillside, but formerly it was much steeper, and many a
horseman must have blessed the memory of the benefactor, as
he remounted his nag after accomplishing the descent. Nowadays it is a light matter to wheel one's cycle to the crest of the
hill, and an easy run thence through Byfield till we once more
meet the river in Town Charwelton,—Town Charwelton for
Church Charwelton is a mile away down stream, and we must
not visit it till we have completed our pilgrimage to the most
northerly of all the springs whose waters combine to pour through
London Bridge. But it is a far cry from London Bridge to the
first bridge over the infant Cherwell, to which we must give
more than a passing glance. For on your machine you will
ride past it and not over it, and if you have not your eyes about
you, you will have left the river far behind before you discover
that you have crossed it. The reason is that it here flows
under the road in the darkness of a modern culvert, which
said culvert is continued under the ancient bridge itself. Built
as long ago as the thirteenth century this bridge is as strong and
solid as ever : there it stands, just wide enough for the passage
of a string of pack-horses, with its two pointed arches and its
sturdy cutwater, the wise provision of the roadmakers of that day
against perils by water ; for the road then passed the river by a
ford, and even yet in times of flood the bridge is still the refuge
of the foot passenger. The natives proudly call it "the highest

bridge in England : " for " England " read " Northamptonshire," and you need not tax them with idle boasting, for here we have attained a level of nearly six hundred feet, and the highest ground to be found in the whole county is barely two hundred feet higher.

A striking contrast to this weather-beaten relic of the past is the brand new red brick bridge over the Great Central Railway, which is crossed a few yards further on, and then we bear away to the left along an open field road till at a solitary farmhouse we reach the goal we are looking for. Deep down in the cellars of his house the farmer could show you not many years ago a spring of limpid water bubbling forth from below, but now the spring has been bricked over, and though sometimes heard is seen no more. This is the source of the Cherwell ; in the farmyard it has already formed a head, and a mile lower down is formidable enough to be honoured with the bridge.

Just across the watershed to the north is Fawsley, and though strictly beyond our limits, so slight is the détour from the direct road to Church Charwelton, that the temptation to transgress is irresistible. For Fawsley is one of those country homes which help to elevate, and I may say idealise our conception of England and the life of Englishmen. We cannot help feeling that it is in no small measure to such places as Fawsley that all that is strongest in English character and English institutions is due : it will be an ill day for the country when they and their traditions are swept away. Fawsley has been the home of the Knightleys since the time of Henry the Fifth. Hampden's son-in-law, Sir Richard Knightley, has already been mentioned as one of the leading spirits in the councils of the Parliamentary leaders at Broughton before the war. Similar gatherings at his invitation took place at Fawsley, and here, remote from prying eyes, his father, Richard Knightley, Esq., and himself would entertain such guests as Hampden, Pym, St. John, Lord Saye, and his son, Nathaniel

Fiennes, Lord Holland, and the Earls of Bedford, Warwick, and Essex. This was not the first occasion on which the Puritan tendencies of the family had been manifested. Another Sir Richard, who succeeded to the estate in 1566, took an active part in the agitation against the bishops, which gave birth to the rabid " Martin Marprelate " controversy. He even went so far as to allow one of the private presses of the agitators to be set up in his house, and " The Epitome," one of the Marprelate manifestoes, to be printed here. For these proceedings he was cited before the Star Chamber and fined £2,000, but thanks to the friendly offices of Archbishop Whitgift the fine does not appear to have been enforced.

Fawsley, like Edgcote, lies secluded from the work-a-day world. From the Daventry road a field way shaded by immemorial elms conducts you to the park, a wide expanse of hill and dale, of ancient forest and open lawn The house stands on a peninsula between two broad stretches of water—a stately well-knit pile, but somehow less captivating than Edgcote. Edgcote, moreover, eighteenth century as it is, is of one date ; solid comfort was the ideal of its builder, and there is nothing to break the unity of the impression it produces. Fawsley, on the other hand, has been much altered and added to, even as late as the last century. The most interesting feature of the existing mansion is the spacious hall built by Sir Richard Knightley in Henry the Eighth's time. Strangely enough the fine oriel window, ordinarily found at the end of the daïs, is here placed at the lower or gallery end. On the roof of this window a small chamber has been contrived, though the staircase which once led to it has disappeared. In the well-filled library, besides the books which ought to be found in any country-house of long standing, are some time-honoured theological treatises, dear to the Puritan ancestors of the family—volumes which remind us that the venerable John Dod spent the last twenty years of his life as vicar here, and a short walk from the house takes us to the church

where he ministered. On entering the church through a
singularly narrow Early English doorway, you are at once struck
by the width of the space that is left unencumbered by
pews ; it is indeed little more than the family chapel, for the
whole parish is the family domain and the parishioners are few.
Far less room than usual is therefore required for the accommodation of the living, and all the more left for the monuments
of the dead. Of these, as is natural when the history of a
family extends over five centuries, there are many, the altar
tomb, and alabaster effigies of the Sir Richard Knightley, who
died in 1534, and his wife being the most conspicuous.

It is a pleasant walk through the fields to Church Charwelton, where the church and manor-house, now the residence
of the rector of the parish, have survived the village that once
existed here. John Rous, the Warwickshire antiquary, writing
in the latter part of the fifteenth century, mentions it as one of
the villages which owed their destruction to the grasping policy
of the landowners, who were now converting arable land
into pasture, and making enclosures on a large scale for
the more profitable business of sheep-raising. We have
already alluded to this innovation in connection with Sir Henry
Lee, of Ditchley. Rous complains that whereas Church
Charwelton was formerly a considerable village, and famous for
providing ample accommodation for persons journeying between London and the Midlands, they now had to turn out of
their direct road to find quarters in Town Charwelton, and
that even here similar danger was threatened.

The church is well worth a visit for the sake of the fine series
of brasses and monuments of the Andrew family, who at one
time held both the ancient manors comprised in this parish,
viz., Thorney manor, which had belonged to the Abbey of
Thorney, in Cambridgeshire, and Bittlesden manor, which had
belonged to Bittlesden Abbey, in Buckinghamshire. Thorney
manor-house, now called the Hall, is situated on the Cherwell
a little way above the bridge in Town Charwelton ; it is still a

picturesque old structure, and retains traces of its former consequence in its extensive fishponds.   Bittlesden manor-house is the house near the church already mentioned: it has a fine oak panelled room, with a still earlier oak frieze carved with grotesque figures.   The house was partly rebuilt by the Adams family who succeeded to the Andrews about 1620, and

Fenny Compton.

remained here till the beginning of the nineteenth century: a tombstone in the church to Thomas Adams, linen-draper, of London, who died in January 168$\frac{8}{9}$, illustrates the custom then so general (and commendable) of putting the younger sons of a county family into trade.   Thorney remained with the Andrews till 1648, and both manors are now part of the Fawsley inheritance.

I feel that I must crave the reader's indulgence for taking up his time with these details, but the two Charweltons and Fawsley form a group so engaging and so eloquent of a bygone age, that it is impossible to pass them over with the scant tribute of a line or two. We have, however, many miles to travel and many things to talk about before we get to the end of this chapter, so without further delay we must now regain the Daventry road and retrace our steps as far as Byfield, where the turn to the right will take us past Wormleighton, with its Spencer tombs, to Fenny Compton at the foot of the Edge-hills. A snug, pleasant place is this, the prevailing colour being still that of the rich brown native stone, but perhaps the passing stranger will be more struck by the appearance of the church spire than by anything else. It looks as if it had some-how grown shorter, and you might conjecture that it is the result of some freak of fancy on the part of the builder, but in point of fact its stumpiness is due to economy rather than design. In the eighteenth century it was struck by lightning, and was rebuilt without replacing the damaged stones. From the "fenny" country—the fen is not much in evidence now—it is a climb of some three hundred feet to the summit of the Dassett or Dercett hills. At Burton Dassett, a mile away to my right, stands the ancient beacon tower, from which the tidings of Edgehill fight were flashed to the shepherds of Ivinghoe, forty miles to the south-east, and by them signalled on to London. But I cannot see the beacon as I climb the hill between the tall hedgebanks, their heads crowned with festoons of white convolvulus, and their feet hidden amid masses of tall pink willow-herb. So over the crest and down through the trim village of Avon Dassett and the deep rich meadows beyond, till another ascent at Warmington bids me once more dismount. The village nestles umbrageously at the foot of the hill, but the church crowns the summit, and a long flight of steps must be climbed in order to reach it from the road. As I walk round the

Warmington.

exterior of the church, I am attracted by a singular building of
two stories projecting from the north wall of the chancel, and
partly covered by thick masses of ivy.   There is a strange
weird look about its crumbling masonry, as though it were
silently protesting against the many lawless uses to which it has
been put, since it could no longer serve its original purpose.
What that was we may guess if we enter the church, and pass
through a small door in the chancel wall.   We now stand in a
dimly-lighted chapel containing a stone altar, and a winding
stair in the corner conducts us to an upper chamber, which
once served as a dwelling for the ministering priest.   In
the south wall of this chamber is a window overlooking the
high altar of the church, through which he might keep
watch.   Two-storied buildings of a similar character exist
at Cropredy and at Edgcote.   Among the gravestones in
the churchyard to the south of the church, is one to the
memory of Captain Alexander Gaudin, with the significant date
—October, 1642.

Indeed as we ride along Camp Lane past Nadbury Camp to
the crest of Edgehill we have no thoughts for any other date
than this—to be precise, Sunday, October 23rd, 1642, for
on this day, as everybody knows, was fought the first battle
between King and Parliament, and the Civil War began
in earnest.   The long line of the Edgehills forms the
Warwickshire portion of that steep escarpment which
facing the north-west overlooks the great central plain
of the Midlands.   So gradual is the ascent on the other
side, that the traveller coming from the south or south-east is
astonished to find himself suddenly and without any warning at
the brink of an almost precipitous descent, a descent which
the high roads both here at Edgehill and throughout the
Cotswold are compelled to negotiate by careful windings and
zigzags.   One of these roads at Knoll End, the point we have
now reached, descends to Kineton ; another, a couple of miles
further on, makes its way down by Sunrising House to Stratford.

The extensive view from the hill I shall not attempt to describe; it has been done over and over again in the guide-books.

> " Like a tall Rampart ! here the Mountain rears
> It's verdant Edge ; and if thy tuneful Maids
> Their Presence deign, shall with PARNASSUS vie.
> Level, and smooth the Track, that leads to thee !
> Its adverse Side a Precipice presents
> Abrupt, and steep ! Thanks, MILLER ! to thy Paths,
> That ease our winding Steps ! "

So sang the Rev. Richard Jago in the 2459 lines of ponderous blank-verse which he printed in 1767 under the title of *Edge-hill or the Rural Prospect delineated and moralised.* The reader will probably think the delineation quoted enough for him. The village at the bottom of the hill is Radway, and Radway Grange, the fine Tudor mansion with its park climbing the hillside, still belongs to the descendants of the " Miller " apostrophised above. This was Sanderson Miller, an architect and antiquary of taste, who succeeded to the estate in 1735. His most famous works are the house at Hagley, designed for the first Lord Lyttleton, and the County Hall, at Warwick. He was visited at the Grange by some of the most distinguished men of the day, and the family tradition relates that once when Henry Fielding was among the guests staying in the house he read the manuscript of *Tom Jones* aloud to them in the dining-room, in order to get their opinion upon it before offering it to the publishers. It is even asserted that several traits in Squire Allworthy's character were derived by the novelist from that of his host. Another visitor at this time was William Pitt, the elder, and a clump of trees in the park is recorded to have been planted by him. The church formerly stood at some distance to the west of the village, but it was removed to its present situation in 1865 in order to make it more accessible. In the tower is the effigy of Captain Henry Kingsmill, who was slain in the battle by a shot from a field piece ; tradition says that this happened as he was ascending the hill on a white horse, and so became a conspicuous mark for the Roundhead gunner.

The battle of Edgehill belongs to the History of England, but the right book is not always at hand, and the reader who has accompanied me so far may not be displeased to hear the tale once more. The King, he will remember, was marching upon London from Shrewsbury, while Essex was hastening in the same direction from Worcester with the view of intercepting him. For some miles the two armies had been advancing parallel to each other without either being aware of the other's presence. The night before the battle Charles spent at Sir William Chauncy's, at Edgcote, as before mentioned, and here about three o'clock in the morning he was roused by an express from Rupert, with the intelligence that the camp fires of Essex had been seen from the Dassett hills in the valley in front of Kineton. He at once issued the order that his army should assemble at daybreak on the summit of Edgehill. It was some time before the whole of his forces reached the rendezvous from their various quarters, and he did not himself arrive at Knoll End before noon. Here he reconnoitred the enemy's position through a field-glass. Essex had drawn up his army in a strong position, protected by furze brakes and brushwood, at some little distance from the foot of the hill. The Royal troops were now formed along the edge of the hill, which was not then covered with thick woods as it is now. In the centre was planted the Royal Standard, and the Tower, or "Round House," which now forms such a conspicuous landmark, was built by Sanderson Miller in 1750 to mark the spot. Here the King took his station with the Earl of Lindsey in command of his regiment of foot guards. On the right was Rupert and his horse; on the left Henry Wilmot, afterwards Earl of Rochester, with another detachment of cavalry. Essex was too good a general to attempt to attack an army in such a position, while for the King, in a district disaffected to his cause, and with the hostile garrison of Banbury in his rear, an engagement was a necessity. Accordingly, about one o'clock, he gave the order to descend the hill, and advance to the attack. It is said that as he passed the church the bells were ringing for evening service, but the vicar, the Rev. Jeremiah Hill, must have had a poor congregation on that afternoon. By three o'clock the fighting had begun. Rupert in the first of his ill-starred charges utterly routed the Parliament's left wing and drove the panic-stricken fugitives pell-mell into the streets of Kineton. Here, instead of re-forming and taking the enemy's centre in flank or rear, he allowed his troopers to waste their time in plundering the baggage waggons, till it was too late to be of any service. On the left Wilmot likewise charged, and drove back the Parliament right till he was stopped by some hedgerows and ditches about half a mile in front of Little Kineton, when, after hard fighting, he was driven back to the rising ground near the modern farm of Lower Westcote. "This," says the present vicar of Radway, who has made a minute study of the fight in all its details, "and other disputed points have been elucidated of late years by the deep cultivation and deep draining of the land, which has brought to light bullets and other débris of the battle which had lain buried in the ground." Meanwhile, in the Parliament's centre, the regiments of Essex and Holles stood firm to receive the attack of the Royal Foot Guards. "Here again," continues the vicar, "the Royalists drove back their enemies at the first onset, though they had, after crossing the Radway brook under fire, to breast the higher ground of the ridge on which Essex had posted his troops. The rising ground and ridge were naturally covered with furze and brushwood. Through these the King's troops drove their opponents, but when they came to the old hedgerow between the present farms of Thistleton and Battleton, which houses do not appear to have existed in those days, Essex's musketeers, who were drawn up behind it, barred the King's advance. The carnage in front of the hedge must have been great, as hereabouts the largest portion of the débris of the battle has been brought of late years to view." Fully occupied as they thus were in front, the Royalists were simultaneously harassed in the flank and rear by the small regiments of Balfour and Stapleton, which were the only cavalry that still remained in the field. It was in this struggle that the gallant Lindsey fell mortally wounded, and Sir Edmund Verney, of Claydon, who bore the Royal Standard, was struck down and the Standard captured. It was soon afterwards recovered by the adroitness of an officer of the Life Guards, Captain Smith, of Skilts, near Tamworth. Picking up an orange scarf which had fallen from one of Essex's soldiers, and accompanied by one or two comrades similarly disguised, he slipped in amongst the Parliamentary troops, and finding the Standard in the hands of Essex's secretary, told him that "it were shame that so honourable a trophy of war should be borne by a penman." The secretary thereupon surrendered the trophy to the captain, who succeeded in carrying it back to the King. Darkness was now coming on, and though Rupert's troops were now straggling back to the field, it was impossible to collect a sufficient force of horse to charge the enemy again ; both sides therefore drew off, and though both sides claimed the victory, the result remained undecisive. Thus were the expectations disappointed of the many who thought that a single battle would suffice to decide the issue of the war.

In the evening the King's carriage (it seems that the country roads were then good enough for great personages to travel in carriages ; Essex's carriage was captured in Kineton by Rupert) was brought down the hill from Knoll End, by a track still known as King Charles's Road, to a spot beyond the village now marked in the maps as King's Ley Copse. Here Charles passed the night, and on Monday morning, according to local tradition, he walked into Radway and breakfasted at a farm-house, which was still standing as late as 1882. The two armies were then again drawn up in order of battle, but neither side cared to assume the offensive, and as the evening came on Essex retreated to Warwick, while the King fell back towards Oxford.

Many local traditions of the fight have doubtless been irretrievably lost, and in these days when village boys and girls quit their homes as soon as they can for the excitement of town life in the shop or factory, any that remain are less likely than ever to survive; but they are always worth listening to when they can be arrived at; and when they have been faithfully handed down in the same family for generations, they may be accepted with little hesitation. The vicar of Radway in his *Rambles round the Edge Hills* has preserved three traditional anecdotes which were related to him " by a man over seventy who heard them from his grandmother, who lived to be over ninety. She heard them from her grandfather, who was a boy when the battle was fought." I have not space for them here, but I quote these words to show how carefully the oral record of striking events was once preserved in the country side. I must, however, present the reader with a brief account of the battle as given about 1833 by an aged labourer residing on the spot, and recorded by Beesley. The old man was standing on the hill near the Tower: " the King," he said, " was on the hill here; the others came Kineton way. They fought in two companies; one along the hill at Bullet Hill [Knoll End] where the road comes up; but the main in the vale at Battleton and Thistleton. They on the hill drove the others down into Kineton; while they at Battleton and Thistleton made head, and forced the King back to the hill." This shows that a very accurate general idea of the battle had been current on the spot for two hundred years.

If the way-farer is genuinely desirous of an intimate acquaintance with Edgehill and its associations he cannot do better than take up his quarters there for a night or two, and I can assure him that he will find capital entertainment at one of the houses opposite to the Tower. Years ago I should have sent him on a mile further to Sunrising, a spot I have already mentioned in connection with the battle.   Here was a noted coaching inn well known to the traveller for its dinners and its port, and thanks to its remote and romantic situation a favourite resort of newly married couples.   But alas, its hospitable doors have long been closed: the house is now much altered, and has become a private residence.   Its very name has been changed and what was once the Sunrising Inn is now Edgehill House.   Yet "inn" or "house," it still looks down upon the fertile valley which from very ancient times has been known as the Vale of the Red Horse.   The name is derived from the figure of a horse cut in the red soil on the side of the hill, and this horse was "scoured" annually on Palm Sunday at the expense of the particular freeholder, who held certain lands in the manor by this service.   This horse was destroyed at the time of the enclosures in 1798, and the annual fair which was held in connection with the scouring was in danger of becoming extinct.   This, however, would have been a contingency highly detrimental to the custom of the worthy host of the Sunrising ; another horse was therefore promptly carved out in a field adjacent to the inn, and the annual merrymaking got a further lease of life.   Whether this modern horse still exists or not, I cannot say, but in any case it is of little interest.   It is of more interest to inquire into the origin of the old one ; but what that was can only be a matter of conjecture.   The story that it was cut by the Kingmaker in memory of the horse he slew on Towton field, is extremely improbable, since the valley was called the Vale of the Red Horse long before his time, but the fact that the battle of Towton was fought on a Palm Sunday may have connected Warwick and the Yorkist victory with the Palm Sunday scouring. The simplest solution of the mystery is that of the Rev. Richard Jago at the end of the first book of his redoubtable poem. After dismissing (in a dozen magniloquent lines) the recondite poetic fancies that the horse was due to a freak of Nature, lightning, planetary influence, the lair of Pegasus, the impression of "the red-hot seal of some huge Polypheme "—he arrives at the common-sense suggestion that after all it is nothing but the symbol of the Saxon conquest corresponding to the White Horse of the Berkshire downs. Thus, as the broad expanse of hill country stretching from Faringdon to Edgehill is bounded by the Vale of the White Horse on the south, so it has the Vale of the Red Horse for its boundary on the north.

CHAPTER VI

A WILD heath once covered the high table-land that lies between Edgehill and Chipping Norton. Isolated stretches of it still survive here and there, but for the most part it has been broken up into grass enclosures and cultivated fields. As late as the early part of the eighteenth century it had not ceased to be a happy hunting ground for the antiquary or the seeker after buried treasure, and Dr. William Stukeley, who explored this district at that time, bears witness to the many sepulchral monuments of the pre-Roman period which it then contained. Of these the most important is the stone-circle at Rollright, which we shall come to presently. The Dobuni, the tribe to whom these monuments are ascribed, seem to have occupied the hill country between the Cherwell and the Warwickshire Avon. An ancient road, a well-trodden highway of this people, runs from Edgehill past the Rollright Stones to Stow-on-the-Wold, where it meets the famous Foss Way. It keeps to the high ground in a remarkably direct course, but twice it is compelled to dip, first to cross the infant Stour at Traitor's Ford, and secondly to cross the Evenlode at Adlestrop. Here and there along the sides of this road may be observed isolated upright stones—a fact which suggested to Dr. Arthur John Evans, who some years since made a thorough investigation of the Rollright Stones and their Folklore, that the road might have been used as a "Via Sacra," leading as it did to the ancient sepultures and monuments scattered over the hill-top. The whole length of this road from Edgehill to Stow is about twenty miles, the first half of which is now a rough country lane, and of this the two miles from Epwell Down to Traitor's Ford is a mere cart track, where cycling is difficult or impracticable.

For the first part of our journey, however, riding is fairly easy. Leaving the Sunrising on our right, we may, if we please, dismount a couple of miles further on and follow a tangled lane to the edge of the declivity. Hence, there is a vast prospect—to use the old-fashioned term—across the vale towards Shipston, Ilmington, Stratford, Kineton and far beyond. At our feet lies the village of Tysoe in its triple division: the church has the same remarkable windows in the upper part of the nave arcade, which we noticed at Swalcliffe. Windmill hill to the left hides from us Compton Wynyates, whither we are bound. On the further side of the road, as we resume our ride, is a curious medley of tumbling grassy hills, some of them reaching an elevation of over 700 feet, among which the quaint little village of Epwell lies snugly tucked away. This place is an ancient chapelry of Swalcliffe, and the miniature fourteenth century church forms a striking contrast to the larger churches of the district: the entrance is through the tower, which is singularly placed at the west end of the south aisle. There are also many picturesque bits of domestic architecture scattered about the village, which will delight the artist but we have still a couple of miles to go before we reach our destination, and must hasten on.

The Marquess of Northampton's house of Compton Wynyates or Compton Vineyatys—so called from the vineyard which once existed here—must be one of the most difficult places in England for the stranger, unassisted by maps or finger-posts, to find. It lies deep down in a fold of the hills, which here have but a single opening, towards the north-west—a situation sheltered and secure, and of all others one to appeal to the builder of four centuries ago. I hardly know whether to advise the visitor to approach it for the first time through the opening

Compton Wynyates from the Moat.

in the hills, or whether to descend upon it from above, but in either case I can promise him that the sight which awaits him will be unique. If he is able to suggest a parallel I shall be glad to hear of it; for my own part I know of none. On the south, at the foot of the hills is a beautiful garden, the creation of the present Marquess, aflame with flowers of every colour, the plants distributed, as they should be, in large compact masses, and not dotted about in driblets—now a pinch of this, now a pinch of that, and now a pinch of this again—in the fashion affected by so many modern gardeners: beyond, a smooth stretch of well-kept lawn and then the house of red brick—the brick of Hampton Court or the gate house of a Cambridge College. The employment of brick as a material for building in this stone country is surprising, but an explanation is at hand. Sir William Compton, the faithful friend and servant of Henry VIII., among numerous other marks of the royal favour, received the gift of the castle of Fulbrook, a brick edifice of Henry the Sixth's time situated on a knoll between Stratford and Warwick. This he pulled down and used the materials to build his new house at Compton Wynyates; and so strong was the mortar of those days that the twisted chimneys which still rise over the highest part of the house are said to have been transported whole.

Sir William Compton is the first of the family of whose career any details have come down to us, but his ancestors had lived here from the time of Edward the First, if not earlier, and had been men of mark in the county. In their days a thriving village had existed here, but like Charwelton, it was one of those which were swept away by the enclosures, and Sir William himself is recorded to have enclosed and imparked no less than two thousand acres. It was a time when great houses were springing up all over the land, no longer mere fortresses, though capable of being put in a posture of defence, but solid substantial edifices destined to be the home of the family for generations. No longer were the windows made on the inner side only, looking into the court, while the outer walls were merely pierced with cross-bow slits and loopholes. Here at Compton windows abound everywhere, and the many mullioned windows of the exterior bespeak the airy spacious rooms within, giving the whole the impress of comfort and hospitality. Sir William, who died in 1528, nearly twenty years before his sovereign, retained the royal favour till the last. His great-grandson William, first Earl of Northampton, married the heiress of a wealthy London Alderman, Sir John Spencer, and the family became more prosperous than ever. It was his son Spencer, the second earl, who led two thousand of the best trained men in the royal army to Edgehill. Of his six sons the third, William, was the gallant defender of Banbury, and the hero of another exploit which we shall come to directly. The youngest, Henry, was the militant bishop of London, who, when the princess Anne fled from White-hall at the Revolution, rode before her carriage attired in a buff coat and jackboots, with sword by his side and pistols in his holsters.

But before I say any more about his descendants, I must notice the only link which connects the first Sir William with Oxford. Between the years 1521 and 1529 Balliol College was engaged in erecting a new chapel—the very building which was unfortunately destroyed in the middle of the last century to make room for the present edifice. Here was an opportunity for the munificence of benefactors, a munificence which took the appropriate form of stained glass windows for the new chapel. It must, however, be admitted that charity in this case was not wholly without its reward, seeing that it was customary for the window presented to include the "portraiture" and arms of the donor, together with an inscription recording the donation. Now in Dugdale's *Warwickshire*, published in 1656, is a charming engraving of a knight and his lady kneeling opposite to each other "in their surcoats of Arms," with their children standing behind them ;

Compton Wynyates. The Entrance Front.

there are also two armorial shields.   The legend beneath is as
follows :

" Willelmus Compton, Miles cum pia consorte sua hanc fenestram
vitrari fecit An. Dni. 1530."

Dugdale tells us that this engraving was taken from the window
set up in Balliol Chapel in Sir William's time, and when
Anthony Wood wrote his account of the college some years
later than Dugdale, he described the chapel windows and the
Compton window among them.   Since then sad havoc has
been made of the Balliol windows, when or how, who knows ?
Portions of the old windows have, however, been preserved in
the windows of the modern chapel, including a few fragments
of the various portraitures and legends enumerated by Wood.
In his time the Compton window was the third from the
east on the south side, and when I was writing the present
chapter I naturally wondered whether any fragments of it
survived : if so they might easily be identified by the aid of
Dugdale's copy.   Search was rewarded by the discovery of two
such fragments : in the third window from the east on the *north*
side were the two armorial shields, and in the centre compart-
ment of the rose window over the organ was the kneeling figure
of Sir William Compton and his two sons.   The figure of
Lady Compton and her daughter, as well as the legend beneath
the figures, have vanished.

From this excursion, of special interest to an alumnus of
the college, I return to Warwickshire.   When the civil
war broke out Compton House was garrisoned for the
King, and though its lord was slain at Hopton Heath, in
March, 1643, it remained undisturbed till June, 1644, shortly
before the fighting at Cropredy, when it was captured by a
party of Roundheads under Colonel Purefoy.   In their
possession it remained till the end of the war, though a spirited
attempt to recover it by surprise was made by Sir Charles and
Sir William Compton in the following winter.   On a moonlight

night these gallant brothers made a sudden dash from Banbury, stormed the outworks, cut the ropes of the drawbridge, which then spanned the moat, and got possession of the stables and outbuildings before the garrison could recover from the shock. The outbuildings then stood to the left of the present entrance; they have since been cleared away and new stabling erected beyond the church. Some of the soldiers of the garrison who had their quarters in these outbuildings were overcome without resistance; but parties from the house coming up to the rescue, the assailants, after a fierce struggle of three hours' duration, were at last driven back, and compelled to abandon the attempt. The garrison had thus been able to ward off the attack from the house itself, and the damage was fortunately confined to the outbuildings.

The church, which stands at a short distance from the house, was at this time, says Dugdale, "totally reduced to rubbish." The monuments of the builder of the house and his wife, and of his grandson Henry, first Baron Compton, were broken up and thrown into the lake, from which the fragments were afterwards fished up and replaced in the church.

By this time the traveller who has followed me from Edgehill will be glad to find a comfortable inn, and such a one he will find in the George at Brailes, a familiar resort of the country squires of former days, and even now much frequented by hunting men. As we thread the shady lanes that lead us thither from Compton Wynyates, which here and there give us a view of the well-wooded country on either side, it is hard to realise that this part of Warwickshire is called the Feldon, that is, the land from which the timber has been cleared away, to distinguish it from the woodland district of the Forest of Arden, which lies to the north of the Avon. Brailes Church, from its size and massive tower, is known as the "Cathedral of the Feldon," and it well deserves the name. As we turn a corner of the lane the tower comes into sight, the central object in a vast amphitheatre of meadow, wood, and hill. The church stands in the highest part of the village, not far from the inn. Nothing can be finer than the exterior; the lofty tower, 120 feet high, and wide in proportion, the long clerestory rising above the aisles, the open foliated parapet on the south side, with a cornice elaborately carved with grotesques beneath, and the rich orange tints of the stone, command our wonder and admiration. Enter the church, and alas! the scene is changed. The expectations raised by such an outside are doomed to disappointment; the plaster has been ruthlessly scraped from the walls, almost every trace of the sanctifying hand of time has been removed, and the whole has a strange, cold look, from the contrast with the exterior all the more repellent.

There is not much else, always excepting the comfortable inn, to detain us at Brailes. Brailes House, in which the last survivor of the Sheldon family recently died, is now a forlorn and deserted mansion. Up to the beginning of the nineteenth century the Sheldons were only second to the Comptons in local importance. They had a fine house at Weston Park, four miles to the south-west, and the landlord at the inn will show you the names of some of them cut with a diamond on the window panes, and also an old rent book of the family, which shows that their estates were spread over half-a-dozen parishes. The most famous of them was Ralph Sheldon, the squire of the seventeenth century. He was an indefatigable collector of books, manuscripts, and antiquities. Readers of Anthony Wood's autobiography will remember how often he would walk over to Weston from Oxford to visit his friend and patron, and how many happy weeks he spent there arranging and cataloguing the library. Weston enjoyed the distinction of possessing this fine library for a century after the death of its collector, but when poverty comes in at the door, books fly out of the window, and in 1781, when the squire of that day slept with his fathers, it was brought to the hammer at Long Compton. Ralph's copy of the first folio Shakespeare, and a large collection of old plays, were among its chief treasures.

Brailes Church.

The former now belongs to Lady Burdett-Coutts, and many of the latter are in the Malone collection in the Bodleian.

Just beyond Weston, on the further side of the Shipston road, is Little Wolford, famous for its interesting fifteenth century manor-house. You may make an afternoon's excursion there from Brailes, or take it on a ride to Four-shire-stone, which marks the meeting place of the shires of Gloucester, Worcester, Warwick and Oxford. The manor-house is of the typical form characteristic of its date, a hall in the centre, with a projecting wing on either side. One of the wings has been pulled down; the remaining one is of stone below and half-timber work above; the central part is all stone. In the hall, which preserves its screen and gallery, hang rusty weapons and accoutrements, and a curious instrument of iron, which the farmer's wife tells you is an eel-drag, with which the eels were dragged up from the ponds. She will also affirm that "King Charles" dined in the hall, and will show you the oven in which he was concealed from his pursuers. You may believe as much of this as you like, but you will refrain from hinting at your scepticism to your guide, or you may miss the draught from the chalybeate spring down in the field behind the house, with which your departure is graced.

But I am not going to Wolford to-day. It is time to resume our pilgrimage along the " Via Sacra," and I must leave Brailes by the Banbury road in the opposite direction, and climb the hill till I come to the spot where the gallows once stood, and where a remnant of the original heath is still left. The Brailes people call it Gallows Hill to this day. The rough track to the right is the ancient road I am in search of: for several miles it forms the boundary between the counties of Oxford and Warwick, and before the days of shires may well have marked a still more ancient division of the land. I follow its course down to Traitor's Ford, and surely if ever there was a name suggestive of antique story this is one. But I have been quite unable to hear of any story connecting any traitor with the spot,

Little Wolford Manor.

nor does anyone appear to be able to give any explanation of the
name. Can it have any remote connexion with the treachery
of the Whispering Knights to which we shall come directly?
The only legend connected with the place I could pick up was
told me by the landlord of the Unicorn at Great Rollright.
The great bell, he said, which now hangs in Brailes Tower, was

The Four-shire Stone, Moreton-in-the-Marsh.

dug up here. Perhaps this story arose from the fact that when
the bell was being taken away to be recast, I know not how
many years ago, the conveyance broke down on Gallows Hill,
and the bell lay by the roadside for a long time before it was
removed.

There is a bridge now over the Stour at Traitor's Ford, and
it is a long climb on the other side up to Great Rollright.

From the top there is an extensive view towards Shipston and Chipping Campden, while close at the foot of the range lie the villages of Long Compton, already mentioned, and Little Compton, where Bishop, afterwards Archbishop, Juxon had a manor, to which he retired during the Commonwealth. His manor-house is still inhabited, though it has long passed into the hands of another family. Up here on the wold we have entered upon a fabled land. Close to us on our left is the spell-bound circle of the Rowldrich, on our right the King-stone, which would bow its head when the "eldern-tree" was cut on Midsummer Eve, and down below the circle are the Five Knights still whispering treachery against their lord. These stones, the silent chronicle of a long-forgotten time, how much could they tell of the true story that lies hidden beneath the legends, for so many centuries the heritage of these hills! Did the mysterious people who reared these megaliths belong to the Celtic or to some still earlier race? That the legends associated with them have Celtic affinities is not to be disputed, but for all that the monuments may be older than the legends, just as the legends themselves are older than the name by which the monuments are known; for, as Dr. A. J. Evans was the first to point out, the name Rollright, which appears in Doomsday as Rollandri, is nothing more than a corruption of Rollandriht, *i.e.*, the right or jurisdiction of Roland. Now Roland the Brave, the Paladin of Charlemagne, was, as everybody knows, the legendary champion of Christianity against the Paynim, and since he does not appear in this capacity earlier than the middle of the ninth century, it cannot be till some time after this date that his name came to be connected with these monuments. The same thing took place on the continent: in northern Germany the name *Rolandsäule* was attached to the ancient stone pillars which stood in the market-places of various towns: but this is a story which I cannot enter upon here; for a full discussion of the subject, and for a most suggestive review of the legends connected with the

Rowldrich, I must refer the reader to Dr. Evans's paper on the subject.[1] I will only add that the name points to an importation of the Rowland romance from the continent in the ninth or tenth century.

As for the legends connected with the King-stone and the stone circle, or King's men, as they are or were current among the natives, I cannot do better than quote the summary of them given by Dr. Evans as follows: "A certain King—the name is not, as a rule, remembered—had set forth at the head of his forces to conquer all England.   But as he went up the hill on which Rowldrich stands there appeared to him the Witch to whom the ground belonged.   The King was now within a few steps of the crest of the hill from which the village of Long Compton would be visible in the combe below, when she stopped him with the words, 'Seven long strides shalt thou take, and—

> If Long Compton thou canst see,
> King of England thou shalt be.'

The King who now thought his success assured, cried out exultingly :

> 'Stick, stock, stone,
> As King of England I shall be known !'

So he took seven strides forward, but lo! and behold, instead of his looking down on Long Compton there rose before him the long mound of earth which still stands before the King-stone, and the Witch said:

> ' As Long Compton thou canst not see
> King of England thou shalt not be.
> Rise up stick, and stand still, stone,
> For King of England thou shalt be none,
> Thou and thy men hoar stones shall be
> And I myself an eldern-tree.'

---

[1] *Folk-Lore* for March, 1895.

Thereupon the King and his army were turned into stones where they stood, the King on the side of the mound and his army in a circle behind him, while the Witch herself became an elder tree. But some day, they do say, the spell will be broken. The stones will turn into flesh and blood once more, and the King will start as an armed warrior at the head of his army to overcome his enemies and rule over the land."

The fairies would dance round the King-stone on moonlight nights. Dr. Evans talked with an old woman whose husband had actually seen them. She herself remembered a hole in the bank by the stone from which they used to come out for their dance, and many a time when a girl she and her companions had placed a flat stone over the hole of an evening to keep the fairies in, but they always found it turned over next morning. As for the Whispering Knights, they were traitors, who remained behind the rest of the army and were plotting treason when they were turned into stone by the Witch. They had become a kind of oracle for the young girls of the neighbourhood: the same old woman related that "years ago, at the time of barley harvest, when they were often out till dusk in the fields near the Whispering Knights, one of the girls would say to another, 'Let us go and hear them whisper.' Then they would go to the stones, and one at a time would put her ear to one of the crevices. But first one would laugh and then another, and she herself never heard any whispering." Another aged dame told Dr. Evans "that the stones were thought to tell of the future. 'When I was a girl we used to go up at certain seasons to the Whispering Knights, and climb up on to one of the stones to hear them whisper. Time and again I have heard them whisper—but perhaps after all it was only the wind.'"

But, the reader may ask, putting aside all these stories, with what object were these stones originally erected? The shortest answer that can be given is that they were all sepulchral in intention, and intimately connected with the sepulchral cult of those who set them up. Thus the Whispering Knights are a dolmen, and like all such monuments, including the one at Enstone, half a dozen miles away, was originally covered by a mound pierced with an entrance passage. As for the circle it probably contained several interments, the remains in each case being cremated and enclosed in an urn; but though Ralph Sheldon dug here industriously more than two hundred years ago he could find nothing, nor is there any record of any one having been more successful since. As for the King-stone, it is doubtful whether it is the survivor of a group, or whether it always stood alone; in either case, perhaps it marked the resting-place of a chief. The legends which speak of the stones as having been once endowed with life no doubt descend from the remote days of ancestor worship, when the stone set up at a man's grave was regarded as in some mysterious way personifying the departed, or at least as enshrining his spirit; while the custom of making offerings of food for the use of the dead is probably at the root of the story of the baker, who, to test the truth of the popular belief in the impossibility of counting the stones, put a penny loaf on every one, but when he came to count his loaves always found one stone without a loaf.

Our scene now changes, with scant respect for the stately march of time, from the days of the ancient Britons to those of James the First, for so it is with wayfarers like ourselves—we must needs follow where the way leads. And now it leads us into a remote corner of Oxfordshire that can boast one of the most notable houses of a district where notable houses are not rare. Turning off the road to the right a mile beyond the Cross Hands—a house of entertainment well known to followers of the Heythrop—we skirt the summit of Adlestrop Heath, whence the golfer, as he shoulders his weapons at the close of a well-fought day, sees the sun sink behind the long dark ridge of the distant Cotswold. Another mile and we are face to face with the tall grey front of Chastleton. So tall and so imposing is this *façade*, with its soaring gables and great square flanking towers, that the ancient church which stands hard by seems to shrink into insignificance beneath its domineering neighbour. Nevertheless, church and house together, in their setting of green meadow and woodland, form a stately and impressive group. Reminding one of Wroxton, and built at the same period, Chastleton House has a distinct individuality of its own. Wroxton lies in a hollow, and is approached by a long curving shrubbery drive: Chastleton is built high up on the slope of a hill, with nothing but a square court of modest size between the house and the road. The long sweeps of lawn and the terraced walks of Wroxton, suggestive of Capability Brown and the landscape style of gardening, are unknown at Chastleton, where the old trim garden, with its clipped yews and formal beds, remains undisturbed. Chastleton, in fact, view it from without or from within, remains what it was, the home of the larger country squire. Enter the house, and in a moment you are back in the days of the Stuarts: here is the hall with its screen, its daïs, its bay window, its armour and its family portraits: you half expect to find your host mending fishing tackle or the implements of hawking, and his talk to be of Worcester or Edgehill, till the butler brings you a cup of canary to refresh you after your long ride from Oxford. As you pass from room to room, old panelling, old tapestry, and old furniture of every kind abound. It so happens that among the family papers is preserved an inventory of "all and singular the Goods, Chattles and Debtes" of the builder of the house taken after his death in 1633, and there you may read how "the Great Chamber" contained, amongst other things, "one draweing table with a frame, & one court cupbord of Walnut tree one smale square table, eight needle worke chaires of Irish stich, one large needleworke chaire with a backe," and how "Mr. Sheldon's Chamber" (it was not far for Mr. Sheldon to ride over from Weston, and some of the books still in the library may have been purchased under his advice) had "one field bedstead with taffata curtaines, valence & testerne, one Downe bed & bolster and pillowes one taffata cov'let one Mattrice & one Rugge & Blanketts." It is a little disappointing to find that no list of Mr. Jones's " bookes in the library" is given; they are all lumped together as worth £10, while his " wearinge apparrell " is valued at exactly double that sum.

At the very top of the house you come to the long gallery which runs the whole length of the north side. These galleries were a common feature in old country houses, and in bad weather, when open air exercise was impossible, must have been the scene of many an indoor pastime. Sometimes they served a more serious purpose, as at Broughton and Compton Wynyates, where they were used as barracks during the war. At both these houses they have since then been portioned off into separate bedrooms, but here at Chastleton no such innovation has been allowed, and the whole space is as open and unencumbered as of old. The elaborately moulded plaster ceiling of its waggon-shaped roof had suffered here and there from decay, but Miss Whitmore Jones, the present owner of the estate, has recently had it perfectly restored on the original lines by clever local workmen, and when the freshness of the plaster has toned down the new work will be indistinguishable from the old.

The Chastleton estate was purchased at the beginning of the seventeenth century by Walter Jones, a well-to-do woollen merchant of Witney, who built the present house. He came of an old Glamorgan family, which, like the Andrews at Charwelton, had not scrupled to put its younger sons into trade. The vendor was the notorious Robert Catesby, and tradition asserts that a part of the purchase money was expended in maturing the never-to-be-forgotten Gunpowder Plot. The last of the Joneses died in 1828, and Chastleton then passed into the family of the present owner, Miss Whitmore Jones. The story of the way in which this happened is worth hearing, and was as follows. At the close of the eighteenth century the representatives of the

family were two brothers, John and Arthur Jones, the former a
bachelor, the latter a widower without children. They had no
near relations, but they had kept up an intermittent intercourse
with some distant cousins of the Whitmore family—a family
connected with their own by marriage a hundred years earlier
—and they began to think that somewhere among the Whit-
mores an heir might be found. Miss Whitmore Jones shall
continue the tale in her own words: "In the winter of 1812

Dovecot at Chastleton.

Arthur Jones was attending a fair at Chipping Norton and was
hailed from the window of a carriage, which was so blocked
in the crowd that it could not proceed; its occupants were
an elderly gentleman, a bluff hearty sailor, and his very handsome wife. 'I am sure you are Jones of Chastleton,' said the
gentleman, 'I am William Whitmore of Dudmaston; we are
posting home from Teignmouth, and have got entangled in this
crowd.' Arthur Jones was delighted with the *rencontre*, and

insisted that they should turn their horses' heads and accompany him to Chastleton. This they did and stayed a day or two, mutually pleased with one another. They then proceeded on their journey, and a few days after they got home, Mr. Whitmore received a letter from Arthur Jones (written at his brother's request), inquiring whether his second son, John Henry, was provided for, and if not, offering to settle Chastleton upon him, provided he took the name and arms of Jones. Of course the offer was thankfully accepted, and from that time young John Whitmore, then a boy of 14, paid an annual visit to Chastleton as the acknowledged heir."

To return to the seventeenth century: in the Civil Wars the Joneses were staunch Royalists. Opening from one of the bedrooms, called the "Cavalier" room, is a secret chamber, the door of which was formerly concealed behind the arras with which the room was hung. On one occasion, at least, the security of this hiding-place was put to the test. Among the fugitives from Worcester field on Sept. 3rd, 1651, was Arthur Jones, the grandson of Walter, the founder of the family. Late that night after thirty miles of stiff cross-country work he reached his home, and, putting his tired-out horse into the stable, was admitted to the house by his wife. Scarcely had he had time to eat and drink when the sound of horses' feet was heard approaching, and their riders were soon clamouring at the door for admittance. Arthur Jones hurried to the secret chamber while Mrs. Jones went to the front door, which a voice outside commanded her to open in the name of the Parliament. There was nothing for it but to do as she was ordered, and a party of soldiers thereupon entered the house, and compelled her to conduct them over it; they were on the track, they said, of a fugitive malignant—no less a person, as it afterwards appeared they imagined, than the King himself. When they came to the "Cavalier" room they searched it thoroughly, but fortunately did not find the secret door. Whether their suspicions were aroused, or whether the room seemed to them the most comfortable one in the house, they signified to their hostess that they intended to pass the night there and directed her to send them up some supper. The selection of this room was most unfortunate; there was no other exit from the secret chamber, and we can imagine the dismay with which the anxious lady received this announcement. However, her resources were not yet exhausted. She duly sent up the supper, but at the same time took care to mix enough laudanum with the wine to give her visitors a good night's repose. When they had well eaten and well drunk, she stole up to the door and listened for the result. Ere long the heavy breathing of the sleepers assured her that all was safe; she then entered the room, opened the door of the hiding-place, and conducted her husband downstairs. He proceeded at once to the stable, and finding that his own horse had not recovered from its fatigue, he mounted that of the commander of the party and rode off. When the pursuers awoke next morning they discovered that their prey had eluded them, and that too with the aid of the best of their own animals. As to the identity of the malignant who had made so free with their property, they were, however, none the wiser. They still believed him to be the youth Charles Stuart, and after threatening Mrs. Jones with all manner of pains and penalties they galloped off.

Barn at Broadwell, near Stow-on-the-Wold.

CHAPTER VII

THERE is nothing now but the green valley of the Evenlode to separate us from the Cotswold. Few natural districts have their frontier more clearly defined. The hill country of north Oxfordshire and south-west Northamptonshire is, it is true, geographically but a continuation of the same range, but from whatever side he enters it the traveller who penetrates into the Cotswold proper is conscious of having passed into a new region. The long stretches of upland, the winding valleys, the clear trout-streams, and the grey venerable hamlets dotted along their banks, the very vegetation, the weather-beaten ashes of the hills, the sheep-downs fragrant with wild thyme and burnet, and the deep rich water-meadows below, with here and there a thick covert of oak and hazel, are all marks of a strange land, marked off by its peculiar genius from the outside everyday world. If you come by the railway from Cheltenham up the valley by the great reservoirs, you issue from the tunnel at the top to find yourself with a touch of the enchanter's wand in the midst of such scenes as I have described. Further on, at Notgrove station, you have climbed to a height of more than seven hundred feet; then you descend to cross

the Windrush at Bourton, and so wind through the curious
pass of Maugersbury to join the Evenlode at Chipping Norton
Junction.   This is one of the two railways which in latter days
have penetrated these silent wolds.   The other leaves the
Banbury line at Andoversford and runs southwards through the
Chedworth plantations and across the Foss Way to Cirencester.
The traveller may have a rapid glance at all the various features
of the landscape: vast rolling sweeps of cultivated down,
patches of ancient sheep-walk, dingle, water-meadow, and woodland are passed in quick succession: with one or two exceptions,
the villages are unseen, for, like the high roads, the railways have
managed to avoid them.   As in other hilly countries, the large
enclosures are divided by loose stone walls, but here they are
so low that on a horse well used to them you might gallop as
far as the eye can stretch without a stop.   Saving the eastern
frontier, which belongs to the Heythrop country, two packs,
the North Cotswold and the Cotswold, divide this great tract
between them.   The late Arthur Gibbs knew it well.   "How
exhilarating," he writes in his charming *Cotswold Village*,
"is a gallop in this fine Cotswold air in the cool autumnal
morning! and what a splendid view you get of hounds! . . .
What is the charm which belongs so exclusively to a fast and
straight 'run' over this wild, uncultivated region?   It does not
lie in the successful negotiation of Leicestershire 'oxers,'
Aylesbury 'doubles,' or Warwickshire 'stake-and-bound' fences,
for there need be no obstacle greater than an occasional four-
foot stone wall.   Perhaps it lies partly in the fact that in a run
over a level stone-wall country, where the enclosures are large,
and the turf sound, given a good fox and a 'burning scent,'
hounds and horses travel at as great a pace as they attain in
any country in England.   Here, moreover, if anywhere, is to
be found the 'greatest happiness for the greatest number,' the
maximum of sport with the minimum of danger; the fine, free
air of the high-lying Cotswold plains; the good fellowship
engendered when all can ride abreast; the very muteness of

the flying pack; . . . the long sweeping stride of a well-bred horse; the unceasing twang of the horn to encourage flagging hounds beaten off by the pace and those which got left behind at the start; lastly, the *glorious uncertainty*! Can it last? Where will it all end? Shall we 'bang into him' in the open, or will he beat us in yonder cold scenting woodland, standing boldly forth on the skyline miles ahead? All these things add a peculiar fascination to a fast run over this wild country."

The woodland proper is confined to the valleys, and there would be a dearth of fox-cover on the hills, where the older timber consists chiefly of long rows of ash lining the enclosures or the roadsides; but this deficiency has been provided for by large plantations of fir, which diversify the landscape in all directions; and in early spring their dark green masses form a striking contrast to the rich brown of the newly-ploughed fields, the pale grey of the fallows, and the lighter green of the spring-ing wheat. According to the Gloucestershire proverb, a long-tarried-for result is said to be as long coming as Cotswold barley, and in fact the crops are usually calculated to ripen a month later than those raised in the vale. Wheat, barley, and black oats are still extensively cultivated, but arable farming is not more remunerative on the Cotswold than elsewhere, and many acres have dropped out of cultivation and are reverting to their original state. What that was may be seen on many of the steeper slopes which have never been touched by the plough; here the sheep are still nibbling the short, crisp turf, and casual flocks of wool still decorate the furze. Till the days of the enclosures in the first half of the eighteenth century the arable land was confined to the immediate neighbourhood of the villages, and the uplands were one vast expanse of open sheep-down, where throughout the long summer days the shepherds tended their flocks, as they still do upon Salisbury Plain. But with the enclosures the shepherd of the hills found that his duties became in no way different from those of his brother of the plains. The sheep, too, became far less numerous, and the old breed has become scarce. For the farmer has had to look for his profit to the mutton rather than the wool, and by crossing the pure-bred Cotswold with the Hampshire Down, he has produced an animal of smaller size; and though the fleeces are less heavy, the mutton is of superior flavour and more appreciated by his customers. For a graphic picture of the old Cotswold breed we may turn to Michael Drayton's laborious lines :

> " The sheep our Wold doth breed
> (The simplest though it seeme) shall our description need,
> And shepheard-like the Muse thus of that kind doth speak.
> No browne, nor sullyed black the face or legs doth streak
> Like those of Moreland, Cank, or of the Cambrian hills
> That lightly laden are ; but Cotswold wisely fills
> Her with the whitest kind ; whose brows so woolly be
> As men in her fair sheep no emptiness should see.
> The staple deep and thick, through, to the very graine
> Most strongly keepeth out the violentest raine—
> A body long and large, the buttocks equal broad
> As fit to undergoe the full and weightie load."

Sainfoin is largely grown as fodder for sheep and cattle on the Cotswold, as well as on the chalk downs; for this handsome plant thrives best on a calcareous soil, and the blaze of brilliant pink produced by acres of it in full bloom is a distinctive feature in the landscape—a cheering prospect descried from afar by the glad eye of the cyclist as he journeys over the wolds in the early summer. The sainfoin is a native plant, but it began to be grown as a regular crop on the Cotswold two centuries and a half ago, many years before turnip fields came into fashion. Its cultivation is said to have been introduced into England by the squire of Daylesford of the day.

Daylesford, the home of Warren Hastings, lies on our left as we descend the hill from Chastleton to cross the Evenlode at Adlestrop bridge. The mortal part of the great statesman lies beneath the altar of Daylesford church, for though he was buried outside the old church, the new church, erected in 1860, was extended eastwards to include his grave. In the church-yard stands a square stone pedestal supporting an urn, with the simple inscription "Warren Hastings."

Who does not remember the story as told by Macaulay? how one bright summer day young Warren, "then just seven years old, lay on the bank of the rivulet which flows through the old domain of his house to join the Isis. There, as three-score and ten years later he told the tale, rose in his mind a scheme, which, through all the turns of his eventful career, was never abandoned. He would recover the estate which had belonged to his fathers. He would be Hastings of Daylesford." His ancestor, the *patronus* of the sainfoin, had impoverished the estate in the service of his King, and some score of years before Warren's birth it had passed into other hands. At last, in 1788, the great statesman realised his ambition; he re-purchased Daylesford, rebuilt the house, and lived there till his death in 1818. How he spent his days as a country gentleman, dividing his time between farming and literature, fattening prize-cattle, and attempting to naturalise exotics, both animal and vegetable, may be read in the pages of Macaulay. His widow survived him for nearly twenty years, and not long ago there were many surviving in the neighbourhood who remem-bered her.

It is a long climb of three miles up to Stow-on-the-Wold—on the Wold, indeed, for it lies at a height of nearly 800 feet, and its tower is a conspicuous landmark for ten miles round. From the other hill-town of the district, its neighbour, Chipping Norton, on the Oxfordshire table land, it differs in that on every side to it the approach is steep.[1] From the north and east you may positively go down-hill into Chipping Norton, but from whatever side you enter Stow you must reckon with a stiff pull-up of at least a mile. Shortly after leaving Adlestrop bridge we may digress half a mile to the left as far as the old church of Oddington. This very

[1] Except by the road from Broadway on the north-west.

interesting church now stands in solitary grandeur hard by a coppice tenanted by rooks, and quite deserted by the village which long ago migrated up the hill, to a spot nearer the common fields. Here a new church has been built, and except for an occasional funeral the silence of the old church is seldom disturbed. We who have purposely left our road to seek it out in its seclusion may be counted among its disturbers. Happier they who, in an April stroll by the Evenlode through meadow and spinney, bright with marigolds and primroses, burst upon it unexpectedly, and stand fettered by the sudden spell. There is nothing to mar the quiet beauty of chancel, nave, aisle, and tower, nothing but the cawing of the rooks to break the silence. That aisle, once the nave of a small Norman church of the common Cotswold type, received later the tower at its eastern end, and then, in the prosperous times of the early Edwards, the new nave and chancel arose, and ever since it has been but the side-aisle of the larger church.

As we ascend to Stow, we may turn round and survey the Oxfordshire hills that we have now left behind. Opposite are Chipping Norton, Rollright, and Adlestrop heath: to the left Brailes hill bounds the horizon, and further to the left still rise the heights which conceal Chipping Campden. It was from these slopes that in the autumn of 1643 Rupert and his cavaliers watched the Lord General's army marching down from Chipping Norton on its way to the relief of Gloucester. Unprovided with infantry and artillery, he could do no more than face them and retire, and though he made another stand at Eyford, a few miles further on, he was compelled to fall back upon the Royalist quarters. After passing the night at Naunton, Essex pushed on through Brockhampton to the hills above Prestbury, whence he took a distant survey of the King's forces, as they lay round the beleaguered city. The news of his arrival soon spread, and the fires which presently broke out in the Royalist encampments showed him that his march had attained its object, and that the siege had been raised.

The cyclist who has no fear of hills may make the "Talbot" at Stow his headquarters for several days. Roads, all of them excellent, converge upon this airy height from all points of the compass. In half-a-dozen hours or less, he may, if he is so

Moreton-in-Marsh. Curfew Tower.

disposed, reach Cirencester, Gloucester, Tewkesbury, Evesham, Warwick, Banbury, or Burford ; but if, like the writer, he is ever ready to seize an excuse for wandering from the direct route, he will find in the many diverging byways ample material to keep him nearer home. There is something in the very names of the villages which, as was once felicitously said, makes the traveller feel that life is still worth living. Stow-on-the-Wold itself, for instance, suggestive of isolation and defiance, and then we have Barton-on-the-Heath, Moreton-in-Marsh, Bourton-on-the-Water, Bourton-on-the-Hill, to say nothing of the less romantic but not less stimulating names of Upper and Lower Slaughter, Upper and Lower Swell, Temple Guiting, Guiting Power, Turkdean, and Aston Blank, or Cold Aston. Of these Stow and Moreton lie on the great Foss Way, the rest are retired from any main road; but it is a matter of common observation that in central and southern England at any rate, easiness of access was a very secondary consideration with the early Saxon settlers. As for the Foss Way, its Gloucestershire portion lies in a remarkably direct line between Cirencester and Moreton, and it is still one of the best kept roads in the county. You may see it stretching away over the hills for miles, flanked by its broad grassy margins, between which, in its more level parts, it still elevates itself with all the pride of a Roman causeway. Before the days of Macadam these wide grass margins, still cherished by the horseman, had their use for wheeled traffic as well; they were, in fact, the usual summer road, the repairable track in the centre being reserved for the winter, when rain and mud rendered the grass impassable. On the Cotswold, however, the side roads were not always practicable even in the summer: an eighteenth century writer on Rural Economy complains that in order to save the labour of hauling materials for the repair of the central road from a distance, the stone was dug up on the spot, and the pits thus made rendered the side roads unsafe. As in Oxfordshire, a harder stone is now brought from a distance,[1] but a multitude of these pits still remain by the roadside.

A stranger might be surprised to find so many high roads leading to a town now so unpretentious as Stow, but when he has been told of Stow Fair his wonder will cease. This fair was formerly one of the most celebrated in this part of England.

---

[1] From Clee Hill in Shropshire.

A charter of Edward the Fourth authorises its being held twice in the year, on May 1st, the Feast of St. Philip and St. James, and on October 13th, the feast of the Translation of Edward the Confessor.   Since the New Style came in the fair has been held on May 12th and October 24th.   But its ancient glory has long departed, and it is now principally a horse fair, where large droves of half-wild ponies from Wales are sold to the English dealers.   At these times the Celtic tongue, once the familiar speech of the British slaves of Roman masters, may be heard again in the streets.   It may readily be imagined that so important an event formed a red letter day in the calendar of the surrounding villages, and that Stow Fair took rank with other great festivals as a notable date.   The story goes that sometime in the middle of the last century, a Cotswold yokel emigrated to Australia, and on arriving at his destination was asked his age by the official whose duty it was to note down the particulars of the personal history of the newcomers : " Thirty, last Stow Fair, sir," replied the man ; " What ! " said the officer ; " Thirty, last Stow Fair, sir," came the answer again, as who should say " What, never heard of Stow Fair ! "   Here is another story of the Fair dating from earlier in the same century, which shows that the manners and customs at such gatherings are much what they were.   An inhabitant of the adjacent hamlet of Maugersbury, called Hewer, who it seems was somewhat addicted to playing ducks and drakes with his money, started early one morning for the Fair.   His wife, who was a thrifty woman, was not able to leave home so soon, but as soon as she had got through her morning's work, she determined to follow her husband and keep a watchful eye upon his vagaries.   Not being able to find him in the crowd she sat down on a tombstone in the churchyard to rest.   Seated hard by was another woman wrapped in a shawl and nursing a baby.   " I wish you would hold the baby for a few minutes, while I go and have a look at the fair," said this woman to Mrs. Hewer, " and here, you may as well have the shawl too."   With this she departed,

At Broadwell, near Stow.

and the anxious Mrs. Hewer was left saddled with both baby
and shawl.   She had not been in charge long, when a man
hurried into the churchyard, threw a small packet into her lap
and as hastily departed.   Being a prudent person Mrs. Hewer
slipped the packet into her pocket, and kept it there till she had
delivered up her charge to its owner.   Then she went away and
privately opened the packet : her astonishment may be imagined
when she found that it contained her husband's purse, and what
was more, all its contents absolutely intact.   What kind of
a reception Mr. Hewer met with on his return home from the
fair has not been recorded.

" Stow on the Wold, where the wind blows cold," whatever it
may be like in the depth of winter, is a bright cheerful place
enough on a fine spring morning.   On the green, at the western
extremity of the great square, beneath the budding elms, stand
the stocks—once a terror to evil-doers, and the surrounding
houses have all that quiet, comfortable appearance which distinguishes an old-fashioned country-town.   On the south side
is the churchyard, where the rooks are now clamorous at the
summit of the grove of horse-chestnuts, and from their nests
they may survey their favourite feeding grounds stretching for
miles across the wolds.   The air is keen and invigorating, and
impatient as we are to set off on our expedition, we must first
step into the church and look at the great picture of the
Crucifixion over the altar.   It was painted by Gaspar Crayer, a
Flemish artist and pupil of Rubens, and was presented to the
Rectory of Stow in 1838.   The church was rebuilt in the
thirteenth century, and the arcade, together with one or two
good Early English windows in the north aisle, are of that date.
The clerestory is of course perpendicular, but the tracery was
removed from its windows in Charles the Second's time.   At
the rebuilding Edward the Confessor became the patron saint,
but the original dedication had been to a local hermit of the
same name, who was believed to have founded the church in
the ninth century.   In fact, down to the sixteenth century, the

House in Market Square, Stow-on-the-Wold.

town was known as Edwardestow, or Stow St. Edward, and
when the present appellation came in, just as wool in the local
dialect became 'ool, wood, 'ood and woman, 'ooman, so wold
became 'old, and in some of the Civil War tracts the name is
actually printed Stow the Old. This was sometimes with
amazing perversity again corrupted into "Stow o' the 'ole"—
a corruption once attended by an unforeseen disaster. In the
severe winter of 1772, when the snow lay deep on the ground,
a party of five soldiers of the Buffs received orders to march to
"Stow in the Ole." They reached the foot of the hill about
sunset, and on inquiring the way to the town they were directed
to proceed to the top. Believing not unnaturally that their informant was attempting to put a trick on them, they refused
to ascend, and darkness coming on, and overcome by fatigue,
they all perished in the snow.

To return to the church: in the chancel lies Captain
Hastings Keyte, one of the Keytes of Ebrington, a family
connected by marriage with the Hastingses of Daylesford: as
the inscription on his tomb informs us he was slain "ex parte
regis" at the battle of Stow, the last open fight of the Civil War,
where that gallant veteran Lord Astley laid down his arms.
He was marching to join the King at Oxford with 3,000 men
whom he had collected in the north-western Midlands, but
when he reached the Avon he found the governors of Gloucester
and Hereford, Sir Thomas Morgan and Colonel Birch, waiting
to oppose his progress. For some days they succeeded in
thwarting every attempt he made to cross the river, but
eventually changing their tactics they withdrew to Campden,
and on the 20th of March, 1646, Astley crossed at Bidford,
and as he marched through the vale by the line of the Roman
road that joins Bourton and the Foss with Alcester, the enemy
lay watching him from the top of the hills. About nine
in the evening he passed them without much opposition, for
Sir Thomas Morgan was expecting the instant arrival of Sir
William Brereton from Cheshire with reinforcements, and

Birch had advised him "not to tempt God by fighting over-much, when it may bee hee would would afoard vs more meanes." An hour or two later, however, Brereton not arriving, he grew impatient, and persuaded Morgan to give the order to advance. "Come, sir," said he, "God will give vs noe more meanes : yett I am confident hee will deliver them into our hands." Astley had drawn up his men on some un-enclosed land about a mile to the north of Stow, and Brereton and his horse having by this time come up, the Roundheads charged him about an hour before dawn. After one or two repulses they were victorious, and Astley, together with many other officers, was taken prisoner. One of his enemies related how "being taken Captive, and wearyed in this fight, and being ancient (for old ages silver haires had quite covered over his head and beard) the Souldiers brought him a Drum to sit and rest himselfe upon, who being sate, he said (as was most credibly enformed) unto our Souldiers ; Gentlemen, yee may now sit downe and play, for you have done all your worke, if you fall not out among yourselves."

We may now cross the Foss and take the Tewkesbury road. A drop of some three hundred feet brings us to one of those green retreats which, from the earliest times, became the chosen homes of those who penetrated into these wilds. What need to wander further? Celtic or pre-Celtic, here the pilgrim would set up his staff: here the Roman had his villa, and the Saxon his farmstead : here the Tudor squire erected his modest manor-house and here in latter days has risen the stately mansion of the modern lord of the soil. I am now standing on the bridge by the mill at Upper Swell: the clear stream beneath me meanders through the delightful grounds of Abbotswood, past Bowl Farm, once owned by Sir Robert Atkyns, the earliest historian of the county, past Lower Swell, where the water is glorious in summer with masses of yellow mimulus, till it joins the Wind-rush a mile below Bourton. But first it is joined by a brook from the north-west which threads a valley almost more

Upper Swell Manor.

romantic : a valley which conceals Eyford and the Slaughters, of which anon. On the right a few paces above the bridge stands the church, and hard by is the fine grey manor-house of early Stuart times. As usual, since these "capital mansions" have been handed over to the farmer, the rooms have been divided up by modern partitions, but you can still see the great Renaissance mantel-piece, and form a picture of the ancient splendour of the place, to which you would fain restore it. The church is a good example of the twelfth century Cotswold type to which I have before alluded. These churches survive here and there in the remoter villages, where the population did not outgrow them, and where there was no money to indulge in the ambitious reconstructions of the fifteenth century. They are small aisleless edifices, with Norman south door and Norman chancel arch, and were originally without any east window. Internally the east wall was ornamented with statues and frescoes ; externally it was blank, and the chancel was lighted by small windows in the side walls. In almost every instance, however, this characteristic feature has been destroyed by the insertion of an east window. Here, at Upper Swell, it is a large modern window in the Early English style, and its contrast with the good splayed Norman windows still remaining in the north and south walls, and quite large enough for the church, only serves to emphasise its intrusion. The lower part of one of the windows in the south wall appears to have been cut off by a transom : as a matter of fact it is a small, square, low-side window formed at the base of the original one. A similar church of even greater interest existed at Lower Swell, a mile down the stream, but alas ! in that iconoclastic age, the middle of the nineteenth century, its historical significance was entirely destroyed. It had committed the offence of becoming too small for the needs of the growing generation, and sentence was forthwith passed upon it. It was in fact condemned to lose its distinction and its identity, and to be degraded to the position of a mere appendage. This result was brought about

M

by the following rough and ready expedient : two large openings were cut in the north wall of the ancient church, and the edifice which constitutes the present nave and chancel was tacked on to it. Apparently it did not occur to the parishioners that the obvious remedy was to build the larger church on another site, and to allow the existing church to remain what it had been for so many centuries. One rude piece of ornamental work it had, which still remains : over what was once the chancel arch may be seen a series of curious symbolical carvings, said to be unique and a veritable puzzle to the learned.

We may reach Lower Swell by a pleasant field-path which skirts the grounds of the modern house of Abbotswood, but the windings of the stream above the bridge look so attractive that I am first of all going to take a ramble in that direction. I soon arrive at Donnington Mill, where, on turning the corner, I suddenly come upon a spacious expanse of water, now tenanted by a family of moor-hens. This small lake might claim to be the head and source of the stream I am exploring, but I suspect that it is fed by underground channels connecting it with a stretch of water two miles higher up in the secluded hollow of Hinchwick. The by-road which crosses the valley at the head of the lake leads to Condicote, one of the very few Cotswold villages situated on what was once the open down, and far from any stream. It has a bleak, poverty-stricken air, in marked contrast to the homely comfort of the riverside villages, and it has few attractions to offer the visitor besides its church. This is a worthy fellow to the two we have just been considering, with its richly ornamented Norman door and chancel arch, and the western exterior, with its two original string-courses and flat central buttress, has been little tampered with. There are two ancient British camps in the parish, and several tumuli—tumps we call them in the west—are scattered over the adjacent hill-sides. The churchyard this morning is perfumed with blue violets ; I gather a bunch of them and continue my journey to Hinchwick—a name of sufficient

importance to be inscribed on sign-posts, and therefore
stimulating to the curious mind. It now denotes, so I discover,
little more than a large modern farmstead with extensive yards
and outbuildings; but in earlier days it must have been a
settlement of some consideration—at least so I gather from
the grass-grown mounds, and long lines of boundary wall,
which I pass about half-a-mile before I reach the farm. But
in any case it was worth while to make the journey, if only to
explore the remote woodland dell, through which the upper
stream I mentioned just now makes its way. I follow the road
which has been cut along one side of the dell at a considerable
height from the bottom, till I arrive at an entrenched mound,
which may well have been a fencible outpost of the earliest
settlers in these wilds. On one side the ground is broken, and
the depressions suggest that a community of pit-dwellers may
have had their habitation here; but the only habitation now
visible is the old grey homestead—Warren Farm, they call it—
on the opposite knoll. As I pass by Hinchwick on my return
a boundary stone in a meadow near the road reminds me that
I am here at the eastern extremity of an oblong patch of
Worcestershire, one of those detatched fragments which still
survive like islands in the midst of another shire. Most of
these islands have been merged in the surrounding county by
the operation of modern Acts of Parliament, but in this part
of the county some half-dozen remain unabsorbed. The
island in question comprises the parish of Cutsdean. The
queer little lone village lies at its other extremity, and its history
is typical of such outlying patches in general. It is a chapelry
of the parish of Bredon in Worcestershire, at least twelve miles
distant, and was given by Offa in the eighth century to the
monastery which his grandfather had founded there: it afterwards belonged to the priory of Worcester, but has always
remained parochially attached to Bredon.

I now gain the Tewkesbury road, which takes me back to
Upper Swell, and so by the footpath aforesaid past Bowl Farm

to the Golden Ball at Lower Swell. This hostelry deserves
mention as one of the few Cotswold inns where a cup of good
cider is to be obtained.   This light and wholesome beverage,
the staple drink of the vale, can only boast of a fitful
popularity in the hills, where the attractions of the heavier
and headier malt liquors still reign supreme.   It will be a happy
day for the cyclist when cider, sound and well made, is everywhere to be had, and when the base counterfeits so often sold
under the name have been abolished.   Thus refreshed I follow
the Gloucester road over the hill till it dips down into the
narrow valley which contains the Slaughters.   I am now at
Eyford, and I have been led here by its associations with an
illustrious, if wayward, statesman, who had no small share in
moulding his country's destinies.   There is a fine modern
house at Eyford now, but in the closing years of the seventeenth
century Charles Talbot, Duke (the only *Duke*) of Shrewsbury,
had here what a letter of the day calls "a little house."   About
this time he purchased the estate of Heythrop near Chipping
Norton, but, before he began to build there, it was to Eyford
that he retired from the cares of state, "being delighted," says
Sir Robert Atkyns, "with the solitaryness of the Place, and
the pleasantness of the neighbouring country for recreations."
Here on his progress from Warwick to Oxford in 1695—the
same journey during which, as we saw in an earlier chapter,
he visited Woodstock—William III. deviated from his route to
dine with the Duke, "and was pleased with his entertainment,
for he thought himself out of the world."   Macaulay had
evidently read the story in Atkyns, and his spirited version of
his authority shall be added.   The Duke had been accused by
Sir John Fenwick of tampering with the Jacobites, but the
King had refused to listen to the charge ; and after describing
how unnerved he had been by "a tenderness which he was
conscious that he had not merited," the historian continues,
"Shrewsbury left town, and retired to the Wolds of Gloucestershire.   In that district, then one of the wildest in the south of

the island, he had a small country seat, surrounded by pleasant gardens and fishponds. William had, in his progress a year before, visited this dwelling, which lay far from the nearest high road and from the nearest market town, and had been much struck by the silence and loneliness of the retreat in which he found the most graceful and splendid of his English courtiers."

In the evening his Majesty rode on to Burford. Whether he returned to Stow and there struck the direct road, or whether he went round by Bourton-on-the-Water, the scanty notes of his progress which remain do not tell us. For ourselves we shall pursue the footpath through the plantation by the brook side to Upper Slaughter. As we enter the village we have the church above us on the right, and two most comfortable looking old houses, with spacious and well-kept gardens, across the water on the left. Such gardens assuredly can never suffer from drought, and water-gardening should be a fine art; for the two Slaughters have an equal right with their neighbour, Bourton, to be known as "on the water." At Lower Slaughter and at Bourton the stream, spanned by numerous bridges, flows through the centre of the main street, which in the former case is reduced almost to the dimensions of a footpath; and in this they differ from Bibury, another water village which we shall visit later on, for here the stream skirts the road and the houses are on one side only. If now we turn up through the church-yard, and pass through the upper part of the village, we shall find ourselves in front of the manor-house (now a farm-house) —one of the most beautiful examples of its kind in the whole of the Cotswold. The Elizabethan front with its fine transomed windows, string courses, and long line of dormers in the roof, is most striking: most attractive, too, is the projecting porch with chamber over it—an addition of rather later date. The oldest part of the house is the basement, which has a fine groined roof of the fifteenth century. The manor was church property till the dissolution of the monasteries; when it passed

Manor House, Upper Slaughter.

into the hands of the Slaughters—even then a family of ancient
lineage—who rebuilt the house and resided in it for nearly
three centuries. Their name they had no doubt long before
taken from their native village ; we hear of a Gerald de Slaughter
as far back as the twelfth century, and still earlier, in a charter of
the tenth century, the name occurs as Slohtranford, while in
Domesday it has become Sclostre. As to the origin of the
name history tells us nothing : was this quiet nook the scene of
some bloody victory over the Dobuni, or were the captives
brought down to the brook side to be immolated like the
priests of Baal at the brook Kidron ? Nor do we know much
more of the later history of these pleasant places : that the old
family should have dwelt in the manor-house for three hundred
years, and left us nothing more than a few monumental
inscriptions, a few entries in the register, and a few dry legal
records of conveyance is disappointing : what a picture of
country life during all those eventful years they might have left
us, had any of them kept a journal or preserved their
correspondence ! As it is, the only fact I can find worth setting
down here has no connexion with this family—it is that in
February, 1800, was sold in London the large library of
George Galwey Mills, Esq., of Slaughter House : it realised
£4258 6s. 6d. : surely Mr. Mills and his books must have been
a loss to the village when he went away to take a government
appointment beyond the seas.

Ruminating thus, I take the footpath through the meadows,
now aglow with marigolds, to Lower Slaughter and Bourton.
There is something spruce in the appearance of Lower
Slaughter, something that bespeaks the presence of a wealthy
and generous squire. The houses are old, and gaze cheerfully
at each other across the clear trout stream, but they all have
the air of comfort and neatness, and the gardens are trim and
well-cared for. The squire's mansion adjoins the neat little
modern church, which like the solitary Clapton on the hill
summit to the southward, is now a chapelry to Bourton. A

mile below the Slaughter brook joins the stream from the Swells, and together they flow into the Windrush some couple of miles below Bourton. The Windrush—in spite of its romantic sound, the name is a corruption of the earlier form Wenrisc (779) or Wenris and Waenric (949)—rises at Cutsdean, and after passing the Guitings and Naunton flows through the main street of Bourton, and thence through rich water-meadows, past Burford and Witney, to join the Thames at Newbridge. It vies with its western neighbour, the Coln, as a trout stream, but this is a topic I must not venture upon; I must be content to refer the reader to the lively chapter in *A Cotswold Village*, entitled "When the May-fly is up": he may there be initiated into the mysteries of the "green-drake" and "olive dun," and learn under what conditions the fish "quap up," and when "the springs be frum."

Compared with Lower Slaughter, Bourton may aspire to the rank of a small town, and the numerous miniature bridges which span the water seem to assert its superiority. It abounds in shops and clean-looking inns, and what with its cricket-club and cottage-hospital, and general air of prosperity, I should not be surprised to hear that a neighbouring resort of fashion was the glass wherein its noble youth did dress themselves. However this may be, the importance of Bourton is not a thing of yesterday. To the left of the main street are the remains of a large camp, possibly of pre-Roman origin, and in any case not unlikely to have been adapted as a stronghold by Plautius in his campaign against the Dobuni. At a gap in the rampart, part of which is still standing, the Court-leet of the Liberty used to meet: the jury were then called over, and the court adjourned to the village for the transaction of business.

At the further end of the village the road bears to the left and ascends through Little Rissington to the Stow and Burford road which runs along the top of the western ridge, and a magnificent run down to Burford it is, but to-day I am only going as far as the Merrymouth Inn, three-quarters of a mile beyond the point where the road enters Oxfordshire. This inn is another of the favourite meets of the Heythrop, whose country embraces this eastern side of the Cotswold, and if you are in search of bracing air and a pleasant centre for excursions you may find comfortable and elevated quarters here. As to the origin and antiquity of this cheerful designation I refrain from committing myself, but the fact may be considered that in 1316 a certain John de Muremouth (the spellings Merimouth, Mirimouth, and Murimouth are also found) was lord of the manor here, and there is reason to suppose that Adam de Murimouth, the Chronicler, who graduated as D.C.L. in 1312, belonged to the same family.

On the right of the road before we reach the inn an interesting survival of old village life must be noticed. Throughout the length and breadth of England enclosure acts have long swept away the old open-field system of cultivation, but here in this remote Gloucestershire parish of Westcot a small piece of it still remains. Here are the strips separated by their balks of turf, just as they are described by Mr. Seebohm. Many years ago an attempt at enclosure was successfully resisted, and the land in question is still cultivated by the farmers and other villagers on the old system, the strips held by the same cultivator being scattered and non-contiguous.

From the Merrymouth it is a quick descent through Idbury, with its interesting church and stalwart houses to Bledington on the Gloucestershire side of the Evenlode, and but a mile from the busy station of Chipping Norton Junction. Not that I am going to have recourse to the railway to-day. Bledington Church is too remarkable to be left unvisited, and I must make my way back to Stow by the road. The distinction of Bledington Church is that though the iconoclastic hand of the Puritan has been heavy upon it, it has escaped the no less destructive alterations of the modern church restorer, and its historic continuity with the past therefore remains unviolated. There must have been some well-to-do parishioners here in the fifteenth century, if we may judge from the extensive alterations then made in the church. The clerestory was then built, windows were inserted in the nave and south aisle and filled with stained glass, many fragments of which remain, and the tower was built, not outside, but *inside* the west end of the nave, and carried up through its roof. At the

Icomb Church.

same time the projecting chapel on the south side of the chancel was added. In contrast to all this perpendicular work the narrow and low Early English chancel arch has a very singular effect; there is also a good Early English piscina and east window of three lights with internal shafts. Then there are the old oak seats with their carved bench ends, and the welcome absence of garish tiles and "cathedral" glass.

As for the village itself it lies low, and has withal the deserted melancholy air of one which has seen better days. Its situation no doubt has been against it, for people do not come here to settle as they come to its thriving Oxfordshire neighbour across the river; the joys of Kingham living have, however, been the theme of a subtler pen than mine, and to the lover of birds and books I need say no more. On my left as I climb up to Stow lies Icomb, formerly one of those Worcestershire islands, which belonged to the Priory of Worcester, but now incorporated with Gloucestershire. The interest of Icomb centres in the fine old fifteenth century mansion called Icomb Place, which, strange to say, was always outside the island, and claimed to be extra-parochial. After having been occupied for many years as a farmhouse, it has been restored by its present owner, who now resides there. At the time when it was built the manor belonged to the Blaket family, and in the church is the recumbent effigy of a knight in the plate armour of the day; this is said to represent Sir John Blaket, who fought at Agincourt and died in 1431. My Oxford readers, who are familiar with the beautiful Wilcote Chapel at Northleigh Church, will be interested to hear that the foundress married this Sir John Blaket as her second husband. The daughter of Sir John Trillowe, of Chastleton, she first married Sir William Wilcote, and founded this chantry at Northleigh for the welfare of the souls of her two husbands, and her two sons by her first marriage. On the altar tomb in the chantry chapel are the alabaster effigies of herself and her first husband. Icomb Church, charming as it looks in Mr. Griggs's sketch, has, alas! been through the furnace of restoration, and has little of interest left beyond the Blaket tomb.

Norman Doorway at Guiting Power.

CHAPTER VIII

ONE of the prettiest walks in the whole of the Cotswold is
that up the valley of the Windrush from Bourton to Temple
Guiting. If possible I would choose either a bright spring day,
when the marigolds are in flower, and the ear is keen to catch
the welcome call of the earliest cuckoo, or a cool midsummer
morning, when the air is balmy with the fragrance of the elder
blossom and the new cut hay. If you would enjoy this ramble
to the full, you must take it leisurely, and had best have a
whole day at your disposal. There will be ample exercise
both for eyes and ears : you must have time to sit and watch
the little eddies made by the rising trout, the wary water-vole
nibbling his salad with swiftly quivering jaws, and the nimble
stoat bounding through the long herbage on the trail of
the rabbit that crossed your path a minute since—time again

to listen to the cheerful note of the blackcap, one of the latest
songsters in these upland valleys, or the soothing murmur
of the turtle dove in the lofty ashes that shade the stream. It
is true that at the end of your walk you will find yourself eight
miles from the nearest railway station, but at midsummer the
chances of being benighted in an unknown land are remote,
and if you should not care to go further, you may be housed at
the Plough, and wile away the evening with the books which
stand upon the parlour shelf; for (O rare inmates of the roadside inn!) here are the *Life of Garrick*, Colley Cibber's
Apology, and other monuments of the past, relics, perhaps, of
the library of some long departed Cotswold squire.

But I am anticipating matters—our walk begins at Bourton.
For the first mile and a half we must keep as near the railway
as possible; then, after passing a picturesque mill, the path
leads through a hanging wood on the right bank of the stream.
Now, at the end of June, our way is gay with hawkweed,
ragged robin, and moon-daisies, while now and again we come
upon a clump of yellow flag, or great masses of waving sedge;
and here and there great bunches of withered leaves tell of the
pink saffron that will bloom in the late summer. Presently
the valley becomes wider, the hills on either side higher, and
the path winds now through level meadows, now through
thickets of ancient thorns, now through shady woods of oak
and ash till the Stow and Gloucester road is crossed at Harford
bridge. Here we have a mile of the stone wall country, the
favourite haunt of the whin-chat, and a pair of these birds
appear to regard our intrusion with some anxiety, the cock, as
he flits here and there to watch us safely off his premises,
keeping up his curious note, "fu—tic tic." We have now
arrived at Naunton, the first of the three villages on our walk,
and a prosaic little place enough, though if we are to believe
Samuel Rudder, the second of the county historians—he
printed his Folio at Cirencester in·1779—one of the healthiest
in England, boasting as it did an annual death-rate of less than

one per cent. Its distinction on this count has not, however, resulted in investing it with any great attraction, and when we have looked at all that remains of the capital mansion, to wit, a cyclopean dove-cot, square, with four great gables, but in these latter days destitute of doves, we may leave the village without a sigh and continue our pursuit of the Windrush up the green valley that takes us to the Guitings. The curious student indeed, should his curiosity have led him into the byways of seventeenth century poetry, may tarry to search for some memorial of Clement Barksdale, once rector here, and author of *Nympha Libethris, or the Cotswold Muse*.

> " The Cotswold Muse so called to do her right
> For rustic plainness, not for any height."

Perhaps he may have read in Rudder of certain brass plates affixed to the north wall of the chancel, and will go into the church to see them. He will find them, but not *in situ ;* the church has been swept and garnished, and they have been most improperly (for was not Barksdale rector ?) relegated to the tower. The first of them, a little plate less than six inches by four, was set up by the rector in his sixty-first year (he lived till his seventy-ninth), and appeals to our traveller with startling directness : " D. S. Clemens Barksdalius Artium magister Evangelii minister Quotidie orans Quotidie moriens Jubet te, Viator, Cœlestem Cogitare Patriam." The other he inscribed to the memory of three of his children who predeceased him. If any memorial was ever set up to himself (and as rector he was buried in the chancel) it has disappeared.

Under the Commonwealth Barksdale kept a private school at the neighbouring village of Hawling, where he had many of the sons of the surrounding county gentlemen as his pupils. Here he wrote the *Cotswold Muse*, " presenting some extempore verses to the imitation of young scholars." The book is a collection of short poems, but has little local colouring about it. There is one " Upon the Scholars succeeding Soldiers at Sudeley Castle": another pair are "Sudeley to Rowill," and "Rowill to Sudeley." Rowill or Roel

> (" Madam see here your Roëll Muse
> Exults for joy your name to use "

writes the poet to Lady Chandos) is a hamlet of Hawling where Lord Chandos of Sudeley had a house to which he retired when the Roundheads were in possession of the castle. At the Restoration Barksdale was presented to the livings of Naunton and Stow, and resided at Naunton, where, says Wood, he left behind him the character of a frequent and edifying preacher, and a good neighbour. " He was a good disputant, a great admirer of Hugh Grotius, a frequent preacher, but very conceited and vain, a great pretender to poetry, and a writer and translator of several little tracts, most of which are meer scribbles." I should hardly call this an unfair estimate of the man, at any rate, as regards his pretensions to poetry, but it seems to have given offence to his descendants, for Wood in his diary under May 21, 1695, records: "at the hither end of Magd. bridg, came out of the hole between it and the near herb-house one [Clement] Barksdale and told me I had abused his grandfather and followed me muttering till I came to Magd. Coll. corner. I was faigne to hold up my cudgell at him."

Above Naunton we keep to the stream, and the towering woods of Guiting Grange soon rise before us. This was a Grange of Bruern Abbey,[1] and a few remains of a chapel— supposed to have been a mortuary chapel for the inmates—can still be traced in a field at some distance from the house, while " Trinity ford " and " Bier-way piece " remain to indicate the road taken by the funeral procession. We may leave the Grange on our right and strike across the fields to Lower Guiting or Guiting Power. The church stands at the end of the village, the faithful witness of the fortunes of its inhabitants ; we will turn aside and try to read them there. All

---

[1] In the Evenlode valley, near Kingham.

is now the picture of seemliness, but in 1902 the crumbling fabric reflected only too faithfully the decayed condition of the village. For in recent years the population of Lower Guiting has diminished by nearly one-half, and some thirty cottages now stand untenanted and in various stages of dilapidation. But in old days it was as prosperous a village as any of its compeers : here settled the Norman lord, and here he built the Norman church of the Cotswold type we already know so well. Two richly-ornamented doorways of this period still remain, and a transition Norman chancel arch with similar ornamentation survived till the alterations of 1820. In the twelfth century, or early in the thirteenth, the beautiful Early English chancel was built ; and in the fifteenth, when the wool trade was at its height, the tower was added, and the walls of the nave raised to receive the present low-pitched roof. So far all was well, but with the nineteenth century came the enclosures, and the large profits which followed the new style of farming. With increase of prosperity came increase of population, and it was determined to enlarge the church in the approved fashion of the day. Accordingly at an interval of twenty years (in 1820 and 1844), the north and south transepts were thrown out from the nave and connected with it by two depressed arches without pillars. It was on the earlier of these occasions that the old chancel arch was replaced by a depressed arch to match the new ones ; and on the later that the Norman south doorway was removed from its place opposite the north door and built into the south wall of the new transept, where it stands at present. Towards the close of the century came the days of agricultural depression, and church and village became partners in decay. Three years ago the former presented a melancholy spectacle. The nave and transepts in their squalid deformed condition were alone used for service : for fifteen years the chancel had been boarded off and was fast going to ruin. But at last, mainly owing, as the brass plate in the rebuilt chancel records, "to the quiet determination and persistent effort" of the present curate in charge, money was collected, and a restoration worthy of the name has been carried out. It was found absolutely necessary to rebuild the chancel, but the conservative spirit in which the work was undertaken is evidenced by the following inscription on a small brass plate affixed to the priest's door: "At the restoration in 1903 this chancel doorway and small window were not disturbed."

Close to the church is another of the beautiful old Cotswold manor-houses, and as we leave the village to rejoin the Windrush at the hamlet of Barton, the little tributary brook is crowded with yellow mimulus, which flourishes here in the same luxuriance as at Lower Swell. There are two charming old houses at Barton, both, since the flight of the smaller gentry from the country side, occupied as farmhouses.

From Barton the path runs along the side of the down above the stream, one of those wide stretches of grass still used as a sheep walk. The grass is of that peculiarly bright green hue which suggests "blues" and "burnets" to the entomologist. He will look anxiously about him for *Arion*, the "large blue," which is known to frequent certain favoured but secret spots among these hills, and he will call to mind how he used to read in his Stainton, still treasured and never to be superseded, of its kinsman *Acis* that "the Rev. Jos. Greene took two specimens (not good) of this rare species in a chalky field near Lower Guiting, on the Cotswolds, the beginning of July 1849." But neither Arion nor Acis are to be seen to-day, and we soon plunge into a thick wood from which we emerge into the quiet meadows sentinelled by the church and mansion of Temple Guiting.

If William III. thought himself "out of the world" at Eyford, but three miles from Stow, what would he have said to Temple Guiting? A more peaceful village it would be difficult to find; there is no inn, the great house is untenanted,

N

the children are at school, and their elders in the fields: the cottage doors stand open, and it is with some difficulty that you at last come upon an inhabitant, who encourages you to proceed another mile on your journey to The Plough, at Ford. Thither then we shall proceed in due time, but Temple Guiting has too much individual character about it to be neglected for the sake of mere creature comforts, and an hour spent in loitering here will not be lost. So screened is the village by thick plantations, that the traveller might pass within a few yards of it without suspecting its existence. The Windrush falls through the grounds of the great house into the meadows we have just left, having the church standing aloft on one bank and the mansion on the other. It is hardly necessary to say that the prefix Temple comes from the Templars who held lands here under the Norman Lacies and their descendants, and on the suppression of their order by Edward II., were succeeded by the Hospitallers. For an account of any local vestiges that may remain of these orders, and of the fulling mills said to have been established at Barton by the Templars, we must await in patient expectation the *Victoria County History of Gloucestershire.*

With Oxford, Temple Guiting is linked by a double bond; the manor was purchased in 1517 by Bishop Foxe of Winchester, and given to his recent foundation, while at the dissolution of the Hospitallers their estates, together with the rectory and the advowson of the living, were granted by Henry VIII. to Christ Church. The society of Corpus Christi are still lords of the manor and owners of most of the parish, including the deserted mansion. It is sad to see this house standing empty, and its gardens overgrown: what a home of recreation and research might it make for a celibate President and Fellows in the long vacation! Thus Temple Guiting would once more boast its Templars—though a fellowship of students instead of soldiers, while for the rest, doth not Rudder pronounce the place to be fine country for hunting, abounding in game and enjoying a very healthy air? Oxford men may also like to know that this house once had the distinction of containing the famous Pusey horn. In the eighteenth century the college tenants were a family named Allen, and one of the last of these, Mrs. Jane Allen, was a descendant of the Puseys. The Allens were succeeded as lessees by the Talbots, a family whose connection with the village began about 1740 and lasted till about twenty years ago. About this time Dr. George Talbot, a son of Lord Chancellor Talbot, of Great Barrington, was appointed to the incumbency, a man who left his mark on the place in more senses than one. His virtues, which include the refusal of a bishopric, are recorded on the tablet erected to his memory in the church. These may have made him the idol of his flock, but for posterity the church itself is his most eloquent memorial. He spent a thousand pounds in " beautifying " it according to the taste of his day, and it remains an astonishing example of the enormities which the taste of the day was capable of. From contemporaries the work met with nothing but praise : " this church," says Rudder, " has been beautified in a more elegant manner than is often seen in village churches ;" " Dr. Talbot," writes Ralph Bigland about the same time, " in 1745 entirely remodelled the inside in a high style of modern decoration with a flat roof and surrounding cornices." This is, it is true, more guarded language, as befitted an eminent antiquary and Garter King-at-Arms ; the " high style of modern decoration " was probably not altogether to his taste. The best that can be said for it is that the work is solid, practical, and appallingly heavy, and perhaps had better remain unaltered as a historical curiosity ; even the tower has been loaded with four stout square, squat pinnacles, which have managed to rob it of any grace or dignity it may once have had.

And now across the fields to our inn in the pretty hamlet of Ford, just where the road from Stow to Tewkesbury dips to cross the head waters of the Windrush. The Plough is now kept by one Mr. Jesse Wiggett, a name familiar for generations in this part of the Cotswold. His house is a rambling, picturesque building, apparently about three hundred years old, though he himself is inclined to date it from Adam. After seven long miles up and down over the hills from Stow, with not a house to be seen for the last six of them, the smoke curling up from the kitchen chimney of the Plough must have been a welcome sight to the traveller in the days when there was no railway to take him to the Vale of Severn by circuitous routes and easy gradients; in those days he must perforce drive or trudge across the hill country, be the weather what it may, and he would be little inclined to decline the hospitable invitation, which may still be read upon the gable of the inn facing the road, and which I transcribe *verbatim et litteratim* :

> " Ye weary travelers that pass by
> With dust & scorching sunbeams dry
> Or be he numb'd with snow & frost
> With having these bleak Cotswolds crost
> Step in & quaff my nut brown ale
> Bright as rubys mild and stale
> Twill make your laging trotters dance
> As nimble as the suns of france
> Then ye will own ye men of sense
> That neare was better spent six pence."

Whether or no Mr. Wiggett's ale still keeps its character, I am unable to say, owing to a personal preference for his Herefordshire cider ; and I must leave the " weary traveller " who has accompanied me thus far to decide the point for himself. But ale or cider drinker he will do well to take up his quarters under Mr. Wiggett's roof for the night, that is if he means to continue the walk to our next headquarters, the ancient market-town of Chipping Campden. Of the literary entertainment he will find at the Plough I have already spoken ; but he must not linger over it too late, for we must be up and away betimes, no longer sauntering by the brook side, but across the high wild hills and rough uneven ways which lie

between us and our destination. In a mile or two we strike
the ancient track locally known as Buckle Street, which here
skirts the edge of the western escarpment of the Cotswolds at
an altitude of some 1050 feet. Below us on our left is Middle
Hill, where that eccentric antiquary Sir Thomas Phillipps
brought together that wonderful library, which he afterwards
removed to Cheltenham, and a little further we are confronted
by a tall square object, the angles of which are formed by four
circular projections, rising to battlemented turrets, looking
for all the world like a castle belonging to some colossal set
of chessmen. This is Broadway Tower, or as the country folk
call it "Broaday Monument"—a landmark conspicuous for
miles the whole country round. Mediæval as it looks from its
massive construction, if not in its details, it is little more than
a century old. At the end of the eighteenth century the
ground on which it stands belonged to the Earl of Coventry,
and the story goes that the Countess wishing to see whether
the spot could be seen from Croom Court, the family seat
near Worcester, caused a bonfire to be lighted here. The fire
being plainly visible, she persuaded the Earl to build a tower
here, and the foundation stone was accordingly laid on August
29, 1800. The tower is now inhabited by a labouring man and
his family, but some thirty years ago was rented by a well-
known Haileybury master, who spent many an airy vacation
here entertaining congenial parties of friends. They found
the situation and mode of life highly conducive to the
formation of a healthy appetite, and scorning the only drawback to their felicity, namely the difficulty of obtaining
provisions, they bravely carried them up from the village at
the foot of a steep hill more than a mile long. The view they
had on a clear morning was superb : at their feet the vale of
Evesham stretched to the Malvern Hills—a range always striking when viewed from a distance—to the south-west lay the
Forest of Dean with the Black Mountains towering behind it ;
north-west rose the Licky Hills, and, further still, the Shropshire

Clee and the Long Mynd, whence their eyes ranged eastward
to the Wrekin, the spires of Coventry, and the red roofs of
Stratford.

We may now descend to Campden either across the fields
by the Fish Inn—a small isolated public built in 1771, or
follow the Stow road as far as the old sign-post known as
the Four Cross Hands. These "Hands" point to "Woster,"
"Oxford," "Gloster" and "Warwick," and bear the date 1669,
together with the initials of the public-spirited setter-up of the
post, one Nathan Izod, a member of a family which has for
generations owned and farmed land in the vicinity. It will be
observed that the miles indicated, being computed miles, are
considerably longer than our modern ones. The Warwick road
is the one which takes us down to Campden.

Of the five Cotswold towns with which this volume is concerned, Chipping Campden, Stow, Northleach, Burford and Cirencester, Chipping Campden is undoubtedly the most distinctive
and the most expressive. Outwardly but little changed for some
three hundred years, a silent yet eloquent witness of the past,
the old town lies retired in a fold of the hills, apart from any
main road, and unmolested by the railway which hides itself in
the valley a mile away. The long wide street, its houses of
native stone, most of seventeenth century date, and some much
older, finds its fitting termination in the church, the pride and
glory of the town and the imperishable monument of its greater
days. For Campden was once the great emporium of the
Cotswold wool, and its church is one of those splendid buildings of the later middle ages which owe their existence to the
piety and munificence of the great wool merchants. Here
lived William Grevel, ancestor of the houses of Warwick and
Willoughby de Broke, whose fame was such that his brass in
the church calls him the flower of the wool merchants of all
England ; when he died in 1401, he bequeathed a hundred
marks towards the building of the church which was then in
progress, and in which he had doubtless taken a leading part.

Grevel's House, Chipping Campden.

The dwelling-house which he built for himself with its Gothic doorway and fine panelled bay windows two stories high still stands on the north side of the main street and is still inhabited.

By the time of William Grevel the wool trade had probably been flourishing at Campden for the best part of two centuries. Before the Norman Conquest it is not likely that sheep-farming on any large scale was carried on. The few fleeces raised on each manor would suffice to supply the rough cloth or frieze that formed the ordinary dress of the lord and his dependants. The yarn was spun and woven at home, and the labour of each community was self-sufficing. But with the advent of the wealthy Norman landowners, the waste land of the manor was no longer allowed to remain without its profit. The wolds now became, as they continued to be for six centuries, vast sheep-walks, and the produce of the countless flocks that grazed them far exceeded the wants of the scanty population. The wool was grown for sale, and England soon became the principal wool-producing country in Europe. A story told by a contemporary chronicler shows that at least as early as the beginning of the twelfth century, the Flemish traders were in the habit of travelling to England for their wool. In 1114, certain canons from Laon crossed over to England in order to collect subscriptions towards the rebuilding of their church. In the same ship were several Flemish merchants with more than three hundred marks of silver in their purses. On their voyage they were attacked by pirates, "whereupon (I quote Professor Ashley's version) the aforesaid merchants in despair of their lives, offered their bags and purses with all their money to Our Lady, and cast them on her shrine, beseeching her with pity and tears, promising that if only she saved their bodies from the hands of the pirates, she should keep all their money for the restoration of her church." A wind thereupon rose and scattered the enemy, and the monks were in charity about to give back some of the money to the merchants, "but they as soon as they saw that they had escaped death, forgot their fear, and without permission each one took his bag and purse, leaving nothing to Our Lady but idle words of thanks. But now let all who give their property to God and take it back again, listen to the revenge which the just Judge her Son took for his Mother. They had journeyed over almost the whole of England, and had spent all their money in buying vast quantities of wool, which they had stored in a great building on the coast of Dover ; but behold, on the night before the day on which they intended to cross, the building suddenly took fire and was burnt down with the whole of their wool. Then when they had lost all their property and had become destitute, they too late repented of the insult they had offered to the Queen of Heaven."

It is unlikely that these ungrateful merchants with their long train of sumpter mules or pack-horses neglected to visit the Cotswold towns, though the trade was as yet in its infancy. By the time of William Grevel, 250 years later, Englishmen had begun to export their wool themselves, and visits of foreign buyers must have been the exception. In 1363 the Staple, as the licensed mart for the sale of English products was called, was, after several changes, definitely fixed at Calais, and here buyers from all parts of the continent would congregate. We can in imagination draw a picture of the appearance which the High Street of Campden would have presented at this period about shearing time. Droves of pack-horses laden with wool consigned to Grevel and other merchants, would be seen slowly filing through the town to the Woolstaplers' Hall, a fourteenth century building still standing, with its adjacent warehouses. Here the wool would be sorted and made up into bales of the orthodox size call sarplers and pokes, while samples would be passed from hand to hand, to be criticised and appraised by the assembled merchants : bids would follow and a considerable quantity would change owners, as corn does now-a-days

in a modern corn exchange. Before Grevel's time most
of the bales thus sold would have sooner or later found their
way to the continental market. But in his time a change had
begun, the effect of which was to diminish the foreign exporta-
tion of the raw material, and which ended in stopping it
altogether. This was the rise of the native clothing trade.
Anxious to improve the domestic manufactures, Edward III.
encouraged the settlement of Flemish artisans in this
country, and under their influence cloth of an excellence
hitherto unknown except as imported goods began to be
made in several parts of England. In Gloucestershire, the
home of the new industry was the valley of the Stroud Water
and its numerous affluents, and we can have no doubt that a
large proportion of the Cotswold wool, which had formerly been
shipped to Flanders, was now manufactured into cloth at home.
At last the home made cloth itself began to be exported, till
the clothing industry became so flourishing that under Elizabeth the export of wool in the raw state was altogether forbidden. In the long run, this changed state of affairs, conducive
as it was to the general prosperity of the country, proved fatal
to the prosperity of Campden. Though conveniently situated
as a centre for the collection and distribution of the raw
material, the town was deficient in that abundant supply of
water-power which attracted the new manufacturing interest to
the copious rivulets of the Stroud valley, and with certain
qualifications to be noticed directly it became from the accession of the Stuarts onwards a purely agricultural country-town.
Just at this crisis in its fate a munificent benefactor appeared
upon the scene, to whom many of the most beautiful features
of the town as it exists at present are due ; but to him we must
return presently ; we must first finish the story of the industries
of which it has been the home.

What may be called the second period in the industrial
history of Campden began some time in the eighteenth century.
The extensive ribbon trade of Coventry encouraged the

establishment of subordinate branches of the silk industry in the neighbouring localities, especially those in which water power was available. Among the latter the Cotswold district would hold a prominent place, and accordingly a silk mill was opened at Blockley, three miles to the south of Campden, by one Henry Whatcott in Anne's reign. Exactly when the silk mill was opened at Campden, or how far the industry succeeded there, nobody seems to know, but at any rate it lingered on till the middle of the nineteenth century, when the collapse of the Coventry ribbon manufacture proved fatal to its further existence. I should say that the particular stage of the industry carried on at Blockley and Campden was that technically known as silk-throwing, that is, the conversion of the raw material into twisted threads suitable for weaving : the weaving itself being done at Coventry. The silk-throwing gone, the silk mill was abandoned to all kinds of base uses, and the decline in the fortunes of the ancient borough proceeded apace.

A borough, indeed, it soon ceased to be ; the useless and effete corporation was abolished in 1883, and in 1891 the population which had stood at 2,357 in 1851 had dwindled down to 1,736. In 1901 the returns showed a further diminution of ten per cent., and it seemed that Campden would soon present a spectacle only less desolate and decayed than Northleach, its quondam rival, when an event occurred which has given a fresh turn to the wheel, and from which it may be confidently expected that its townsmen will date a third period of prosperous activity.

This was the migration from London in 1902 of the Guild of Handicraft under the inspiration and direction of Mr. C. R. Ashbee. After fourteen years' work at Essex House, a fine old Queen Anne mansion in Mile End Road, Mr. Ashbee was enabled to realise his idea of the advantages which would result to the life and work of the Guild from a move right out into the country. Few places could make a stronger appeal to the disciples of John Ruskin and William Morris—and those who know anything of the Guild know that it is to the teaching and ideals of these masters that it owes its inception—than Chipping Campden; and when an opportunity occurred of obtaining a footing here by the purchase of the old silk mill, the members, almost unanimously, agreed to make the move. Thus Campden gains as an access to its numbers a body of educated and intelligent craftsmen, while the craftsmen have exchanged the tainted atmosphere and crowded spaces of the East End for the fresh air and freedom of the wolds.

The Guild of Handicraft has been organised on the co-operative principle. After eighteen months' probation a workman may become a full member; he then has a voice in its management, and participates in its profits, for it is an established principle that if the enterprise is to be successful it must not only be self-supporting, but must earn dividends. The ranks of the craftsmen are recruited from pupils who learn their trade in the various workshops. These embrace many of the domestic arts, other than those connected with food and clothing. There are jewellers, metal smiths of all kinds, enamellers, woodcarvers, cabinet-makers, printers and book-binders. The designs are frequently those of the workmen themselves, and one of the most valuable traditions which they have received from Morris is that a thing should be useful as well as beautiful, that it has not fulfilled the demands of true art if its utility is lost amid an elaboration of merely decorative flourishes.

Nor is the Guild forgetful of its members when the hours of the workshop are over. An arts and crafts school has been established, athletic clubs formed, a bathing lake constructed, and a Craftsman's Club instituted, where books and newspapers may be read, and where essays on literary and artistic subjects are welcomed and criticised. In the winter there are dances and social parties; a brave attempt has even been made to tread the learned stage, and I suppose that the Town Hall,

A Courtyard at Chipping Campden.

Chipping Campden, is the only place in which Jonson's *New Inn* has been witnessed, since it was "most negligently played" and "more squeamishly censur'd" in the poet's own day.

O fortunatos nimium sua si bona norint, *Campdenides*! In the modern Arcadia the voice of Pan is too often silent, and it would be difficult to rate too highly the accession to the small country town of a company of eager and enthusiastic workers—men whose interest in life is not sapped by the crushing monotony of merely mechanical labour. Already, too, there have been signs of what may be called the conservative influence of the presence of the Guild. New cottages have been built in the spirit and character of the High Street, and old houses until recently in ruin have been carefully repaired, and given new life. Indeed it was none too soon to show what may be done in this direction, for the solid house of grey stone, the pride of Campden for so many generations, is already threatened by the vulgar style of the present day: already several cases have occurred in which red brick has been used when stone was to hand, and in which grey stone slates have been stripped from the roofs to make room for garish red tiles. Let the men of Campden take timely warning, and see to it that their priceless heritage is not lost to them for ever. In Mr. Ashbee they have a fellow townsman whose sympathies are entirely with the architectural traditions of the place, and under his advice (I need hardly say that he is an architect by profession) neither will any outrageous novelty intrude itself, nor will any pains be spared to preserve everything worthy of preservation. His own residence, the ancient Woolstaplers' Hall, is a striking instance of what may be done in this direction: the removal of modern partitions has restored to its former proportions the fine open timbered, 14th century room in which the wool business was transacted ; the cottage built by him for Mr. Izod, a member of the family already mentioned, opposite the Roman Catholic Church, is another, and at Broad Campden, a hamlet a mile to the south, he has obtained a long lease of a curious Norman chapel, long a prey to ivy and choked by nettles and brambles, and till recently used as a dwelling house. Not that this desecration is of modern date, for there is evidence that the chapel had been converted to secular uses, even before the Reformation, and it is possible that the rise of the great church of Campden in the fifteenth century may have rendered its further maintenance unnecessary. Mr. Ashbee has taken steps

Norman Doorway at Broad Campden.

to rescue this venerable relic from further destruction ; and intends to deal wisely with it in future.

The impression made upon the stranger by the great church of Campden is best described as that of a perfect combination of unity, magnificence, and strength : in this respect it is not surpassed by any one of the many churches mentioned in this volume. Moreover, the unity of the effect is enhanced by the solemn uniformity of the colouring of the exterior, which is a

rich dark brown unbroken either by creeping plants or by
patches of unweathered stone. But the greater our admiration
for the exterior, the greater will be the shock to our feelings on
entering the building : it is the old story of nineteenth century
atrocities,—scraped walls, encaustic tiles, stained deal, and flat
ceiling. The reader, I fear, must be getting weary of my
frequent lamentations on this subject, but the fault is not mine,
and this instance is too flagrant to be passed over in silence. In
justice, however, it must be added that the last restoration is not
wholly responsible for the present state of affairs. A hundred
years earlier the seemly oaken benches carved with the arms or
marks of the wealthy woolstaplers had been swept away to make
room for the unsightly high pews so dear to the later Georgian
era. For these, at any rate, there was nothing to be said, but
that at the same time the paving of black and white marble
and the many flat gravestones which it contained should have
been ruthlessly torn up, is unpardonable. The slabs containing
the famous brasses were of course respected, but it was
judged expedient to move them into the chancel. Considering that, except in the case of Grevel, these slabs were
believed to cover the graves of the persons they commemorate,
the justification of such removal is not apparent.

The singular arcades of the nave, consisting of lofty octagonal
fluted pillars supporting very depressed arches, we shall meet
again at Northleach. They are a mark of late Perpendicular
work, and although, as mentioned above, rebuilding was in contemplation at the death of Grevel in 1401, almost the whole of
the present church must have been built at a later date than
this—probably some time in the latter half of the fifteenth
century.

The south chapel is the burying place of Baptist Hicks, first
Viscount Campden, and his descendants. The long list of
benefactions bestowed upon his adopted town by this splendid
patron, may be read in Stowe's Survey of London : among the
smallest are the handsome carved pulpit, and the fine brass

Church Street, Chipping Campden.

lectern still in use in the church; while most conspicuous among the rest are the Almshouses on the right as we leave the church and the market hall in the centre of the High Street. For pure craftsmanship in stone masonry it would be hard to find anything finer than these noble Almshouses, and they bear emphatic witness to the truth that however humble the edifice, it need never be either flimsy in construction or paltry in design. These benefactions would alone suffice to immortalise his memory, but it is also fitting that his bodily likeness should be preserved by the magnificent monument in this chapel erected by his widow. There they lie in marble for all time, himself and his wife, attired in coronets and robes of state, the central figures of a striking scene. For on their right in the act of stepping forth from the open doors of a marble sepulchre are two strange shapes hand in hand, their limbs wrapped in flowing shrouds and their heads crowned with coronets. These are Juliana daughter of Baptist Hicks, and her husband Edward Lord Noel, who succeeded his father-in-law as second Viscount Campden : the scene depicted is that of the Resurrection, my Lord gracefully handing his lady from the tomb. From them descends the present Earl of Gainsborough. There are also marble busts of their daughter Penelope Noel, a " most beautiful and virtuous lady " to whose memory Milton's friend, Alexander Gill, dedicated an elegy, and of their son's first wife Lady Anne Noel, daughter of the Earl of Denbigh.

Sir Baptist Hicks was the youngest son of a Gloucestershire man, who had set up business as a mercer in London. His shop was at the sign of the White Bear in Cheapside, and when Baptist succeeded to the business he made money so fast that he was able to advance large sums to King James, and the Scottish nobles who frequented the Court. In this connection his elder brother Michael (the ancestor of Sir Michael Hicks-Beach), who held a post about the Court, was able to render him much assistance. Indeed it seems to have been to his extensive money-lending transactions even more than to his regular

Chipping Campden Church.

business that he owed his large fortune, though his experience of the canny Scot was not always satisfactory, if we may judge from a remark in one of his letters to his brother still preserved among the Lansdowne MSS. " I fynde Scottyshe men are fayre speakers and slow performers being rydd of them I will cross them out of my bookes." It was in 1609 that he bought the manor of Campden, and about 1613 he built the splendid mansion to the south of the church, the scanty remains of which are among the first objects to arouse the curiosity of the stranger. In point of fact beyond the curtilage wall and a few out-buildings there is nothing left but a fragment of wall containing one side of the entrance, together with a couple of windows, and two pavilions or belvideres, one at either end of the terrace. The house must have been a magnificent one, considering that it cost £29,000 of the money of that time to build. Unfortun-ately no contemporary drawing of it exists, but it is said to have been built in the Italian style—which indeed would be antecedently probable—and to have been crowned with a transparent dome in which a light was kept burning after dark as a guide to benighted wanderers on the wolds. But costly and splendid as it was its term of life was short—Sir Baptist, who had been raised to the peerage in 1628 as Viscount Campden, died in 1629, and his house survived him less than a score of years. The cause of its destruction was the same that proved the ruin of many a stately pile throughout the land —the Civil War. At the beginning of 1645 Campden House was garrisoned by the Royalists under Sir Henry Bard, a good soldier, but a true specimen of the profane and rapacious cavalier, who had risen from the ranks, and who from his plundering excursions in the country round had made the garrison almost equally detested by both parties. These forays, which extended even as far as Winchcombe, where the victims complained they had not even " a Sunday shift of cloathes left them," went on till May. On the 7th of that month the king, attended by his nephews Rupert and Maurice, set out on his

march from Oxford to relieve the siege of Chester : on the 8th
he held a council at Stow, where he spent the night, and on the
9th he passed within sight of Campden on his way over Broadway Hill.   Meanwhile Bard had received an order from Prince
Rupert to draw off his men and join the king's army, but " least
the enemy should make use of the house for garrison when he
had left it," he was further ordered to set the place on fire before
he marched off.   This was forthwith done, and as the rearguard
quitted the high ground to march down Broadway Hill they
took their last look at the blazing ruins of the mansion.   The
owner Baptist, third Viscount Campden, was serving the king
elsewhere, and had no hand in this destruction, for which it is
difficult to think that there was adequate reason, and which is
condemned in strong terms by Clarendon.   It is a coincidence
that a week or two previously Lydney House, on the verge
of the Forest of Dean in the same county, had been burnt by
its owner, Sir John Wintour, and for the same reason.

I have spoken of the third Viscount as the owner, but it
seems that his mother, the Lady Juliana, who did not die till
1680, at the very respectable age of ninety-five, had a considerable interest in the Campden estate. At any rate it is in a steward
of hers, one William Harrison, that the tale of mystery centres,
famous for many generations as the Campden Wonder.   The
story has been told so often, and has so recently been examined
by the most accomplished of our legendary critics, that I feel
some hesitation in dragging it forth once more ; but no account
of the place would be considered complete without it, and I
must console myself with the hope that to some of my readers,
at any rate, it may yet be a novelty.   I shall cut it as short as
possible, with the proviso that it may be read at greater length
in various places, notably in the *Cornhill Magazine* for
February, 1904.

On the 16th of August, 1660, the said William Harrison,
who had been fifty years in the service of the Dowager
Viscountess, and was now an old man of seventy or there-

abouts, left his house at Campden to walk to the hamlet of
Charringworth, three miles distant on the east side of the town,
for the purpose of collecting some of his lady's rents (an odd
time of year, by the way, for collecting rents; perhaps they were
due at the half quarter). Evening set in and the good man
had not returned. His wife, afraid that something was wrong,
then sent her servant, John Perry, to search for him. Morning
dawned and nothing had been heard either of master or man.
Sending a servant had proved useless, so the son of the house,
Edward Harrison, started off, and had not got more than a
mile on the road when he met Perry returning alone : he made
the man turn round, and they ascertained that his father had
called at the house of one of the tenants at Ebrington the
previous evening, and had rested there a short time. This
was all they could hear of him, but on their return journey
they met a woman who showed them a comb and band stained
with blood which she had found that morning in a furze brake
between Ebrington and Charringworth. These they at once
recognised as the property of the missing man, and so far as
they went they pointed to foul play. The brake was accordingly
thoroughly searched, but no other trace of the steward alive or
dead could be found. This was all the comfort that Edward
Harrison could bring home to his mother. Her suspicions not
unnaturally fell upon Perry, and he was accordingly brought
before the nearest magistrate. The story he then told was so
rambling and confused, that he was detained in custody
pending further inquiries. At the end of a week's detention
he professed himself willing to disclose the real facts of the
case. He was therefore once more brought before the bench,
when he told his story as follows : his mother Joan Perry, he
said, and his brother Richard had long been urgent with him
to join them in robbing his master ; he had turned a deaf ear
for some time, but had at last yielded to their entreaties, and
they had decided that no better opportunity could be found
than when the old gentleman was returning home with his

pockets full of his lady's rents.   They had accordingly waylaid him within a short distance of his own house, strangled him, and taken the bag of money from his pocket: his body they had thrown into the "great mill sink" at Wallington's mill hard by.   As for the comb and band he had himself put them where they were found in order to divert suspicion.   On the strength of this confession, Joan and Richard Perry were at once arrested, but they vehemently protested their innocence, and denounced John for wilfully accusing those he knew to be innocent.   John, however, stuck to his story, and even swore that a piece of string afterwards found in his brother's pocket was the very string with which Harrison had been strangled. Meanwhile the "great mill sink" was dragged and other likely hiding places searched, but without result.   At the Gloucester Assizes when the three prisoners were arraigned, the judge refused to proceed with the trial on the ground that the body of the man supposed to have been murdered had not been found, but at the next assizes a less scrupulous judge presided, and although John Perry now told a different story, and declared that he was mad when he made his confession, and that in fact he knew nothing of his master's death, all three were found guilty and sentenced to death.   The execution took place on Broadway Hill within sight of the scene of the supposed crime.   The old woman, who was reputed to be a witch, and to have prevented her sons by her black arts from confessing the truth, was the first to suffer.   Richard's turn came next; he died protesting his innocence, and vainly calling on his brother to make a clean breast of it by confessing the truth.   At last, just before he was turned off, John Perry solemnly declared that he knew nothing of his master's death or what was become of him, but that *they might hereafter possibly hear.*

Were these last words merely a piece of empty commonplace, or had John Perry somewhere at the bottom of his mind an inkling of the truth?   In any case we can have little doubt

that he was afflicted by that peculiar form of lunacy which leads
the patient to accuse himself and others of wholly imaginary
crimes. His conduct has its parallels; the mystery lies in the
sequel. Two years later in the dusk of an autumn evening
good Mr. William Harrison walked into his house alive and
well. How he explained his absence to his astonished family
is not known, but the story which he presently set forth for the
public benefit is so preposterous, that one wonders how he
could ever have expected it to find acceptance. As he was
returning home on the evening of the eventful 16th August, he
was, he said, kidnapped by three horsemen, who carried him
to Deal in Kent, and sold him to a ship's captain. With this
captain he put to sea, and after six weeks' voyage their vessel
was boarded by Turkish pirates. He and certain other captives,
who had been likewise kidnapped, were seized and carried off
by the Turks. After a further voyage in the hold of the
Turkish ship he was landed and sold as a slave to "a grave
physician of 87 years of age," who lived near Smyrna, and
had formerly visited England. He had to keep his master's
"still-house," and had "a silver bowl double gilt" given him
to drink out of. After nearly two years of this kind of life his
master died, and he managed to escape and make his way to
the coast. Here he bribed some Hamburg sailors with his
bowl to smuggle him as a stowaway to Lisbon, whither they
were bound. At Lisbon he was lucky enough to fall in with
an Englishman, who took compassion on him, and procured
him a passage to England; where he landed at Dover, and made
the best of his way home.

In the article already referred to, the absurdities of this story
have been pointed out by Mr. Lang with his usual acumen.
The unsolved mystery is, where had Harrison really been
during these two years? One would have thought that the
natural persons to have instituted an inquiry into the whole
affair would have been Lady Juliana and her son; but they do
not appear to have stirred a finger in the matter. Possibly

they had reasons of their own for leaving the matter alone: possibly Harrison had knowledge of certain facts affecting the life or liberty of influential persons, and this rendered his disappearance desirable till such time as the danger was blown over. No aspersion appears to have been cast upon his personal character. He seems to have returned to his home and to his stewardship, and to have resumed the life of a respectable citizen till his natural days were ended. The unforeseen consequences of his disappearance were terrible; so much so, that had it been voluntary, one could understand a desire on his part to disguise the fact. Be this as it may, the Campden Wonder the story still remains.[1]

In the first half of the eighteenth century Campden was the residence of two men, who rose to more than local reputation, the one as an inventor, the other as a scholar—Jonathan Hulls and George Ballard. Hulls was the son of a mechanic at

---

[1] Wood in his diary under date Aug. 6, 1662, notes the return of Harrison "out of Turkie to his home in the country." Wood evidently suspected that Mrs. Harrison had something to do with her husband's disappearance. From Ralph Sheldon he acquired a copy of the pamphlet published in 1676, which is the main authority for the story: to this account he adds the following note: "John Perry hung in chaines on the same gallowes. Richard and Joane Perry were after execution taken downe and buried under the gallowes. Three dayes after a gentlewoman, pretending to understand witches, hired a man to dig up the grave that shee might search Joan's body [i.e. for the witch-mark]. Shee being on horseback drew up to the grave when 'twas opened, but the horse starting at the sight of the body ran away under the gallowes, and her head hitting against John's feet struck her off from the horse into the grave.

"After Harrison's returne, John was taken downe and buried and Harrison's wife soon after (being a snotty covetuous presbyterian) hung herself in her owne house. Why, the reader is to judge.

"Upon Harrison's returne to London Sir R[obert] Hyde [the judge who had sentenced the Perrys] was at Glocester in his circuit and one that had seen Harrison there brought the news to Gloucester. Which comming to the hearing of Hyde, he became somewhat passionate and commanding his servant to call the messenger chid him for bringing false news and commanded the jailer to commit him to prison."

Aston Magna, a hamlet through which the railway now passes between Moreton and Blockley stations. In early manhood he settled at Broad Campden as a clock repairer, but his genius carried him far beyond the cogs and balances of the rustic timepieces. His studies led him to reflect on the possibilities of steam power as a means of locomotion, and fifty years before the day of Watt or Fulton he may claim to have been the inventor of the steamboat. His boat was tried on the Avon at Evesham, and in the same year he published a pamphlet containing explanations and diagrams of his system. He did not get so far as to place his engine on board an ordinary vessel; his boat was simply a steam-tug with an axis furnished with six paddles at the stern, this axis being connected with another one turned by the engine. Thus it is clear that he mastered the first principle of steam locomotion, viz., the conversion of the straight horizontal or perpendicular motion of a piston-rod into rotatory motion. Unfortunately, his experiment on the Avon was not a success, and owing to want of money and influential support he seems to have become disheartened, and not to have repeated it. Some years later he patented another invention for "discovering and preventing frauds by counterfeit gold," as well as for a novel kind of measuring rule; but his experiments were a heavy drain upon his limited income, and tradition says that like many another neglected genius he died in obscurity in London.

George Ballard was a native of Weston Subedge; he had but little schooling, and the remarkable thing is that the village lad conceived a passion for the study of Anglo-Saxon, and actually copied out a Saxon dictionary of the day and added to it some thousand words of his own collection. Beside this, his taste for old coins is quite a commonplace weakness: no wonder that he should find his way to Oxford, and that he should become the friend and correspondent of that omnivorous antiquary, Thomas Hearne. Perhaps he is best known to posterity by a quarto which he published at Oxford in 1752, entitled "Memoirs of several ladies of Great Britain who have been celebrated for their writings or skill in the learned languages, arts and sciences"; "an entertaining work," says Lowndes, "comprising notices of the lives and writings of 62 ladies commencing with Juliana of Norwich, and ending with Constantia Grierson." Ballard, who was always a man of delicate constitution, died at Campden in 1755, aged forty-nine.

We must not quit Campden without ascending that part of the ridge on the north-west of the town known as Dover's Hill. One of the most picturesque features in the view from this point is Meon Hill, an outlier of the Cotswold rising behind Mickleton village: perhaps the best time to see it is the early morning, when it is lighted up by the slanting rays of the sun. On the summit of Dover's Hill is a grassy plateau, famous for 250 years as the site of the Cotswold Games. Games of one sort or another had probably long been customary in the district in connection with the Whitsun ale, but they were organised on a more elaborate scale on this spot by the public-spirited gentleman who has given his name to the hill. This was Robert Dover, a member of a Norfolk family, who began life as an attorney at Barton-on-the-Heath, a Warwickshire village some eight or nine miles to the south-east, and better known to fame as the local habitation of the Sly family, but gave up his profession early and settled at Stanway, where he built a house in which he resided till his death in 1641. Indignant at the Puritan attack upon the old English sports and pastimes, the cessation of which he declared only drove the country people to the pot-house, he "being," writes Wood, "full of activity and of a generous free and public spirit, did, with leave from K. Jam i, select a place on Cotswold Hills in Gloucestershire, where those Games should be acted. Endymion Porter Esq. a Native of that County [he was lord of the manor of Aston Subedge] and a Servant of that King, a Person also of a most generous Spirit, did, to encourage Dover, give him some of the

Meon Hill.

King's old Cloaths, with a Hat and Feather and Ruff, purposely
to grace him, and consequently the Solemnity." In what is
presumably the royal Hat and Feather, Mr. Dover appears in
the foreground of the frontispiece to a collection of poems in
his honour issued in 1636, and entitled "Annalia Dvbrensia :
Vpon the yeerely Celebration of Mr. Robert Dover's Olympick
Games vpon Cotwold Hills " ; the rest of the picture is filled up
with representations of the various sports and feastings, and of
the movable wooden castle from which guns were fired to
signify the opening of the games. Another similar, but even
more extraordinary plate of a rustic merrymaking is to be found
in the 1613 edition of *Drayton's Polyolbion*. Here is a flag flying,
inscribed "Heigh for Cotswold," with a ring of men dancing
round it, while others are making music with bagpipes and a
pipe and tabor, and another group are doing justice to the
good cheer of a well-spread board. Drayton's lines, though
they refer rather to the local shearing-feasts than to Dover's
festival, are worth quoting :

" But Muse, return to tell, how there the shepherds' king
   Whose flock hath chanc'd that year the earliest lamb to bring,
   In his gay bauldric sits at his low grassy board,
   With flawns, curds, clouted-cream, and country dainties stor'd :
   And, whilst the bag-pipe plays, each lusty jocund swain
   Quaffs sillibubs in cans to all upon the plain,
   And to their country-girls, whose nosegays they do wear,
   Some roundelays do sing : the rest the burthen bear."

Dover's meeting, as it came to be called, was, says Wood, attended by the nobility and gentry from sixty miles round, and
continued to be held regularly "till the rascally Rebellion was
began by the Presbyterians, which gave a stop to their Proceedings, and spoiled all that was generous or ingenious elsewhere." Such, too, were the sentiments of Ben Jonson, who
contributed to the *Annalia* an epigram to his "jovial good
friend, Mr. Robert Dover, on his great instauration of his
hunting and dancing at Cotswold." The games, he writes,

" advance true love and neighbourhood,
And do both church and commonwealth the good
In spite of hypocrites, who are the worst
Of subjects. Let such envy till they burst."

However, the meeting was revived at the Restoration, and the
envy of the hypocrites, if any, must have been suppressed.
In the next century, if we may judge from *The Spiritual
Quixote* there was some cause for scandal. Jerry Tugwell, in
his unregenerate days, had many a time been at Dover's meeting,
and won a hat there at cudgell-playing, but he was now to learn
from that ardent enthusiast, Mr. Geoffry Wildgoose, that all
such amusements were nought but the " Devil's strong-holds."
The pair started forth on the missionary tour from their native
village of Mickleton on a lovely May morning, and reached
Dover's Hill in time for Mr. Wildgoose, mounted upon an
inverted hamper, to deliver his first harangue. For the sequel
I must refer my readers to the pages of the romance in question—a satirical rap at the Methodist revival from the orthodox
Anglican standpoint. An incident which happened to the
travellers when they first reached the hills reminds us that they
were still, for the most part, open downs. They fell in with a
pack of hounds and a large party of huntsmen ; the game, however, was neither hare nor fox, but a carted stag which had
been turned out that morning, " Lord B—— of Nottinghamshire " having " taken a seat upon the Cotswold-hills for buck-
hunting."

As for the meeting, it held its own, in spite of protest, till the
middle of the last century. By this time it had come to be
the resort of all the scum of the Black Country, as many as
30,000 people were known to have attended it, and it was said
to have had a demoralising effect upon the whole neighbourhood. Then came the railways, and the disorderly element in
the meeting was further strengthened by the gang of navvies
employed in making the Mickleton tunnel. The abuse was
more easily ended than mended : reform or organisation did

not commend itself to those in authority, and it was determined to put a stop to the games altogether. The last meeting was held in 1851, and the ground was soon afterwards enclosed. Robert Dover lies in the Tracy vault at Stanway, without monument or inscription. Let him live in Drayton's genial lines :

" We'll have thy statue in some rock cut out,
　　With brave inscriptions garnished about ;
　　And under written—' Lo ! this is the man
　　Dover, that first these noble sports began.'
　　Lads of the hills and lasses of the vale,
　　In many a song and many a merry tale,
　　Shall mention thee ; and, having leave to play,
　　Unto thy name shall make a holiday.
　　The Cotswold shepherds, as their flocks they keep,
　　To put off lazy drowsiness and sleep,
　　Shall sit to tell, and hear thy story told,
　　That night shall come ere they their flocks can fold."

Stanley Pontlarge.

CHAPTER IX

I HAVE now detained the reader long enongh for the present among the breezy uplands of the Cotswold. In the present chapter I shall quit the plateau and descend into the fertile plain which lies at the foot of the hills, known far and wide as the Vale of Evesham. Not that I shall wander far from the hill country, but before returning to it I must visit the villages which dot the base of the slopes from Quinton in the extreme north as far as Winchcombe. Between this place and Cheltenham the escarpment, which trends steadily to the south-west, reaches its highest point in Cleeve Cloud, 1070 feet, while in the vale to the north are the outlying eminences of Oxenton, Dumbleton and Bredon.

From Campden I descend to Battle Bridge near the station. How long the place has been so called I do not know, and what the battle commemorated was, can only be guessed. Pierre de Langtoft, in a chronicle written in the reign of Edward the First, records that in 689, Ine, king of the West Saxons, defeated a coalition of British chiefs in a field under " Kampdene," and it has been suggested that this spot is the locality intended. If so, it must have been the last spasmodic effort of the Welsh to assert their independence anywhere to the east of the Severn.

At Ebrington (locally Yabberton) on the opposite hill lived Sir John Fortescue, a member of the Devonshire family of that name, and author of the *De Landibus Legum Angliæ* and other

Ebrington.

works relating to constitutional history. He was Lord Chief Justice of England under Henry the Sixth, and a devoted adherent of the Lancastrian cause. After the final defeat of the Lancastrians at Tewkesbury, he submitted to the new *régime*, and retired to the estate he had purchased at Ebrington, where he died at a very advanced age. On the north side of the chancel he lies in effigy in his judicial robes, coloured to the life. It has generally been inferred that the whole monument was erected as late as 1677; but this is a mistake, owing to a misinterpretation of the Latin inscription set up in that year by the Fortescue of the day. The words "Marmoreum hoc monumentum" must refer only to the marble tablet containing the inscription, and not to the effigy, which is of stone and of a much earlier date. This is clear from the words of Wood, who was at Ebrington in Oct., 1676, the year before the tablet was erected: "Going forthwith into the church, I found in the chancell a raised monument of free stone joyning to the north wall and theron the proportion of a man laying on his back, habited in certaine long robes. It is the constant tradition there that it is the monument of Sir John Fortescue. . . . Fortescue of Devonshire, lord of this mannour, is about to set up an inscription over this monument."

There are also monuments to the Keyte family, who formerly owned large estates in these parts. A gruesome story is told of Sir William Keyte, who lived at Norton House, on the beautiful slopes of the hills near Aston Subedge. Driven out of his mind by dissipation, he set fire to his house one evening in the autumn of 1741 and perished in the flames. Nothing loth to point a moral and adorn a tale, Mr. Wildgoose in *The Spiritual Quixote* narrates the particulars at length to a party of his Derbyshire friends. Another branch of the family lived at Hidcote House, two miles north of Ebrington. The centre and one wing of this fine old manor house is still standing; over the door are the arms of Keyte impaling Spencer, and the initials of Francis Keyte of Hidcote, who married a sister of the second Sir Thomas Spencer of Yarnton. They had a daughter who, according to Wood, was anything but a credit to the family. We have already met with Captain Hastings Keyte, a brother of Francis, at Stow.

It is a stiff climb to the top of Ilmington Downs, where, at a height of nearly 850 feet, the road enters Warwickshire; a few yards to the left of the road is an eminence commanding a most extensive view in every direction. The village of Ilmington lies at the foot of the steep grassy slopes a couple of miles further on. It is a quiet unpretending little place, with a few good old houses and many thatched cottages of the rich yellow stone we first met with at Deddington. It is much frequented in summer by unambitious ruralisers from Birmingham, and indeed boasts a chalybeate spring, which, had the tide of fashion set this way, might perhaps have made it a rival to Leamington. But Ilmington has seen its best days. When the smaller landed gentry were to be found everywhere up and down the country-side, there was more than one family of importance here. On the other side of the hill is Foxcote, a fine eighteenth century mansion, the seat of the Cannings, a branch of the famous Bristol family, since the time of Henry the VI., and still in the possession of their descendant, Mr. Canning Howard, of Corby Castle. Then there were the Palmers at Compton Scorpion, and the Brents at Stoke Lark. The manor-houses of these families still exist. That at Compton Scorpion was the birthplace of Sir Thomas Overbury, whose mother was a Palmer. His father's family resided at Bourton-on-the-Hill, a few miles to the south. These Palmers came to an end in 1763 with one Dorothea Palmer, the widow of the last Squire. If the following story is true, one cannot help thinking that the proposal to put up any memorial to her in the church must have met with opposition from the rector of the day. But, in fact, a small brass plate records that she was by birth a Lyttleton, and in virtue of this descent she quarters the arms of Plantagenet on her shield of arms. The story in question, for which I can find no other authority than local tradition, relates that the old lady (she died in her seventy-seventh year), finding that complaints were made of her failing to attend church, jolted across the fields one Sunday morning in a common farm cart, entered the church, and having anathematised the parson, church and congregation in a loud voice returned home as she had come. For the rest of her days she is said to have kept within the law by appearing once a quarter at a Quaker's meeting.

The old house of Stoke Lark, once the home of the Brents, lies in a retired valley to the west of the village. Like Compton Scorpion, it is now occupied as a farmhouse, but you may still trace its terraced gardens sloping down to what were not long since fish-ponds, but which are now drained and choked with weeds. Another brass tablet in the church depones that the founder of the family appeared at Ilmington about the year 1487 under the assumed name of John Buston. He was one of the Brents of Cossington, in Somerset, but the reason for his disguise can only be a matter of conjecture ; perhaps he had involved himself so deeply in the Yorkist cause as to make concealment advisable. Be this as it may, in ten years' time he found himself in a position to woo and win the daughter and heiress of the lord of Stoke Lark, one George Colchester ; and there his descendants continued to flourish up to the close of the seventeenth century.

A deep rich country lies between the foot of the hills and the Avon to the north and west of Ilmington. The whole is intersected by a network of pleasant lanes, and the hedges are bright in summer with the great willow herb and the large white bindweed, interspersed with the crowded umbels of the tall angelica. I am bound for Mickleton, but instead of riding straight there I resolve to make the circuit of the beautiful Meon Hill, already mentioned, in order to see the picturesque village of Quinton, which lies on its northern side. Here I am but six miles from Stratford ; but I must not wander any further into Shakespeare's country, especially as I under-

The vale of Evesham from Hidcote Boyce, near Ebrington.

stand that another volume of this series is to be devoted
to it.   At Ilmington I was in Warwickshire; here I am
again in Gloucestershire.   But sundry ancient, half-timbered
cottages remind me that I have trespassed beyond the limits of
the Cotswold, and have penetrated into a typical village of the
vale.   Facing the village green is a comfortable old inn known
as the " College Arms."   Wherever any college has large estates,
you may be sure that there it is *the* college *par excellence ;*
the others, if they exist at all, are not worth counting.
At Quinton the college is Magdalen, who have been lords
of the manor for four hundred years, and the diamonds
and lilies are swaying in the wind at the summit of the tall
sign-post that stands in front of the inn.   The church alone is
well worth coming some miles out of your way to see, though
the effect of the interior is marred by the undignified appearance of the cheap deal pews, which are sadly out of harmony
with the venerable Norman and Early English arcades, and the
solid tracery of the windows.   The chancel is spacious, but
its character has been altered in modern times by the insertion
of a large east window in the Decorated style.   Formerly,
as in the case of certain churches, already noticed, the east
end was windowless, and the wall decorated with frescoes:
it is a pity that a historical feature of such distinction
should have been annihilated.   In the nave is an altar
tomb, on which rests the effigy of a knight in plate armour,
said to be that of Sir Thomas Rouse, who died in 1499,
and at the east end of the south aisle, where the sedilia
and piscina of a chapel remain, is another raised tomb with the
fifteenth century brass of Joan Clopton, widow of Sir William
Clopton.   On her husband's death she became an anchoress
and was immured for the rest of her days in a cell adjoining
the churchyard.

   At the detached hamlet of Upper Quinton is an ancient,
mysterious-looking farmhouse, that seems a fitting home for
treasons, stratagems, and spoils, and is appropriately shrouded

in a thick overgrown garden. What plots may be hatched there nowadays, I cannot certainly affirm; but it is not unreasonable to imagine that the victims are largely drawn from the geese which frequent the long open green in large flocks. In fact these grassy levels that lie between the Cotswold and the Warwickshire hills seem to be particularly adapted to the cultivation of this petulant bird, and numbers of them no doubt eventually find their way to the Birmingham Christmas market. So along under the western slopes of lovely Meon, whose praises I am never tired of singing, to Mickleton.

Now Mickleton both on the score of its own merits, and from its associations, deserves more than a passing notice. Even a glimpse from the distant railway of its spire rising out of a mass of clustering orchards, backed by the verdant slopes of Cotswold, which hereabouts are cleft with deep and darkly wooded coombes, must rouse both envy and curiosity. It is not a place where the squire and the parson seem to reign in solitary state. There are many other comfortable-looking houses besides the manor and vicarage, there are village shops, there is a resident doctor, and the whole has all the air of a place where a man might possess his soul (and body) in peace. The manor-house is a fine substantial mansion close to the church: the grounds are fenced from the road by a lofty wall, but the beautiful gardens on the other side of the house lie open to the meadows, and look across to the hills. The manor which belonged to the abbey of Eynsham has, since the Dissolution, twice been held by men of some reputation for learning and scholarship. In 1597 it was purchased by Edward Fisher, whose grandson, also named Edward, succeeded to the estate in 1654. This last Edward, a member of Brasenose College, was well read in ecclesiastical history, and a zealous upholder of the rites and ceremonies of the Church against the Puritans. He was the author of *A Christian Caveat to the Old and New Sabbatharians, or a Vindication of our Gospel Festivals* (1653) and other works.

When he succeeded to the Mickleton estate he found it heavily encumbered, and he had no money to clear it. He therefore retired to Carmarthen, where he supported himself by teaching, but his creditors pursued him, and he took refuge from them in Ireland, where he died. In 1656 Mickleton was bought by Richard Graves, a London lawyer, in whose family it still remains. The grandson of this Richard, another Richard Graves, was one of those benefactors to posterity who devote themselves to the study of the history of their native place. He made extensive collections, which are now among the Lansdowne MSS. in the British Museum, and projected a History of the Vale of Evesham, but died in 1729 at the age of fifty-two, before he had anything ready for publication. He was a valued friend of Hearne's, who gives us a pleasant picture of him: "He was one of the most worthy and most virtuous gentlemen I was acquainted with. He was also a most excellent scholar and antiquary, a man of great modesty and of a most sweet temper, and a great friend to his tenants and to the poor, so that all people are very sorry for his death." On the marble tablet to his memory in the church there is a portrait of him in profile. His eldest son, Morgan Graves, succeeded him at Mickleton: his younger son was Richard Graves, the author of *The Spiritual Quixote*. We have already noted in connection with Dover's meeting that it is at Mickleton that the opening scene of this entertaining story is laid. I like to fancy that I can identify the old elm at the cottage gate of the "honest sociable cobbler," beneath which the villagers were wont to congregate of an evening to discuss the news of the day, as well as "the Angel" frequented by Jerry Tugwell, though there is no inn now called by that name.

The author, like his father and three of his own sons afterwards, was "bred" at Pembroke College; he became a Fellow of All Souls, and in 1748 was presented to the rectory of Claverton near Bath, which he held till his death in 1804 at the age of eighty-nine. At Pembroke he formed a life-long friendship with Shenstone, who became a frequent guest at Mickleton Manor, where Richard's brother Morgan now reigned as squire. It was here that Shenstone made his first essays in landscape gardening, an art which he afterwards cultivated on so elaborate a scale at the Leasowes. The stranger who takes the footpath leading from the churchyard to the foot of the hills will come upon a fine avenue of elms which is carried up the slope towards the aerie-like modern mansion of Kiftsgate Court. This avenue was planted by Shenstone on one of his Mickleton visits, and will long preserve his memory there. But this is not all: in the church, now standing on the floor of the south aisle, but formerly in the chancel and apparently intended for a more elevated position, is a funeral urn with this inscription : " Utreciae Smith, Puellae simplici, innocuae, eleganti : R. G. Una actae memor pueritiae Moerens posuit M.DCC.XLIV." Utrecia Smith was the daughter of the curate of Mickleton, with whom Richard Graves had read the classics until he was old enough to be sent to Abingdon school. She developed remarkable talents as she grew to womanhood, and won the admiration of the two young Oxford students, Graves and Shenstone. " At a time," writes the former in his memoir of Shenstone, " when the ladies did not so generally rival our sex in learning and ingenuity, from the books with which her father supplied her [she] had formed to herself so good a taste of polite literature and wrote so well in prose (and sometimes in verse) that a very ingenious clergyman, bred at a public school, and a Master of Arts in the University, often said he was afraid to declare his opinion of any author till he previously knew hers." I regret to add that the ingenious clergyman after being engaged to Miss Smith for four or five years, broke off the match " for prudential reasons." Poor Utrecia was carried off by small-pox at the early age of thirty ; Shenstone wrote his fourth Elegy, " Ophelia's urn," in her memory. It is addressed to his friend Graves, but is not penned in his happiest style ; there is a stiffness about it which repels rather than attracts, and the number of personifications is excessive : in the course of ten verses we have " fame," " young simplicity," " candour," " innocence," " elegance," " beauty " and " fancy." The best stanza is perhaps the following :

> " Sure nought unhallow'd shall presume to stray
>   Where sleep the reliques of that virtuous maid ;
> Nor aught unlovely bend its devious way,
>   Where soft Ophelia's dear remains are laid."

The reader will exclaim that bad is the best, and by way of compensation I will give him an extract from one of Shenstone's letters to Graves which contains a mention of Utrecia. It also illustrates the difficulties of travelling through the Cotswold before the enclosures ; though it is certainly strange that any one going from Mickleton to Cheltenham should have ascended into the hills at all, much less got anywhere near Stow, instead of following the ordinary road along the bottom of the hills through Broadway and Winchcombe ; but perhaps in those days this road was a mere local trackway impassable from ruts and mud. " I am this moment arrived at Cheltenham after an expensive and fatiguing journey. I called yesterday at Mickleton ; saw the portico, and snapped up a bit of mutton at your brother's ; drank a dish of tea with Miss S—— ; and in opposition to the strongest remonstrances, persisted in an endeavour to reach Cheltenham after five o'clock. The consequence was that, about ten, I found myself travelling back again towards Stowe ; and had undoubtedly wandered all night in the dark [he was presumably on horseback], had I not been fortunately met by a waggoner's servant, who brought me back to the worst inn but one [at Stow ?] I ever lay at, being his master's."

On entering the church we are at once struck by the lowness of the arches of the nave arcades compared with the height of the walls they support ; this, however, is due to the addition of the clerestory in the fifteenth century. The two Norman arches on either side with their curious stiff-foliaged circular

capitals are the remains of the original twelfth century church ;
to these the two western bays with pointed arches are a fourteenth century addition, and the tower and the two aisles with
their splendid east windows of flowing tracery belong to the
same period; the chancel is later, and probably built at the
same time as the clerestory.   Early in the seventeenth century
came the south porch, with the chamber over it in the style of
the Renaissance.   In the north aisle are numerous monumental tablets to the Graves family, together with a long series

Cottages at Weston Subedge.

of hatchments.   The Fisher monuments are at the east end of
the chancel.   Here also is the curious "ephitath" of one
John Bonner of Pebworth, a local worthy contemporary with,
and possibly known to, Shakespeare, whom he survived some
eighteen months.

From Mickleton I continue my ride to Aston Subedge,
along a road commanding lovely views of Bredon Hill and the
Malverns.   Here I am in a land of cherry and apple orchards,
but by far the most interesting thing in Aston is the old manor—
house of the Porters, with its impressive gabled front and ball-

shaped finials. A long gallery runs from end to end under the rafters of the roof, reminding one on a smaller scale of those at Broughton and Chastleton; it is reached by a massive oak staircase, which only wants cleaning and polishing to make it as serviceable as ever. Some of the Porter family resided at Mickleton, where they held a long lease of the manor, granted them by one of the last abbots of Eynsham, which did not expire till the last quarter of the sixteenth century. Angela, daughter of Giles Porter of Mickleton, married her cousin Edmund Porter of Aston. Their son, born in 1587, was Endymion Porter, patron of poets, as Herrick calls him, and as we have already seen, of athletic sports as well.

The road now passes the pretty villages of Weston Subedge, Saintbury, and Willersey. It was as vicar of Weston and of Saintbury that one of the pioneers of the New Learning in England spent the evening of his days. This was the learned and modest William Latimer, the friend of Grocyn, Linacre, and Erasmus. Himself a Fellow of All Souls, he shares with the two former the honour of planting the study of Greek at Oxford. Like Grocyn, he left behind him hardly any written proofs of his scholarship, but both for his intellectual and moral worth we have the unimpeachable testimony of Erasmus : " vere theologus integritate vitae conspicuus," he styles him in one of his epistles, and in another which he addressed to Latimer begging his assistance in preparing a second edition of his Greek Testament for the press, he writes, " suavissimum istum ingenii tui candorem ac pudorem plusquam virgineum agnovi." Latimer, however, excused himself on the ground that he had not touched Greek or Latin for some years and was engaged in other studies. He died in 1545, and was buried at Saintbury. The church of Saintbury is charmingly situated on the green hillside above the village, and in the east window may be seen the figure of an ecclesiastic in the attitude of prayer with the legend " San Nicolas priet pur W. L." This, as Richard Graves of Mickleton considered,

Saintbury.

is probably a portrait of Latimer. Graves also conjectured that Latimer built the vicarage (now rectory) house at Weston " as big as a little college " (in spite of modern alterations it still merits this description), where the initials W. L. were formerly to be seen carved on the stone-work and wood-work.

Bearing to the left at Willersey and crossing the village green with its picturesque old smithy in the centre, I soon enter Broadway and make for the Lygon Arms. The traveller will be wise who makes this fine old seventeenth century hostelry his headquarters for a day or two; nowhere in the course of these excursions will he find more comfortable quarters or a heartier welcome. Broadway is a populous village, and lying as it does on the high road from London to Worcester, its wide street (whence of course its name) was full of life and bustle in the old coaching days; not that it is dull now, particularly in summer; for the place was discovered by the Americans some years ago, and has continued to be a favourite resort of artists both American and other. Among the old houses besides the Lygon, the most interesting is the fourteenth century grange of the abbey of Pershore; it had fallen into decay, but has been rescued in time, and repaired in good taste, and now forms a comfortable private residence. Long ago the attractions of the London road drew the village away from the vicinity of its parish church. This church lies a mile away to the south beside a streamlet which here descends from the hills. It is a fine cruciform twelfth century structure with transition-Norman arcades, and a chancel and transepts of later date. The space beneath the tower was the chancel of the original church. The interior being used for service only on summer Sunday afternoons has a somewhat deserted air, but for that very reason it has escaped the clutches of the Early Victorian restorer, and may look forward without fear to the future. The patron saint is St. Eadburgh, a daughter of Edward the Elder.

Willersey.

A charming field path to the right will take you to Buckland, whence you may wander on along the slopes of the hills to Stanton and Stanway, and even further to Hayles and Sudeley, and a day or two may well be devoted to a ramble along this delightful hillside, with its constant variations of wooded coombe and upland meadow, and its outlook across the broad vale of Evesham to the distant hills beyond. The villages just mentioned are all secluded and unspoilt, and for two or three centuries have worn much the same aspect that they do to-day; but a time of probation is approaching, the new railway will soon be open—and then? But I will not forestall the date of grief; they are all built of the good local stone and are built to last.

To begin with Buckland, bookland that is—a common name enough—in this case it was the abbey of Gloucester that held it by charter or book—and to speak only of the church, the manor house and the rectory. From 1466 to 1510 the rector was William Grafton. He probably built the rectory, for one of the windows of the hall has his rebus, a tun with the graft of tree issuing from it : this fine room retains its original proportions, but at the manor house, behind the church, the hall has been divided up by modern partitions. On the south side of the church in the churchyard is a pre-Reformation altar tomb with quatrefoils on the sides—a rarity outside a church. The east window has three compartments of painted glass, a century older than the stonework, and perhaps the gift of William Grafton : the subjects of the glass are the sacraments of confirmation, marriage, and extreme unction. The panelling of the walls is early seventeenth century work, as appears by the following inscription : "Thomas Izzard and James Sowthern of theyr own cherg have given this wainscot and benchin to church in the yere of our Lord 1615." At Buckland, evidently the yeomen had not by that time ceased to take a pride in their parish church, or to be able and willing to spend their money on it.

Broadway, the Grange.

Stanton and Stanway each have their great house, but
Stanton Court conforms to the ordinary type of Cotswold
manor-house; Stanway House, as we shall see, has distinctive
features of its own. Another fine old house in Stanton is
Warren House, built by one Thomas Warren in 1577; one of
its principal rooms has an elaborate plaster ceiling adorned with
the Warren arms, Tudor roses and fleurs-de-lys. The present
owner of this house assured me that King Charles slept in it
after his escape from Worcester field, and added that he himself
occupied the bedroom used by his Majesty. I am afraid,
however, that this story will hardly fit in with known facts, for,
as readers of the Boscobel tracts are aware, the King accomplished the journey from Mr. Tombs's at Long Marston to
the rectory at Coberley in a single day. Moreover he took
the ordinary road through Campden across the hills, and would
have left Stanton some miles on his right. Nor is there any
evidence that his father, though more than once at Broadway,
and nearer still, ever actually entered Stanton. The church,
originally built by the monks of Winchcombe in the twelfth
century, retains its Norman arcade on the north side of the
nave, but the rest is of later date. One of its most remarkable
features is the west window of the fifteenth century south aisle:
it has two transoms in its upper part, thus forming two tiers of
smaller lights above the larger lower ones. The effect is so
good that the architect responsible for the recent restoration
has inserted two copies of this window in the south wall of the
same aisle.

The estates owned by the great Mercian monasteries in the
Cotswold were enormous. As Broadway belonged to Pershore,
Buckland to Gloucester, and Stanton to Winchcombe, so
Stanway belonged to Tewkesbury, and here its abbots had a
country house. No situation within such easy distance could
have been better chosen. Tewkesbury lies low in the vale, and
in winter time was much exposed to fogs and floods. Stanway
is from two to three hundred feet higher, and could bid

Stanton, with Warren House.

defiance to the waters, while at the same time it is sheltered
from the north and east by the steep background of hill
that rises immediately behind the village.   For recreation,
too, there was the hunting of the stag, which then and much
later was as wild on these hills as it is on Exmoor to-day;
indeed, throughout the country it was only the clearing of
forests, the progress of enclosures, the improvement in farming
and the growth of population, which finally confined this
noble animal to parks, and put the fox in its place as the beast
of the chase.   At the dissolution the manor was granted to the
Tracys of Toddington, and from them in 1771 it passed by
marriage to the family of the Earl of Wemyss.   Stanway
House, the residence of Lord Elcho, is a splendid Jacobean
mansion built by the Tracy of the day.   You enter the grounds
beneath an imposing gatehouse with three gables and an oriel,
and are at once face to face with the great grey front of the
house.   The most striking feature is the huge bay window of
the hall, divided by mullions and transoms into no less than
sixty panes.   The gardens are behind on the slope of the hill,
but the Dutch garden and cascade which formerly existed
disappeared before the school of Capability Brown.   The
great stoneway from which the village takes its name here
descends from the hills to Toddington and Tewkesbury.

These places are, however, outside the scope of this book :
our route keeps to the skirts of the hills, and by nightfall we
must reach our inn at the historic town of Winchcombe.   The
reader has perhaps, never heard of this now unfrequented little
place, and may demur to the epithet historic, but I will ask
him to suspend his judgment for a page or two.   Meanwhile
I must ask him to accompany me up the stoneway till we can
once more look down into the hollow in which lies the tiny
hamlet of Ford and Mr. Wiggett's inn.   We soon cross an
ancient trackway (the place is known as Stumps Cross) which I
suspect to be the very one along which the disguised and
fugitive king rode with Mrs. Lane from Campden to Coberley,

Stanway.

and the next turning to the right will take us to Winchcombe.
It is one of those cross-country Cotswold roads carried from gate
to gate across the enclosures, but I shall soon leave it and
follow a cart track over the down, which makes it necessary
to dismount and wheel my machine. The ruts and rough
grass as I climb an ascent through a cornfield require careful
steering, and keep my eyes fixed upon the ground. On rais·
ing them again the scene disclosed is positively startling :
without being aware of it I have reached the brow of the steep
western face of the hills, and there on the horizon stands the
blue undulating chain of the Malvern range in all its grandeur :
to the north-west appear the distant Shropshire heights, while
the middle distance is filled by Bredon, with Dumbleton Hill
like an outpost planted in front of it. To the left are the spurs
which hide the valley of Winchcombe, while the long ridge of
Cleeve hill rises over all with the brown moorland look of a
stretch of Dartmoor, or even of a Welsh mountain. High up on
the hillside at my feet is Farmcote, a cluster of grey farmsteads
and cottages, forming a hamlet in the parish of Lower Guiting.
The distance (more than four miles) from the parish church,
in early days, called for the alleviation of a chapel of ease·:
shorn of its chancel—the round chancel arch is now built up
—it still presents Early English and Perpendicular features,
and on the north side of the altar is an Elizabethan tomb with
two effigies in native stone, doubtless cut by a local artist, over
which are the arms of the Stratford family, who were long Lords
of the Manor and held other estates in the neighbourhood.
Their name occurs in the Cotswold Muse among the patrons
of Clement Barksdale, and at Hawling there is a tablet to one
of them who seems to have succeeded at an early age to the
family honours, for he is described as "Toparcha," *i.e.*, Lord
of the Manor, and after four happy years profitably spent at
Oxford was cut off by a fever in 1692 at the early age of twenty.
two.

But the fact that so small a settlement as Farmcote was not

suffered to go without a church of its own is one eminently characteristic of the whole district which we have now reached. To one who would attempt the difficult task of reconstructing in the imagination a picture of pre-Reformation England, there can be no better field of study, south of Yorkshire, than the vale of Evesham and the adjacent tract of Cotswold. Within a circuit of less than thirty miles were no less than eight wealthy monastic foundations :—Worcester, Pershore, Evesham, Malvern, Tewkesbury, Gloucester, Winchcombe and Hayles. Almost the whole of the land was in their hands, and when the dissolution came both the tenant farmer and the farm labourer were thriving and contented. The years that followed that catastrophe were years of unsettlement and distress for the rural population—a distress which was shared by the inhabitants of the smaller towns. Nor was the position of the secular clergy improved ; in most parishes the monks were the impropriators of the rectorial tithes, and they were also the patrons of the vicarages. There was therefore every guarantee that the latter would be properly filled, and the parochial duties adequately discharged. I need hardly say that in the grasping and greedy days of the Protectorate these things altered for the worse. It was not till the new order was purged and settled under the wise rule of Elizabeth, and the excesses of her sister had made Papist and Persecutor synonymous terms, that village life again enjoyed something of its former prosperity. It was now that these fine old manor-houses, of which we have seen so many, began to be built. Here and there a wealthy abbot had had a country-house, and in some few places where a lay Lord of the Manor existed (the reader will remember that all along I am speaking only of this particular district) he had no doubt had a decent dwelling. But with these exceptions the villages must have consisted merely of cottages, that of the farmer differing only from the others by its larger size and more extensive outbuildings. Traces of such outbuildings may still be seen around the existing Elizabethan or Jacobean manor-house. Perhaps it is a large buttressed barn dating at least from the fourteenth or fifteenth century, for in those days ample storage room was more essential than at the present day. In the first place each village—I might almost say each household—was self-supporting, and a smaller proportion of the yearly produce was available for transport to the larger towns; the very means of transport, too, were limited and difficult. Instead, therefore, of threshing half-a-dozen ricks at once, and packing off the grain in sacks to the nearest corn-factor, threshing operations would be carried over a much longer period; the harvested produce would be stored in the great barn, and the portion threshed out would be taken to the manor mill to be ground into the flour required for the domestic use. In the second place tithes were paid in kind, and while it was an easy matter for the vicar to collect those due to him and store them in the small barn attached to his own modest parsonage, the monasteries lay at a distance, and the conveyance of their tithe straight from the harvest field, through all their many manors, would have been well-nigh impossible. It was therefore convenient for them to have a barn on the spot, where their share of the produce might be stored till such time as they required it. There must have been constant intercourse between the great monasteries in the vale and the distant villages in the hills : and the traveller in those times must have often doffed his cap to officials in monastic garb passing to and fro on business connected with the farms, or it may be to an abbot and his train making a regular progress through the estates of the foundation.

Of these monasteries the limits of this volume allow us to visit only two, Winchcombe and Hayles, and of these Winchcombe has entirely, Hayles all but entirely, disappeared. Descending from Farmcote through the wood we find ourselves in a green coombe shut in by hills on all sides except the north. On our right is the parish church, in the meadow on our left a square plot enclosed by four ruined walls.

This is the cloister-garth of the once famous Cistercian monastery of Hayles. Nothing else remains; the splendid church, the conventual buildings, the approaches, the gatehouse, the precinct-walls—all have gone; there is nothing above ground but these ruined walls to tell of the vast edifice of which they once formed so small a part. A few years would suffice for the destruction of all that for three centuries had been the object of veneration. Neither here nor at Winchcombe, two miles away, was it any outburst of popular fanaticism, or any violent manifestation of popular hostility, that overthrew the shrines, and pulled down the walls of these two magnificent churches. The demolition was deliberate and systematic; it was a mere matter of business proceeding upon a cool calculation of profit and loss. That these buildings were landmarks in the history of the national church, that they were the supreme efforts of constructive art, was quite beside the question; it was enough that on utilitarian grounds they stood condemned; neither of them was needed either for a cathedral as at Gloucester, or for a parish church as at Tewkesbury; why then should they any longer cumber the ground? Rather let them be swept away at once and their materials put to some more profitable use. So, at any rate, thought the man who was responsible for their destruction, Thomas, Lord Seymour of Sudeley, Lord High Admiral of England, and brother-in-law of the King. Both abbeys had been granted to him at the dissolution in 1539, and he was not the man to lose any time in making the most of his acquisition. It would no doubt be unfair to condemn him on this count alone; nine out of ten men in his day, estimable citizens enough according to their lights, would have done the same, but for Thomas Seymour it is impossible on any count to feel either sympathy or respect. So thoroughly were his orders in each case carried out that not a single stone of either church remains, and it has been only in recent years that excavations have discovered their foundations, and given us indisputable evidence of their former splendour.

As for the conventual buildings at Hayles, they might be put to some practical use, and the abbot's lodging on the west side of the cloisters, together with some of the domestic offices adjoining, was spared and converted into a dwelling-house. In Sir Robert Atkyns's time this was the seat of the Tracy family : it survived till the middle of the eighteenth century, but has now entirely disappeared.

An admirable ground plan of the church, based upon the recent excavations, is exhibited in the small museum near the custodian's cottage.   This will give the visitor a good idea of its position and proportions : he will notice that the cloisters and the abbey buildings were placed on the south side of the church ; this was their usual position, unless, as at Tintern, there were special reasons for placing them on the north.   The abbey was founded in 1246 by Richard, Earl of Cornwall, brother of Henry the Third, and afterwards King of the Romans, an able statesman, to whom the chroniclers have done but scant justice.   At the consecration ceremony in 1251, an immense gathering assembled, including the King and Queen, and thirteen bishops, each of whom said mass at a separate altar, the celebrant at the High Altar being the great bishop of Lincoln, Robert Grosseteste.   But the crowning distinction of the abbey was the possession of the Holy Blood—"the blode of Crist, that it is in Hayles "—a relic which made it famous throughout the length and breadth of the land.   This was presented in 1267 by Edmund, the son of the founder, and for its proper reception an apse with five polygonal chapels was added at the east end of the church, which had hitherto terminated in a straight wall.   Here, at the back of the High Altar, stood the shrine which contained the Holy Blood—a shrine visited every year by thousands of pilgrims from all parts of the country.   The "George " at Winchcombe, was the pilgrims' inn, and the gallery which runs along one side of the yard, is still called the pilgrims' gallery. The yard was probably larger in those days, and the gallery ran right round it, as is still the case at the

"New Inn" in Gloucester. The paved way over the hill by which the pilgrims passed from Winchcombe to Hayles is also in existence, and is still the shortest route for walkers. The shrine itself was destroyed as completely as that of St. Thomas at Canterbury, but the base on which it stood, a structure eight feet by ten, still remains intact beneath the soil, and was uncovered by the explorers in 1900. The last abbot was Stephen Sagar, and in his time an old monk, about eighty years of age at the dissolution, had had the charge of the

Bell-turret, Hayles Church.

sacred relic for forty years. "Some years ago, writes Mr. Bazeley in his paper on the abbey, "the matrix of a beautiful seal was found in Yorkshire with the figure of a monk. . . holding in his right hand the phial containing the Holy Blood, and in the other the asperges with which he sprinkled with holy water the pilgrims kneeling before the shrine. It bears the following inscription : 'Sigillum fraternitatis monasterii beatae Mariae de Hayles.' Probably Abbot Sagar, when he went some years later to his brother, Otho Sagar, vicar of Warmfield, to die, and be buried in his church, took the seal with him, and it was subsequently lost." At the dissolution, the Commissioners viewed the "supposed relic called the Blood of Hayles," and upon examination judged it to be "an unctuous gum coloured." Among the tombs ruthlessly broken to pieces by Lord Seymour's agents was the "noble pyramis," or altar-tomb, that covered the remains of the founder, nor was any greater respect shown to the graves of his wife, Sanchia, Queen of the Romans, and of his sons, Henry, murdered at Viterbo, and Edmund, his successor in the earldom.

The small parish church of Hayles, as is the case at the old Llanthony, stands close beside the abbey. Originally built in the twelfth century, it passed, on the foundation of the monastery, into the possession of the monks and was much altered by them: the fragments of the original church which remain are the shafts of the chancel arch, and the two pilasters which support the south chancel wall.

The traveller who goes from Hayles to Winchcombe by road will have to cross the line of the new railway twice, but if he takes the short cut, which I have called the pilgrims' way, he will avoid it altogether, for it is carried from Cheltenham round the base of the projecting hills, and the Winchcombe station will be a mile away from the town. In either case he will cross the Isbourne by the bridge at the town-end, and pass up the quaint old-fashioned street to his inn. I have called Winchcombe an historic town, and Leland wrote that it was of old-time "mighty large." It was, in fact, one of the chief towns of Mercia, and a residence of the Mercian kings. Nor did it decline in importance during the seven centuries and a half that its great Benedictine monastery flourished. Its abbot was one of the three Gloucestershire abbots who sat in the House of Lords, the other two being the abbots of Gloucester and Cirencester. The abbey precincts were fortified—an exceptional privilege—and at the dissolution its estates were valued at a sum equivalent to more than £11,000 of the money of our own day. Of this magnificent foundation, however, beyond a few pavement tiles and a doorway now built up into the parish church, the visitor will not find a trace. When it passed into the possession of Seymour, the conventual buildings became a common quarry, and so thoroughly did he carry out the demolition of the church that its very site was forgotten, and when Browne Willis visited Winchcombe in 1714, in the hope of gaining some information about it, all he could find was a tradition that the central tower had been large and fine. It was not till 1892 that excavations revealed the foundations of the nave to the east of the present parish church, and the measurements of the base of the central tower, 40 feet each way, showed that the tradition of its grandeur was not exaggerated. Owing to difficulties connected with the ownership of the soil the choir and transepts could not be uncovered, but tablets were set up at either end of the central line of the church, and a cross to mark the centre of the space beneath the tower.

Founded by Kenulf, King of Mercia, at the close of the eighth century, and restored in the tenth, after the Danish ravages, the abbey church was burnt down in the twelfth century and rebuilt in the style of architecture then prevailing. Hence we may conclude that when the final destruction came, it was in the main a Norman building of the same character as the neighbouring churches of Gloucester and Tewkesbury. Like Hayles it had its shrine, and its pilgrims, and though the relics they came to worship were less sacred, they were so efficacious in the working of miracles, that they were a source of vast revenue to the foundation. These were the bones of Kenelm, the boy saint to whom, and to the Virgin Mary, the abbey was dedicated. His story is so intimately bound up with Winchcombe that it must be told.

On the death of Kenulf in 822, his son Kenelm, a boy of seven years, succeeded to the throne of Mercia. Winchcombe was then the Royal residence, and there the little king began his reign under the guidance of his tutor, Askobert. Fortunately, or unfortunately for him, he had an elder sister,

Quenride, who cast envious eyes upon the lad and sought to supplant him on the throne. With this end in view she attempted to take him off by poison, but so saintly was the holy child that the noxious drugs had no power over him. Her next move was to whisper evil counsels in the ear of his tutor, the mercenary Askobert, and endeavour to win him over to her designs. In this she succeeded, and one fine morning Askobert invited the boy to accompany him on a hunting expedition to the forest of Clent, in the north of Worcestershire (rather a long distance off, we may remark in passing). Kenelm was, of course, delighted with the proposal, and off rode the villain and his victim. When they reached the forest the miscreant cut off the child's head, and buried the corpse beneath a thorn. It should be said that at the moment that he severed the head from the body a white dove came forth from the neck, and straightway flew up to heaven. Quenride now reaped the fruit of her misdeed—for a time. But it so happened that a year or two later as the Pope was celebrating mass at the High Altar of St. Peter's, at Rome, a dove flew into the building and dropped a slip of parchment upon the altar. His Holiness, observing a certain writing upon the parchment, attempted to read it, but without success, a thing which was not wonderful seeing that the language was English, then an unknown tongue in the Holy City. At last an Englishman was found who could read and interpret the writing, which ran thus: "In Clent in Cowbache Kenelm Kinges bern lith under a thorn heuade bireued," that is, "In Clent in Cowbach Kenelm King's child lieth under a thorn, his head taken from him." Thereupon the Pope lost no time in sending these strange tidings to the Archbishop of Canterbury, and orders came down to Winchcombe that a search should be made for the murdered child's body. Accordingly a party of monks set off for Clent and arrived at the Cowbach, where a white cow, herself long a devotee of the saint, guided them to the thorn. Here they found the body, and were about to take it back with them to Winchcombe when a difficulty arose. The monks of Worcester put in a claim to the body as having been found in their province, while the Gloucestershire men as vehemently asserted their claims as fellow townsmen of the saint. At last they agreed that weary as they were they should all lie down to sleep, and whichever party woke up first should be considered to be destined by the will of Heaven to be the possessors of the relics. It chanced that the Winchcombe monks were the first to awake, and they were well on their way with their precious burden before their brethren of Worcester were aware of their departure. The return journey was managed without adventure till they reached a point high up on the hillside, over against Winchcombe town, and some two miles distant therefrom.[1] Here the good monks found themselves overcome with thirst, and offered up prayers that for the love of Saint Kenelm some refreshing drink might be granted to them. Immediately, a second miraculous spring (for another had already appeared under the thorn in Clent) gushed forth from the hillside, a spring which was long famous for its wonderful healing properties. The spring was covered with a well-house, which may be seen to this day, and a chapel was erected hard by, which was only pulled down in the last century. But to return to the convoy; thus refreshed the procession filed up Winchcombe Street on its way to the abbey, and here a terrible thing happened. The wicked Quenride, with her psalter in her hand, was watching the approach of the procession from a window of the palace; as appropriate to the occasion she had chosen for recitation the 109th psalm, in which the psalmist calls down the vengeance of heaven upon his adversaries. To render the

---

[1] It is singular, by the way, that the party should have taken the trouble to climb the slopes of the Cotswold instead of keeping to the vale, but perhaps this is only an earlier instance of that preference for the roads of the hill region which we have already noticed.

charm more effective, when she reached the end of the psalm, she began to recite it backwards, and had just reached the 20th verse [1] as her brother's corpse was borne beneath her window. But she got no further with her reading, for at this moment her eyes fell out upon the open psalter, and the book stained with her blood was thereafter piously preserved among the sacred treasures of the abbey.

It may be thought a somewhat ungracious proceeding on the part of historical critics to cast any doubts upon the veracity of this edifying tale. The hard fact, however, remains, that about the very time that she is represented as suffering condign punishment for her misdeeds, Quenride, or Cwoenthryth as she herself spelt her name, was actually making atonement to Wulfrid, Archbishop of Canterbury, for the wrongs her father had done to him : at a Council held in 825 she handed over to the See certain lands in lieu of others which Kenulf had forcibly wrested from the Archbishop ; and a modern window in Harrow Church depicts her in the act of reverently handing over the title deeds. It further appears that she held the position of abbess of more than one convent, and presumably therefore ended her days in the odour of sanctity.

As I pass the "George" on my way to my quarters at the "White Hart," I notice the letters R. K. carved upon the old oak lintel of the archway. These are the initials of Richard Kyderminster, the wealthy abbot in the time of Henry the Seventh. Like many another Winchcombe monk, he studied at Gloucester (now Worcester) College, in Oxford, which was then frequented by members of all the great Benedictine monasteries in the province of Canterbury. Each monastery had its *mansio* or set of chambers appointed to it, and over one of the doorways, on the south side of the quadrangle, is a mitre, with a shield beneath it displaying a W, a comb, and a tun, perhaps a rebus of some

[1] "This is the reward of mine adversaries from the Lord, and of them that speak evil against my soul."

Winchcombe abbot. Richard made an abridgment of the cartularies of his abbey, which was destroyed in the great fire of London, in 1666. Sir William Morton, of Kidlington, who as we shall see presently, was acting as governor of Sudeley Castle in the Civil War during the absence of the owner, managed to procure the book from a Winchcombe farmer. Sir William was afterwards made a judge, and it was burnt in his lodgings at Serjeants' Inn during his absence on circuit: an earlier collection of the charters fortunately survives in the possession of Lord Sherborne. Within the archway is the pilgrims' gallery already mentioned. So on to the White Hart, where I leave my cycle, and determine to climb Langley Hill on the west of the town in order to obtain a bird's-eye view of the neighbourhood. By the wayside grows the larger Burnet-Saxifrage (*Pimpinella major*), a rare plant in the country we have hitherto explored, but abundant all round Winch-combe. From the summit I get just what I wanted—a comprehensive view of the lie of the town and its environs. To the north the coombe opens towards Bredon; to the south it runs up into the ridge that here forms the watershed between the Severn and the Thames; to the south-west the road to Cheltenham is seen mounting the shoulder of Cleeve Cloud, behind which that favourite home of pensioners and pupils is effectually concealed, and across the town to the east the towers of Sudeley are seen rising above the trees of the park. I have no time to do more than take a casual glance at the camp which crowns the summit of the hill. The early settlers were not likely to neglect a position so commanding, so readily fortified, and affording so secure a refuge from the approach of danger. Similar fortifications will be found on nearly all the projecting spurs of the Cotswold: if we begin with Meon Hill on the north and go no further than Randwick, where the escarpment is broken by the Stroud water, we shall count nearly a score; but I cannot linger now over these pre-historic monuments, and I suspect that the reader will be better pleased to accompany me to the Tudor manor-house of Postlip which lies snugly in a fold of the hills to the south.

For many years the house was neglected, but since it became the residence of the present owner, Mrs. Stewart-Forster, it has recovered all its former dignity. The old proverbial saying, " As sure as God's in Gloucestershire," was explained by Thomas Fuller as referring to the number of churches and religious houses in the county; but even in Gloucestershire it is not every manor-house that has its chapel—a distinction that has been Postlip's since the days of Stephen. The story goes that owing to the constant violence and civil strife that marked that king's turbulent reign, the tenants of the Lord of Postlip were afraid to attend the services at their parish church, and begged him to build a chapel where they might have the benefit of his protection. Whether there be any truth in this story or no, it is not contradicted by the chapel itself. It is incontestably a building of the twelfth country—a small church of the Cotswold type, with fine Norman chancel arch and south door. Perpendicular windows have been inserted at the east and west ends, but of special interest, because in an ordinary parish church they would have long disappeared, are the original Norman windows in the side walls, mere slits in the wall without, but widely splayed within. There are no other windows north and south than these—a survival which must surely be almost unique.[1] This survival may be accounted for by the long period of desecration, dating from the Reformation, and continuing till a few years since. Till the present owner took it in hand, had it put into repair, and restored to sacred uses, it was a mere cattle shed and sheep pen, and only the great thickness of the walls and its massive foundations had preserved it from going to ruin. It is now

[1] " Another interesting feature is the small opening high up in the south wall of the nave made to hold the ' Poor soul light,' a lamp lighted nightly to remind all who saw it to pray for the souls of the dead. This custom died out long before the Reformation."

Postlip. Norman Chapel, near Winchcombe.

fitted up for regular services; there is a resident priest at the Hall, and after a silence of three centuries and a half, mass is once more celebrated at the altar.

I return to Winchcombe by the footpath that leads down the valley. The signs of the inns as you enter the town on this side are eloquent of old country life; there is the " Pack Horse " and the " Old Pack Horse," and an ancient gabled house the corner of a street, which styles itself "The Old Corner Cupboard "—in this case one cannot help suspecting that the house is older than the sign. I soon arrive at the church, a fine Perpendicular edifice built in the reign of Henry the Sixth; the depressed arches separating the nave from the aisles are characteristic of the period, and remind us of those at Campden. At the east end may be seen traces of a lady chapel, the presence of which would account for the height of the sill of the east window from the ground. Before the restoration in 1872 the chancel was separated from the nave by a gallery called the Ladies' gallery, whatever that may have signified, and the communion table stood within a railed enclosure quite clear of the eastern wall: round it on the north, east and south sides were seats for the communicants—an arrangement which formerly survived in other churches in this neighbourhood, such as Hayles, and, as I can myself testify, at Deerhurst. At the west end of the church are deposited two stone coffins unearthed in the early part of the last century, and conjectured to be those of Kenulf and the youthful Kenelm, his son.

The only industry now carried on at Winchcombe appears to be the paper manufactory in the Postlip valley, but for many generations the district was noted for the cultivation of tobacco. This business was so remunerative that it was carried on in the teeth of more than one Act of Parliament, and of repeated proclamations against it by the Government. These attempts to suppress it were even met by rioting, which the Sheriff had to put down with a strong hand, and on one occasion it was con-

sidered necessary to send the Life Guards down from London
to destroy the crop. This was in 1667, and Pepys records
"how the life-guard, which we thought a little while since was
sent down into the country about some insurrection, was sent
to Winchcombe, to spoil the tobacco there, which it seems the
people there do plant contrary to law, and have always done."
The reasons alleged for the prohibition were that the home
cultivation was injurious to the interests of the Virginian

At Broadway.

plantations, diminished the Customs revenue, and monopolised
land that would be better employed in raising corn and cattle.
But the tobacco growers did not always proceed to rioting;
sometimes the defence took a humorous turn, as in a tract of
1655, entitled "Harry Hangman's Honour, or Glostershire
Hangman's Request to the Smokers and Tobacconists of
London," in which the said Harry is made to complain that "the
very planting of tobacco hath proved the decay of my trade,
for since it hath been planted in Glostershire, especially at

Gloucester Street, Winchcombe.

Winchcomb, my trade hath proved nothing worth . . . Then 'twas a merry world with me, for indeed before tobacco was there planted, there being no kind of trade to employ men, and very small tillage, necessity compelled poor men to stand my friends by stealing of sheep and other cattel, breaking of hedges, robbing of orchards and what not." And so the surreptitious industry went on, and in Yorkshire, lingered on till the Act of George the Third in 1782.

CHAPTER X

SUDELEY CASTLE is a private residence, and not accessible to strangers, but the late Mrs. Dent's *Annals of Winchcombe and Sudeley* have made both its history and its treasures familiar to all who are interested in the history of the county. When the Dents came into possession about the middle of the last century, the castle was in the ruined condition to which it had been reduced in the Civil War, and such portions as remained habitable had been converted into a village inn. The new owners conceived the idea of restoring it to something of its former grandeur, and so successfully has the work been accomplished that Sudeley is now one of the finest baronial houses in Gloucestershire. The whole of the northern quadrangle has been restored, while the southern one, containing the hall with its magnificent oriel, remains a ruin. At the same time, the parish church, which adjoins the castle on the east side, was again made serviceable : it had been defiled and defaced by the soldiers of the Parliament in 1643, and had remained in a neglected and ruined state ever since. Sudeley has been exceptionally fortunate in having so competent and so zealous a guardian as Mrs. Dent ; her interest in all that bore upon the history of the castle and its belongings ·never flagged, and her active support was always to be counted on in any attempt to discover or preserve the historic relics of the neighbourhood. Besides compiling the *Annals*, she conducted a local periodical called the *Winchcombe and Sudeley Record*,

Sudeley Castle.

in which she brought together many stray particulars concerning the history, folk-lore, and customs of the country side. In any undertaking tending to promote the public welfare she was always foremost, and, from all I have heard, her loss must have been deeply felt throughout the neighbourhood.

From the White Hart the road descends abruptly to the Isbourne, and rises more gently on the other side to the modern gatehouse of the castle, inscribed with the hospitable legend " Amicis Quaelibet Hora." The ancient dame, the keeper of the gate, who has grown grey in the service of the family, will conduct you to the church, and show you the beautiful tomb erected by the Dents to the memory of Queen Catherine Parr. And here I must pause, for the reader will naturally ask, what brought the last wife of the six times wedded monarch so far from courts and camps, to lay her bones on a cold hillside of the distant Cotswold. Thus, then, it was : Sudeley, for the best part of a century a royal manor, had been granted to Thomas Seymour, the destroyer of abbeys, and, as Froude styles him, the hard landlord, the tyrannical neighbour, and the oppressor of the poor. Here he made his country house, and here he brought his bride, the widow of his late master. Poor Catherine, however, did not long survive to taste the joys of Sudeley, or to repent of her latest marriage. In less than two years she was dead, and her body was buried in the church. Her tomb was destroyed at the desecration of the church, and the very spot was forgotten. At last, in 1782, a search was made and a leaden coffin discovered, the inscription on which left no doubt as to its identity : this inscription has been reproduced on the modern tomb, beneath which the coffin is now deposited.

I have said that Sudeley, before it was granted to Seymour, was a royal manor. A story told by Leland explains how it passed into the King's hands. Originally erected in the reign of Stephen, the castle was rebuilt from its foundations in Henry the Sixth's time by Ralph, Lord Boteler of Sudeley, into whose family the estate had passed by marriage. Ralph was a notable sea-captain, and one of the towers he built at Sudeley is said to have derived its name, Portmare, from that of a French admiral taken prisoner by him. He was a staunch Lancastrian, and when Edward the Fourth came to the throne he was summoned to London and forced to surrender his estate. Leland hints, however, that it was the attractions of Sudeley rather than any suspicion of treasonable conduct that influenced the King in this matter, for as Ralph was ascending the hill on his way to London, he turned to take a farewell look at his home, and said "Sudeley Castle, thou art the traitor, not I." Again a royal demesne on the attainder and execution of Seymour, a few years later it became for more than a century the seat of the princely house of Chandos. This was the most glorious period in the annals of Sudeley. The family of Brydges was one of the most powerful in the western midlands : its matrimonial connections were extensive and influential, and its manors were distributed over four counties. Sir John Brydges, who had distinguished himself in the wars of Henry VIII., was one of the most energetic supporters of Queen Mary, and in 1554 he was rewarded with the grant of Sudeley and raised to the peerage as Baron Chandos. The castle soon became famous for its magnificence and hospitality : Edmund, the second lord, was "a generous friend, a noble housekeeper, and a bountiful master": Giles, the third lord, entertained Elizabeth on one of her progresses with the splendour to which she was used. The *genius loci* was not forgotten. On her entrance to the castle an old shepherd presented her with a lock of wool, and made her a speech commending his calling and the ancient industry of Cotswold to her royal favour. Next day there was an "entertainment," in which Apollo and Daphne, in the guise of shepherd and shepherdess, played the principal part, and nothing but the inclemency of the weather prevented the performance of a

more elaborate piece, in which the comic character was to have
been the "Cutter of Cotsholde, that looks as though he only
knew his leripoope [lines he had to speak], amorous he is and
wise carrying a sheep's eye in a calf's head." Grey, the fifth
lord in James I.'s time, "was a noble housekeeper, and
by winning behaviour contracted so great an interest in
Gloucestershire, and had such numerous attendance when he
came to court, that he was commonly called the King of
Cotswold." It was under the rule of his son George, the sixth
lord, that evil days fell upon Sudeley, and the castle, shattered
by the civil strife, was abandoned to decay. His own career
was typical of the fate of his mansion ; beginning happily and
gloriously it terminated in misfortune and obscurity. I shall
return to him directly, but I must first briefly relate the
fortune of the castle.

Its military position, as the chief fortress between Berkeley
and Warwick, was one of the first importance. It could command all the roads, in every direction, across the hills between
Campden and Cirencester ; and at this time, when the royal
garrison at Oxford closed the main London and Gloucester
road to the Parliament, this meant the command of the
remaining available routes to Gloucester, Hereford, and South
Wales. Hence the possession of Sudeley was a primary
object to any force contemplating a demonstration in any of
these directions. As soon as the war broke out, therefore, the
castle was garrisoned by Lord Chandos for the King. But in
January, 1643, when the Cavaliers were busy making an
attempt upon Cirencester, Massey made a dash from Gloucester,
assaulted the castle and reduced it to surrender. It was on this
occasion that the abominations were perpetrated in the church.
The Roundheads did not, however, enjoy their triumph long ;
a week later Rupert carried Cirencester by storm, and Sudeley
was promptly abandoned by its captors. The Royalists now
returned, and in the following September the King, after being
compelled to abandon the siege of Gloucester, took up his

quarters at the castle for some days. We may believe that Lord Chandos was here in person to receive his master, for shortly afterwards he attended him to Newbury Field, where he charged at the head of his regiment and had three horses killed under him. He then followed the king to Oxford, and early in 1644 he sent his lieutenant, Colonel Sir William Morton, to command the garrison at Sudeley. For some months Sir William remained undisturbed, but in June Charles's masterly escape from Oxford, described in an earlier chapter, drew Waller into his neighbourhood. Waller's design, after his final parting with Essex at Stow, was to hang upon the rear of the King's army and follow it to Worcester, but Sudeley was not far out of his way, and commanding as it did the road from London to Gloucester through Warwick—the only one then open to the Parliament—he determined not to throw away the chance of securing it. He therefore sent word to the active and energetic Massey to meet him before the castle, and their combined forces made a vigorous assault upon its defences. The walls, however, proved too strong for such artillery as they were able to bring to bear upon them, and in spite of scanty supplies the governor might have succeeded in holding his own, had not his men proved refractory and obliged him to surrender. Thus, for the last time during the war, Sudeley changed hands, and Morton was sent to London and committed to the Tower: a later incident in his career has been already noticed. I must not omit to mention one circumstance in connection with the surrender of the castle, since it illustrates the flourishing condition of the Gloucestershire clothing trade at this time. The wealthier sheep-farmers had long been clothiers as well as graziers: that is to say, they put their wool into the hands of paid operatives to go through the successive stages of manufacture, and received back the completed product to dispose of as they best could. They must therefore often have had large quantities of cloth on their hands, and when the district became

disturbed by the war, a considerable proportion of their stock
had been brought to the castle for safety. It is said that as
much as £4,000 worth was found there by the victorious
party.

Meantime, what had become of Lord Chandos? When the
news of the loss of Sudeley reached him he was already in
London, and the remainder of his career forms a melancholy
contrast to its brilliant commencement. Disgusted perhaps at
the ascendancy which Rupert had acquired over the King, and
despairing of the success of his party, he had left Oxford and
gone up to London to take advantage of the terms offered by
the Parliament to those who were willing to refrain from
further active participation in the royal cause. That he was a
man of headstrong and uncertain temper is not the less likely
from a subsequent incident : in 1652 he quarrelled with an
intimate friend—Colonel Henry Compton, a member of the
Northampton family—"about a lady he recommended to the
colonel, whose person and fortune were below few matches in
the kingdom." The quarrel ended in a duel, in which the
colonel was killed. Lord Chandos was brought to trial and
found guilty of manslaughter, but he did not long survive his
disgrace ; early in 1655 he was carried off by small-pox. He
was the last of his family to reside at Sudeley Castle, which was
dismantled at the conclusion of the war. Of his brother
William, who succeeded him in the title, but not in the Sudeley
estate, Pepys made an entry in his diary (Sunday, December
21, 1662), which, at the risk of irrelevance, I cannot help quoting : " By and by comes in my Lord Sandwich, and so we had
great store of good musique. By and by comes in my simple
Lord Chandois, who (my Lord Sandwich being gone out to
Court) began to sing psalms, but so dully that I was weary of it."

A delightful day may be spent in rambling about the hillside above the castle, or over the edge to the remoter coombes
towards the Guitings : in this country are Hawling and Roel
farm, with their memories of Clement Barksdale and his pupils,

and Roel Gate, a famous meet of hounds. The territory of
the local hunt was formerly larger than at present. This hill
region, as I have said before, is now divided between two packs,
the "North Cotswold" and the "Cotswold," but previously to
1858 it was all hunted by the "Berkeley," and Lord Fitzhardinge used to bring his hounds to Cheltenham every alter-
nate month during the season : a room at the Lygon Arms,
Broadway, in which he used to dine, is still known as the Earl's
parlour. If in the course of his ramble the stranger should pass
Sudeley Lodge—the place lies in the ancient park of the castle,
and its very name is suggestive of the old hunting days—he will
see on the wall of the house an inscription commemorating a
visit of George III. in 1788, graced with a medallion of that
monarch in profile. The King would drive over occasionally
from Cheltenham to inspect the ruins of the castle ; and on
this occasion he was on his way to Brockhampton Park to view
a famous black horse : it is on record that after his visit to the
stables, his gracious Majesty was invited by his host at
Brockhampton to share the family midday dinner, which consisted of a leg of Cotswold mutton and a batter pudding ;
and the family tradition loved to tell how the royal appetite,
sharpened by the bracing air of the hills, did ample justice
to their humble fare.

Brockhampton I have to pass on my way to Andoversford,
but I must first climb the steep hill that divides Winchcombe
from the Thames basin. As I wheel my cycle up the road,
one of those cross-roads barred here and there by field gates, I
pause now and again to take a farewell view of Winchcombe
and Sudeley, now far below me ; and once arrived at the
summit I soon reach Charlton Abbots, where the beautiful old
Tudor manor-house claims its tribute of admiration. As the
name denotes, the village belonged to Winchcombe Abbey,
and here the monks had a lepers' house, a refuge indispensable
in mediæval times. Whether any traces of it are still left is
doubtful, but an ancient thatched cottage is believed to occupy

its site. Hard by is a spring of beautifully clear water, collected into a circular basin large enough for a bath, whence it flows northwards to the Severn ; at no great distance is another spring, which finds its way southwards to the Thames. So past Brockhampton Park, leaving to the left the quarries where in 1634 the snow and ice lay till August, past Sevenhampton with its interesting cruciform church, and grey cluster of farms and cottages, to the very practical and business-like looking inn at Andoversford.

From the wide sweep of road in front, and the extensive stabling in the rear, one may tell at a glance that the Andoversford inn was a bustling place in the old coaching days. Lying as it does on the great high road to Oxford and London, it was the end of the first stage out of Cheltenham, and glad enough the horses must have been of their rest after their stiff pull up on to the Cotswold table-land. The only public conveyance which now passes the door is the humble Northleach omnibus, but there are two railway stations within half a mile, " Andoversford " (on the Great Western), and " Dowdeswell " (on the Midland), as they are called for distinction. The two lines join at the top of a lofty embankment which forms the background of the inn garden, and for the better discipline of such presumptuous passengers as may wish to pass from one to the other, the Midland trains run through the Great Western Station without stopping.

We have now reached the south-western division—if I may borrow a term from electioneering—of our district, and the reader will have a good notion of the area it includes, if he will draw a line on the map from Andoversford through Birdlip to Painswick and Stroud, thence to Cirencester, Fairford and Burford, and so back through Northleach to Andoversford. The further westward you go the deeper and more numerous become the coombes, and, by consequence, the narrower the ridges which separate them, so that a transverse section of the Stroud and Bisley country, taken from north-west to south-east, would resemble nothing so much as a series of W's compressed together at either extremity. It follows that the routes from east to west, in the centre of the district, are better suited to the pedestrian than the cyclist, and I therefore propose to explore it in somewhat zigzag manner, chiefly from north to south, and lastly to pursue the southern curve of our imaginary boundary line from Stroud to Burford.

Three ancient roads radiate from Cirencester towards the northern circumference of the horizon—and these are all with which we are concerned—Akeman Street towards Bicester, the Foss to Stow and far away beyond, and Ermin Street to Gloucester: midway between the two latter the modern Cheltenham road runs up the valley of the Churn. To-night I will put up at our coaching inn at Andoversford, and start refreshed for a ride down the lovely Churn valley to-morrow morning. The name Andoversford is a puzzle to me; I know that an earlier form is Andiford, but this does not help me much: presently, however, as good luck will have it, I fall in with an aged farmer who is able to give me an explanation. Some score of years since, he said, when he was about fifty, he fell into talk with some old men of the neighbouring village of Shipton Olive, and they told him that in their younger days they had helped to build the bridge which now spans what was once the ford that gives the place its name. Before that there were only stepping-stones, and there "the gentleman used to *hand the ladies over!*"

Before dinner I take a stroll across the fields by the long wall of Sandywell Park, once a deer park; the house, a comfortable early eighteenth century mansion, and the Park wall some twelve feet high, built of dry stones without mortar, and saved from ruin by its flat coping. A little further under the edge of the hill, and looking down the valley towards Cheltenham, is Dowdeswell,[1] the demesne of the Rogers family since the days

[1] " Near Andoversford is a farm called Owdeswell. In old charters Dowdeswell and Owdeswell appear as Fons Dodonis and Fons Odonis.

of Elizabeth. The great house is in the Italian style, but the beautiful old manor-house still stands high up at the southern extremity of the Park. The church nestling on the hillside is cruciform, with a low broach spire of late sixteenth century date, of which you may catch a glimpse as you enter the tunnel on reaching the head of the valley from Cheltenham. At Whittington, on the way back to Andoversford, is another fine manor-house, and an interesting church containing monumental effigies in the armour of the early fourteenth century.

To reach the Churn valley we cross the bridge, and, turning to the left, ascend a very long hill to " Cold Comfort "—cold indeed it must be on a blustering winter's day—and " St Paul's Epistle "—one would like to know the origin of this name— past Pegglesworth Hill, whence you may see as far as Worcester on the north and Marlborough on the south, down to Seven Springs, the source of the Churn, and one of the two claimants to the honour of being considered the source of the Thames, the other being " Thames Head," near Kemble Junction. The decision of course must be purely arbitrary, but if distance from the mouth of the river is to count for anything, undoubtedly the dispute must be decided in favour of the Seven Springs. So thought T. S. E., the author of the Latin hexameter, which you may read on a tablet affixed to the wall that forms one side of the pool :

" Hic tuus O Tamisine Pater Septemgeminus fons.

The Seven Springs gush out from beneath the roots of some aged trees, and form a clear pool, into which you may dip your leathern cup and quench your thirst : the water (experto crede) is excellent.

The villages of Coberley and Cowley lie on the banks of the Churn below the road on our right. Nothing remains of

The places were evidently supposed to be connected with Dodo and Odo, two Mercian chieftains of the eighth century, who founded Tewkesbury Abbey."

Coberley Manor except an old barn and a battlemented wall which separated its garden from the churchyard. But it was a considerable house for many centuries. In the time of Edward the Third it was the home of a branch of the Berkeley family, whose monuments may be seen in the over-restored church. Among them is the effigy of Sir Thomas Berkeley, who fought at Crecy, and who married the widow of one Richard Whittington, of Pauntley, across the Severn. She probably brought with her to her new home at Coberley her young son, Richard Whittington, afterwards so famous as Lord Mayor of London town. The lad was apprenticed to Sir Hugh Fitzwarren, of London, who himself belonged to a Gloucestershire family. The story of Whittington and his cat we have all read in the nursery ; and as we grew older, we have probably regarded it as little less mythical than the story of Jack and the Beanstalk. The following discovery at any rate seems to point to the antiquity of the legend. Like other of the wealthier county families, the Whittingtons possessed a town house in the county town, and when this was pulled down in 1862, a stone was dug up on which was carved the figure of a boy holding a cat in his arms. The work is of fifteenth century date, and apparently formed part of a chimney-piece. It is now in the Guildhall Museum, in London. From the Berkeleys Coberley passed by marriage to an ancestor of the Chandos family, and early in the seventeenth century it was purchased by the Duttons, of Sherborne. The Duttons, who have ever since been one of the principal families in the county, came out of Cheshire in the middle of the sixteenth century, and bought the estate of Sherborne, which had belonged to Winchcombe Abbey. In the time of the Civil War, John Dutton resided at Sherborne, and his brother Ralph at Coberley. At the manor-house Sir Ralph Dutton had the honour of entertaining his Sovereign on two occasions, first, when the King was on his way from Painswick to Sudeley, after the raising of the siege of Gloucester, and secondly, in July, 1644, a fortnight later than the discomfiture of Waller at Cropredy, when Charles was marching through the Cotswold to the west, in pursuit of Essex. We have already alluded to the journey of Charles II. through this district in the disguise of a manservant : like his father, he slept at Coberley, but it was at the rectory and not at the manor-house. These are bare facts, no traditions survive in which they can be dressed, but the imagination has the freer scope.

Cowley Manor is a large modern house, with terraced gardens overlooking an ornamental lake. The small Norman church is close by and conforms to the Cotswold type. The east end is lighted by two small windows in the gable, one above the other, and the wall below is blank ; in each side wall are seven lancet windows. The Perpendicular tower and porch appear to be the only later additions : the former contains a peal of six bells presented by the squire of Queen Anne's day, who was a devotee of campanology, and used to travel about the country with a company of ringers, till at last he had rung away his fortune. Do the churchwardens' books of any parish contain a note of his visit and performances ? We now regain the road just where an old cross road of fearful steepness, even for the Cotswold, descends the hill on our right ; and a mile and a half further there is another : the latter is the old road from Cirencester to Cheltenham, and must have been trying enough even for a steady paced nag or a pack-horse; no wonder, therefore, that when pillions went out of fashion, and the quality took to travelling between Bath and Cheltenham in the family coach, some more practicable road was wanted, and the river valley was utilised for the purpose. It is one of the commonplaces of travel that the modern road (and notably, of course, the railroad) follows the windings of the river valley, whilst the old road is carried across the hills, and the reason is not far to seek. The hills were dry, the valleys were swampy and liable to floods, and when wheel traffic was practically non-existent the want of a more level, but longer valley route was not felt. It is an easy run down to Colesbourne, a clean, neat-looking village with a cheerful roadside inn, where we shall do wisely to lunch. By the way we shall come across two or three other instances of village names compounded with this southern variant of burn, always intelligible from the situation of the place, and I should like to enter a humble protest against the modern fashion of dropping the u, even if I have not the courage to substitute "Sher-bourne" for the prescriptive "Sherborne"; but in the case of Colesbourne and Duntesbourne, at any rate, I refuse to conform to a tendency so Transatlantic. The park lies on the north of the village, and the great house, as at Cowley and Rendcombe, is a modern one. For those who may wish to catch a train at Withington Station, on the Cirencester and Cheltenham line, there is a charming by-road across the downs.

Below Colesbourne the Churn keeps us company on the left all the way to Cirencester, and we soon enter the shady woods of Rendcombe. Unlike its neighbours, Rendcombe lies high on the top of a projecting headland with a deep valley on either side, a natural advantage which has not been neglected by the successive owners of the estate. As the worthy Samuel Rudder remarks, "there cannot be a more healthy situation for the rational and gentleman-like exercises of riding and hunting." Of hunting Rendcombe has seen, and indeed still sees, its full share. Its earliest lords may have even chased the wolf to its distant lair in the as yet unreclaimed wilds, and it is certain that there was abundance of deer during the four hundred years that the estate remained in the hands of a single family. This period ended with the death of Humphrey Stafford, Duke of Bucking-ham, at the battle of Northampton, in 1460. He fought on the losing side, and for a brief space, by Royal gift, Rendcombe fell to the King-maker, on whose attainder it again came to the Crown. Afterwards it came to the Tames—the great wool merchants of whom we shall hear again—then to the Berkeleys,

and at last, at the Restoration, to the Guises, who, deserting
their ancestral home at Elmore, resided here for more than a
century.   It was Sir Christopher Guise who purchased Rendcombe and built the large square uncompromising house, of
which pictures may be seen in Atkyns and in Rudder.   His
son, Sir John Guise, represented the county in Parliament, in
the Whig interest, and, according to Fosbrooke, was "the first
gentleman who went to meet the Prince of Orange."   In this
expedition he was more successful than the Lord Lovelace of
the day, who, as we shall see later, endeavoured to force his
way through Cirencester, but was overpowered by the militia
and sent to Gloucester Castle as a prisoner.   Sir John seems to
have been a fighting-man as well as a politician, but politics were
at the bottom of one, and perhaps both, of his two recorded duels.
In the first, which took place at Barrow's (now Perrot's) Brook,
a mile or two below Rendcombe, he was run through the body
by Sir Robert Atkyns, the historian of the county—"the sword
going in at his navel and coming out at his backbone, he
falling at the same time into a sawpit, and the sword breaking in
his body : " and in the second (which we may wonder he
survived to fight), he disarmed one of King James's officers, in
the College Green at Gloucester.   By the end of the eighteenth
century the Guises had left Rendcombe and returned to their
home on the Severn, but their memory is preserved here, in the
church, by an altar tomb, with the inscription, " Sacred to the
family of Guise distinguished during several centuries by
hereditary worth by active virtue and by the parliamentary
confidence of the county of Gloucester."   The church was
built in Henry VIII.'s reign by Sir Edmund Tame, the
then lord of the manor.   He was the son of John Tame, to
whom Fairford owes its famous windows, and his initials may be
seen on the corbels and in some old glass which remains in one
of the windows of the nave.   Two pillars and a respond of the
Norman church which he replaced are built into the north
wall.

North Cerney Church.

According to one story the ancient glass at Rendcombe (and there is very little of it left) was the glass that remained over after the windows at Fairford had been filled. Be this as it may, the old glass at North Cerney, the next village on our route, is now more interesting. I do not remember to have seen a more striking figure than that of a certain bishop in a window of the north transept here, and it would be difficult to find anything on so small a scale to surpass it as a triumph of skill in this particular art. The fine old Queen Anne rectory, which adjoins the church, bears on its outer face the arms of University College, who are the patrons of the living.

At Perrot's Brook, we may, if we choose, take a by-road over the hill on the right to Ermin Street, but evening is now drawing on, and it will be wiser to keep straight on and find a lodging for the night in Cirencester. We cannot stay now to explore the "capital of the Cotswold": our zigzag journeys will bring us here again, and we must be up and away betimes, and for the first mile retrace our steps along the Cheltenham road, which so far is identical with Ermin Street. We are now in the valley of a tiny tributary of the Churn, and at Stratton we leave the Roman road to climb the hill to Birdlip, and ourselves follow the valley up to Daglingworth. Now this little valley of Daglingworth and the Duntesbournes is the last of those of the east Cotswold type; I have already alluded to the distinction—the eastern valleys are depressions in the open down, the western, deep wooded ravines. By a curious coincidence this distinction exactly corresponds to that between the water areas of the Thames and of the Severn, so that either area is in a way in harmony with the general character of its own river. The general slope of the whole district is from north-west to south-east, and a glance at the map will show that in the western corner the streams descend from similar altitudes in a much shorter distance, and this will go far to explain the difference in question.

On reaching Daglingworth our attention is at once caught by

a picturesque farmhouse on our left, formerly, no doubt, the manor-house (sad to think how hard it is nowadays for the man of humble means, who is neither farmer nor parson, to find a home in an old country village), and hard by in a meadow nearer the road stands a dove-house and certain mediæval ruins much overgrown with grass and weeds. These probably mark the dwelling of a colony, or to speak more precisely, according to

Dovecot at Daglingworth.

Dame Juliana Berners, a *superfluity* of nuns from Godstow, which nunnery had a cell here, and was patron of the living. Their dove-house, entered as usual by a very low doorway, is remarkable as still possessing its revolving ladder. These curious machines have generally disappeared, especially when the dove-house has been put to other uses. It is therefore well worth our examining; and we shall then see that the ladder is attached to two horizontal arms—in a different plane in order to give the requisite slope—which revolve upon a central upright post, so that it can be applied at any moment to the particular nesting holes to be inspected. Of these there are about 550, arranged in tiers round the interior of the house, while two dormers in the roof admit the entrance and exit of the birds. We shall shortly visit a dove-house of another kind, but we must now pass on to the church, which has some interesting details. In the first place, the long and short work at the angles of the building and the extremely narrow south doorway are suggestive of Saxon architecture. Over the latter is a sundial, which shows that it existed as an external doorway before the building of the present porch, itself Norman, with another sundial of its own; then there are one or two curious points to be noticed inside, but under our feet in the porch as we enter is a brass with an inscription too quaint to be left uncopied:

THE DISSECTION AND DISTRIBUTION
OF GILES HANDCOX
WHO EARTH BEQUEATHE[D] TO EARTH TO HEAVEN HIS SOULE
TO FRIENDS HIS LOVE TO THE POORE A FIVE POUND DOLE
TO REMAINE FOR EVER AND BE IMPLOYED
FOR THEIR BEST ADVANTAGE AND RELEEFE
IN DAGLINGWORTH
APRIL THE 9 1638

So we enter to behold facing us three Norman arches, but these, with the north aisle into which they open, only date from 1845. The north wall at that time was plain, and lighted by a small two-light Norman window cut in a single stone. This was removed and given to Barnsley church, a few miles away, where it may still be seen; certain apparently inverted letters were then observed cut upon the stone, and on turning it with the window lights bottom upwards, enough was decipherable to restore the following inscription:

D D
MATRIBVSET
GENIOLOCI
JUNIA

It was in fact a Roman votive altar, half the letters of the inscription having been cut through to form the lights.   Another altar—a Norman one—is now at the east end and is used as a credence table.   This has also a singular history.   Previous to the alterations of 1845, an arch spanned the nave just below the south door, which had once formed the eastern support of a tower erected above the western bay.   In the fifteenth century this tower became ruinous and was pulled down, the present tower being then added at the west end of the nave. The lower story of the original tower, which had probably served as a priest's chamber, contained the Norman altar in question, built up against its eastern wall, which was formed by the said cross arch.   Then, when the floor of the room was removed, the altar remained high up on the western face of this arch till its destruction in 1845, when it was removed to its present position.   Lastly there is a further indication of Saxon workmanship in the three carved stones, now built into the eastern face of the chancel arch.   The Norman masons had, as was discovered when this arch was rebuilt in 1845, inserted these stones with their faces turned inwards into the jambs.   They had probably found them on the western side of the Saxon arch, facing the congregation.   The carved subjects are—the Crucifixion (now the centre of the three), Christ enthroned (on the north), and St. Peter, represented according to the Saxon idea as a beardless youth (on the south).

Higher up the valley lie the two Duntesbournes, Duntesbourne Rous and Duntesbourne Abbots.   The latter, once a manor of Gloucester Abbey, is perched upon a steep slope, at the foot of which is a clear spring that forms the source of the eponymous bourne.   The church (to-day's excursion has its full share of churches, but I trust the reader will be long-suffering) is much modernised, and, all the windows being filled with stained glass, very dark.   Far more interesting is the little Norman church of Duntesbourne Rous, which seems to have been but

Duntesbourne Rous Church.

little altered for the last six hundred years.   The hill on which
it is built has a steep decline from west to east, and there is
therefore room for a crypt under the chancel, lighted by a small
deeply splayed window.   The chancel wall above was blank
after the local peculiarity more than once noticed, but a small
modern window has been inserted.[1]   There is a very curious
low saddleback tower at the west end,[2] and the interior
contains some good old oak pews, and a fine Jacobean pulpit.
Altogether it is one of the most unmutilated churches of its size
in the county.   The manor was, with that of Temple Guiting,
bestowed by Bishop Foxe upon Corpus, and here the college
are also the patrons of the living: it would be pleasant to think
that the immunity of the church was in some degree due to
this circumstance, but I fear that the inference would not be
warranted by a general review of college livings.   We will not
leave the Duntesbournes without noticing a feature characteristic
of the churchyards of these parts.   The inscription on the
tombstones instead of being cut in the stone itself in the usual
manner, is graved on a brass plate which is fixed in a matrix
prepared for it in the stone.   But this like other local industries
is a vanished, or all but vanished, art.   I heard of one old man
at Saperton who could still practise it, but tombstones like
everything else are now procured ready-made from the town
manufacturer.

We shall rejoin the Ermin Street at the Five Mile House,
but shall soon quit it again for Elkstone, an upland village
lying in a lonely depression of the hills, and shut off from the
Churn by a ridge which rises to the height of over 900 feet.
The tall church tower is conspicuous from afar, and the whole
village has a bleak wind-swept look, which marks it off at once

---

[1] Exactly when this window was cut I have not discovered, but about
1870 another window was cut in the north wall of the chancel.

[2] An inscription on the tower records that "This was bilt by John
Halden mason" in 1587, and certainly a tower formed no part of the
original churches of this character.

from the more homely villages in the valley. A Roman villa
has been unearthed where the land slopes to the sun on the
south, but from Roman villas I abstain for the present ; a time
for them will come ere long. Besides the church, the most
notable feature of the village is the large, solid, old-fashioned
rectory, which looks as though it could laugh at the utmost
rigours of which a Cotswold winter could be capable. Once
safe within its walls let the wind howl in the chimney, and the
rain pelt against the window-panes as it will ; it is but to cast
another log upon the fire, and to take down another
volume from the well-lined shelves. On this fine autumn
morning, however, for it is only in imagination that the wanderer can hope to taste the delights of an Elkstone winter, the
library windows are thrown open, the old-fashioned garden
alleys are bright with great clumps of dahlias and sunflowers,
and the mellowing apples have already begun to fall from
the trees. On the farms the last load is being carried from
the corn lands, and the sounds that reach our ears from the
distant stubbles tell us that the partridge shooters are already
busy among the coveys. As for ourselves, since we have
not to handle the pitchfork or the fowling-piece, we can
stroll into the churchyard undisturbed. A long, aisleless,
strong, time-defying church, with a tall, steadfast western tower,
the monster gurgoyles at the angles of which are almost
terrifying in their grotesqueness. But the weird fancy that
found expression in these grotesques did but carry on the
tradition of the Norman builders of the church itself. Walk
round the outside, and look at the corbel-table of the nave
with its array of human faces, stags, and winged horses,
and at the strange monsters, beak-heads as they call them,
around the head of the south door. It will well repay
our interest to stop to look more minutely at this door.
In the centre of the tympanum is the enthroned Christ,
one hand raised in the attitude of benediction, the other
holding the book of judgment (the face has been hacked

away by some zealous Puritan); above the head a hand
is stretched from heaven, symbolical of the first Person
of the Trinity: right and left are the emblems of the
evangelists, the angel, the bull, the lion, and the eagle; above
on the right is the lamb with the standard of the cross, the
emblem of resurrection, and on the left below the yawning
mouth of Tophet. Along the chancel walls runs a cornice
some distance below the eaves, which seems to indicate that
the walls have been raised. If we pass inside we shall be
able to understand why this was done. . Entering under
the tower, we see at once that the church is divided into
three portions; first the nave with a fine old timber roof,
then a central portion separated from the nave by a
Norman arch, and, lastly, a small chancel separated from
the central portion by another Norman arch; the two
latter portions have groined vaulting. The central portion
was the lantern beneath a central tower, and Oxford men
will at once remember Iffley, where this tower still exists;
the general plan of the two churches being in fact very
much the same. The newel staircase, which gave access
to the tower, will be seen on the north side of the lantern space. At an early date,—probably in the thirteentḥ
century,—the arches which supported the tower began to settle
and it was found necessary to pull it down. The tower
being removed, the vaulting over the lantern space was
exposed, and it became necessary to cover it with a roof:
when this was done, in order to keep the ridge of this
roof at the same level right on to the east end, the roof
of the chancel had to be raised, and at the same time
the chancel walls were also raised above the old level
indicated by the cornice which we noticed on the exterior.
The result was to leave space enough between the low
vaulting of the chancel and the new rafters to form a small
room to which the old tower staircase now served as an
approach. The strange thing to us is the use to which this

room was put. Not being required for any sacred purpose it was utilised as a pigeon-house, and a pigeon-house it remained down to modern times. Several other instances of columbaria in churches are upon record, for example, St. Peter's at Marlborough, where the vicar's pigeons lived in the room over the chancel till the middle of the last century. At Elkstone the holes in the wall which admitted the birds are now stopped up, but the forty-three nesting holes are still to be seen in the interior.

On the other side of Ermin Street is Brimpsfield. The Norman church is of the common Cotswold type, consisting of nave and chancel, but a singular tower of Perpendicular date rises above their junction. This tower replaced a thirteenth century bell turret, which rested upon the chancel arch eastwards, and westwards upon two columns which were erected inside the church for its support. When the tower was built the same supports were utilised. The east end is windowless, and it is to be hoped will now be suffered to remain so. South-west of the church, a deep ditch and lofty mounds, reminding us of Deddington, are all that remain of the castle of the Giffards, the Norman lords of Brimpsfield. But while nothing is known of the destruction of Deddington, the circumstances which led to the destruction of Brimpsfield are upon record. John Giffard, second Baron of Brimpsfield, had sided with the King's cousin, Thomas, Earl of Lancaster, against the royal favourites, and had sat in the Parliament of 1321 by which the Despensers were banished. Next year, when Edward was marching westwards against the lords of the Welsh Marches, Giffard attacked and plundered the royal baggage train on Ermin Street, and in revenge for this foray, the King despatched a party of soldiers to demolish Brimpsfield Castle. Meantime, Giffard had made his way to the disaffected lords, and was among the barons who surrendered at Boroughbridge. He was taken to Gloucester, and hanged outside the walls. His father, also named John, the first baron by writ, was the founder of Gloucester College in Oxford for

T

Benedictine monks, a foundation we have already had occasion
to mention in connection with Winchcombe. He took the
part of the barons against Henry III., but after the Battle
of Lewes he quarrelled with De Montfort and fought for the
King at Evesham. A story is told of a ruse by which he managed to gain admission for De Montfort into Gloucester while
they were still friends. One winter's morning two merchants
appeared before the gates of the city riding on woolpacks
thrown across their horses' backs instead of saddles and
covered with long Welsh cloaks. The gates were opened to
them, but no sooner were they inside than they sprang from
their steeds, threw aside their cloaks, and confronted the
astonished keepers of the gates in the guise of two knights
armed from head to foot; the men threw down their keys
and fled, while Sir John Giffard and his friend admitted De
Montfort and his followers.

From Brimpsfield, if the traveller is still in a climbing
humour, he may take the lane that runs southward under
Caudle Green, and descend into the bowels of the earth at
Washford Bottom, whence he may toil up again to Ermin
Street by way of the restored Norman church of Winstone ; or
if he is loth to quit the beautifully wooded ravine he may
follow it down to Miserden, the home of the Sandys family
in the seventeenth century. The stately old house stands on
the hill to his right, and the church contains an exquisitely
finished alabaster monument (attributed to Nicholas Stone)
with the recumbent effigies of Sir William Sandys and his wife.
He may then make his way past a ruined cromlech on his
left to Daglingworth and so back to Cirencester. If, however,
time or fatigue forbid this tempting prolongation of the excursion, he may regain Ermin Street by the way he came (it is but
a short mile), and a rapid run over its excellent surface will
soon bring him back to his inn.

CHAPTER XI

SEVEN miles from Cirencester the Foss Way crosses the Coln at Fossbridge, and here is one of those good old-fashioned roomy country inns, which we are going to make our head-quarters for a day or two. We are now in the centre of some of the most famous vestiges of ancient settlements and civilisa-tion to be found in England. Of the ancient roads the Foss Way and Ermin Street are now two of the best kept thoroughfares in the county, but smaller trackways are numerous and cross the downs in all directions. It will be enough to mention the White Way, leading from Cirencester to Winch-combe, the Welsh Way, which crosses from Ermin Street through Barnsley to Lechlade and was the route by which Welsh cattle and Welsh coal reached the waterway of the Thames, and the Salt Way, which starting from Droitwich mounts the Cotswold at Hayles, and passing through Hawling and Salperton crosses the Foss just north of Stowell Park and runs straight thence through Coln St. Aldwyns to the Thames at Lechlade.[1] The Roman conquest of southern Britain was completed by A.D. 47, and from the fact that very few of the Cotswold camps show any traces of Roman construction it may be inferred that the Dobuni offered but slight resistance.

[1] From the fact that for nearly the whole of its course through the Cotswold, the Foss Way forms the boundary of parishes, it may be conjec-tured that the Saxon conquerors employed it as a boundary line to divide their settlements.

Chedworth Church.

Bath and Gloucester being outside our limits, the only city founded by the Romans with which we are concerned is Cirencester, but the country houses or villas are numerous, and those whose sites have been discovered are probably but a small fraction of the whole number. Some half dozen of the former are within a few miles of us at Fossbridge, and it is a delightful excursion up the Coln valley to Chedworth villa, the finest of them all. On our right the clear, crystal Coln winds through rich green pastures in which the cattle are browsing ; on our left are the Chedworth woods, fragrant in May with vast stretches of lilies of the valley, and now carpeted with their thick clustering leaves. Not long after passing a deserted cottage half concealed by a tangled overgrowth of creepers, a turning to the left brings us to the villa.

Forty years ago you would have seen nothing of the extensive remains which have now been revealed. You might have walked through the undisturbed woodland, little suspecting that the country house of a wealthy Roman or Romanised Briton lay beneath your feet. But a little matter sometimes kindles a great fire : it happened one day that a keeper of the Earl of Eldon had lost a ferret. As he was searching for the animal he turned up a number of dice-like objects which at once struck his attention. On examination they turned out to be Roman tesseræ, and the clue thus given being followed up led to the discovery of the remains we have now come to see. To the uninstructed they will seem to be a confused assemblage of walls, floors, passages and pits. But you have only to buy one of the little guide books sold by the custodian, and confusion at once gives way to order. I do not mean to say that you will at once become a master of Roman architecture and Roman economy—that will take many long hours of study ; but if you go round the villa with the plan in your hand, you will have a good general idea of the arrange-ment of the whole and the meaning and purpose of the various parts. When or how the building was destroyed we can never know, but a lapse of many centuries must be allowed for the accumulation of soil sufficient to bury walls some of which are still nearly five feet high. It is more than likely that the destruction took place before the end of the fifth century, when the Saxon invaders were appropriating the soil and forming their settlements. Had we been here in the autumn of A.D. 404 instead of that of 1904, we should have seen a court resembling a college quadrangle with buildings on three if not four sides. Round the court, and open to it, runs a covered corridor with a sloping roof supported here and there by pillars. Into this corridor or verandah the rooms of the house open : those inhabited by the family are on the east side of the court and look westwards across the valley. On the south side are the offices and servants' apartments : the north side has a long prolongation eastwards and perhaps contains, besides another set of living rooms, the granaries, storehouses, and workshops connected with the farm. The lower story is built of the local stone, the upper of timber : the roof is high pitched and, as well as that of the verandah, is covered with lozenge-shaped stone tiles. The whole building seems designed for comfort and utility : there is no attempt at artistic elaboration, but the work is plain and solid, and the result is good. The builders both in their external and internal arrangements have taken into account the rigours of a northern winter, and the villa seems calculated to last for many a generation. Fire and sword they could not guard against, nor could they be expected to anticipate the advent of an invader to whom all the refinements of Roman architecture and Roman civilisation would be as dross.

A mile above the villa, where the Coln comes sweeping round a tiny headland, the valley begins to wear an aspect of park-like dignity. A fine avenue of limes ascends the hill on our left, and the open road is shaded by majestic beeches and horse chestnuts. But at the same time there is over the whole an air of neglect and vanished splendour which does not

seem to herald our approach to the residence of a modern
country gentleman. It is, in fact, the old story of the mansion
turned farm-house. There by the river stands what was once
the mansion, beautiful even in its decay. While one wing has
been pulled down, and a part of the gardens has been converted into pasture, a magnificent avenue of yews and a lordly
bowling green have been spared. Lighted up by the rays of
the setting sun the whole is a striking picture—the stately walls
and lichened roofs of the house, the dark foliage of the yews,
the limpid river, and the rolling downs beyond. But I have
not yet said who the favoured mortals were who so wisely

Cassey Compton.

chose this sequestered nook for their home. In the parish of
Deerhurst a score of miles away by the Severn side, for
more than two centuries were seated the family of Cassey,
the most famous of whom, Sir John Cassey, knight, was
chief baron of the Exchequer under Richard II. It is
not unreasonable to suppose that it was a branch of this
family who were lords of this manor on the Coln during the
greater part of the sixteenth century; but be this as it may, it
was from these sixteenth century Casseys that the place took
its name of Cassey Compton. On the doings of these Casseys
history is silent: they have left no monuments and no
inscriptions in their parish church (the place, by the way,

is in Withington, and not as the name would lead us to
expect, in the adjoining parish of Compton Abdale); they
remain but the shadow of a name. Nothing still in existence
at Cassey Compton can with any certainty be ascribed to their
handiwork. It was their successors who built the house, laid
out the gardens and planted the avenues. A Wiltshire knight,
Sir Richard Grubham of Wishford on the Wily, bought
the manor about the year 1600, and in 1629 his estates passed
to his nephew John Howe, a member of a Somerset family
and afterwards made a baronet by Charles II. Cassey
Compton now became the residence of the Howes for three
generations, and it is to this period that its palmy days belong.
On the death of Sir Richard Grubham Howe in 1730 the elder
branch of the family became extinct, and Cassey Compton
passed to the younger branch, who by this time had a fine
house of their own three miles away on the hills, which they
felt no temptation to abandon for the old manor-house on the
Coln. The period of its decline must therefore soon have
begun, and in the absence of family records or traditions we
are left to picture in our imagination the golden days spent
there by its possessors during the hundred years that had now
come to an end.

It is otherwise with the Howes of Stowell. John Howe,
afterwards raised to the peerage by George the Second as Lord
Chedworth, who added Cassey Compton to his paternal inheritance in 1730, was the son of that hot-headed Gloucestershire
squire, known far and wide to friend and foe as " Jack Howe,"
who figures so prominently in the pages of Macaulay. Jack
Howe had bought the Stowell estate with its Jacobean mansion
at the end of the seventeenth century, and in his family it
remained till the death of his great-grandson, the last Lord
Chedworth, in 1804. On the accession of George I. he was
dismissed from the public appointments he held, and came
down to Gloucestershire to spend the remainder of his days in
retirement. He had begun his parliamentary career as a

zealous Whig, but on losing his place as Vice-Chamberlain to Queen Mary in 1693 he had turned Tory, and for the rest of William's reign he remained one of the most virulent assailants of the king and his ministers. In 1701, when the dread of the French king, the Pope, and the Pretender was at its height, he lost his election. Macaulay in his most graphic mood describes how "in every market place, on the market day, papers about the brazen forehead, the viperous tongue, and the white liver of Jack Howe, the French King's buffoon, flew about like flakes in a snow-storm. Clowns from the Cotswold Hills and the Forest of Dean, who had votes, but who did not know their letters, were invited to hear these satires read, and were asked whether they were prepared to endure the two great evils which were then considered by the common people of England as the inseparable concomitants of despotism, to wear wooden shoes, and to live on frogs." Next year, however, the first of the new reign, the tide turned and he was again sent up to Parliament, his opponent, Sir John Guise, petitioning in vain against his return. It was in the summer of this same year that Queen Anne made a progress from London to Bristol; on the confines of Gloucestershire, two miles west of Burford, the royal cortège was met by a deputation of county notables, and the High Sheriff was introduced to her Majesty by the new Joint Paymaster of the Forces "the Right Honourable John Howe, Esquire." For the rest of the Queen's reign he remained in favour at Court, and we can imagine that when her successor dispensed with his services, and he finally retired to the seclusion of his country seat, it was not in the most contented frame of mind. He was but fifty-seven, and might have looked forward to several more years of public life. How he spent his remaining seven years at Stowell tradition does not say. Probably the minutes of the local Jacobite clubs would have had something to say on the subject, and for many years after his death racy stories of the sayings and doings of "Jack Howe" must have been rife in the countryside. After the death of the last Lord Chedworth, Stowell was purchased by the great lawyer, William Scott (sometime fellow of Corpus and Camden Reader in Ancient History), who in 1821 became Lord Stowell: it is now the property of his collateral descendant, the third Earl of Eldon.

To talk of Howes and Chedworths is to revive forgotten memories; the name of Scott, borne by those two great luminaries of the law—that noble pair of brothers,—needs no tribute from my pen, and is alone enough to give renown to Stowell. As I climb the steep hill from Fossbridge, and follow the long line of firs that skirts the park, it is of earlier lords of Stowell than either Howes or Scotts that I am reminded. For I am on my way to Northleach, once the great wool mart of the Cotswold, and in Tudor times there flourished at Stowell the great family of wool-staplers, that we have already met at Rendcombe, the Tames. The Gloucestershire estates of this family were large, they seem to have had warehouses at all the principal wool centres, and they can hardly have lived at Stowell without doing business at Northleach.

Northleach lies on the high-road from Oxford to Cheltenham, just to the east of the point where it is crossed by the Foss; and a turn to the right brings me at once into the centre of the town. I am afraid there is no gainsaying the fact that the stranger's first impression of Northleach will be that of a desolate, forlorn-looking place: there is no difficulty in finding a cottage to let, the roofs and windows of the less eligible of these *are* falling in, and I cannot conceal the fact that grass *does* grow in the streets. But matters are not so bad as they were when Samuel Rudder visited Northleach in the middle of the eighteenth century: the population was then rapidly diminishing, many of the houses had fallen down, and the greater part of the rest were going fast to decay. Now if this rate of progress along the road to ruin had continued, one wonders what would now have been left to tell the tale, and I suspect that a turn in the wheel of fortune took place when the great road that runs through the town was remodelled, and began to swarm with all the busy traffic between London, Gloucester, Cheltenham and South Wales. Depend upon it, when the horn of the Royal Mail was heard ringing through the ancient streets, the town awoke from its long slumber, and something of the bustle of old days revived. For even a "flying" coach *must* stop somewhere ; horses and men *must* eat and drink ; and when a posse of freshmen, on their way up to Jesus at the end of the Long Vacation, are calling for their native ale, or my lord in his coach and four, on his way to drink the Cheltenham waters, is stopping to dine, the landlord of the Wheatsheaf must have been making his fortune, and butchers, bakers, brewers, saddlers, wheelwrights, aye, and in those days the necessary barber too, must have had a busy time.

With the advent of railways Northleach again settled down to its repose, not without some protest, one may imagine, on the part of the more energetic spirits. The tremors of the political agitation of the 'thirties and the 'forties seem to have been felt, even in this isolated region. At any rate, by the close of the century, Mr. Gibbs, who knew the Cotswold rustic inside out, tells us that there was a strong Radical element in the place. "Northleach," he says, "is a very Radical town," and he gives an amusing account of a political meeting which he attended here. Not being able to induce the "two hundred red-hot Radicals" before him to listen to a word of the speech he had meant to deliver, he changed his tactics and gave them "Tom Bowling" in his best style : result—unparalleled enthusiasm and handshaking.

If you want to get some notion of what Northleach was in the old time, you have only to look at the church. No mere village church in this part of England was ever built on this scale : like the churches of Fairford and Campden, it was one of those splendid Perpendicular edifices which owe their origin to the munificence of the great wool merchants, some of whom are commemorated by their brasses, where they are depicted

Northleach Church.

clad in their furred gowns, their feet resting on woolpacks, sheep, and pairs of shears. The interior of the church resembles Campden in its peculiar arcades, and in its window at the east end of the nave rising above the chancel arch, but, unlike Campden, it has been well treated by the restorers, and the painful contrast between exterior and interior which struck us there is absent. Puritan zeal was perhaps not so violent here as elsewhere, at any rate it has spared the altars of the two aisle chapels.

The importance of Northleach as a wool mart was due in a great measure to its central position. It is the only Cotswold town which lies right away in the middle of the downs. The others, Burford, Stow, Campden, Winchcombe, Stroud, Cirencester, all lie on, or close upon the edge of the hills, and guard the various entrances from the outer world. Cotswold wool therefore poured into the town from every side, and some of the great warehouses in which it was stored previously to sale existed even as late as Rudder's time. This predominance of Northleach as a wool centre is quite borne out by the letters of a family of wool buyers which have been recently printed by the Royal Historical Society. The wool bought by this family was almost entirely Cotswold wool, and of the Cotswold towns Northleach was the one with which they did most business, and of which the name occurs most frequently in the letters. This family were merchants of the staple, named Cely ; their London residence and place of business was in Mark Lane, but they also had a country-house in Essex. The letters in question, which date from 1475 to 1488, throw a flood of light on the ways of the wool trade in the fifteenth century, particularly in its foreign relations, and also give us some interesting glimpses into the every-day life of a well-to-do middle class family of the day. Thus old Richard Cely writes to son George, then at Calais or Bruges looking after the foreign department of the business, in November, 1479 (in the following extracts I modernise the eccentric spelling of the original) : " Your letter came to me the

Sunday before All-hallows day at dinner-time at London, and Wyll Eston, mercer, and Wyll Medewynter of Northleach dined with me at [the] time ; and the comfort of your letter [George had been ill] caused me for to buy of the foresaid Wyll Medewynter 60 sacks of Cottys [Cotswold] wool, the which is in pile at Northleach, and John Cely hath gathered and bought for me in Cotswold 37 sack by the tod and sack and half sack . . . I am advised for to pack the foresaid wool after Christmas toward Candlemass and I trust in God ye shall be at the packing of the said wool in Cotswold." Besides George, Richard Cely had two other sons, Richard, the eldest of the three, and Robert. While one of the junior members of the firm managed matters at Calais, where the staple was fixed, one of the others would ride down to Gloucestershire to buy the wool. William Midwinter was the principal local dealer at Northleach with whom they did business. Sometimes he made purchases of wool for the Celys in their absence, and then it lay " in pile " till one of the firm should come down in person to superintend the packing, and see that no inferior qualities were substituted for the article purchased, and that no burs or other refuse found its way into the packs. The packing took several days, sometimes weeks : " I have been in Cotswold," writes Richard the younger, on his return to London, in May, 1482, to his brother George, at Calais, "these 3 weeks, and packed with Wylliam Mydwyntter 22 sarplers and a poke, whereof be 4 middle [medium quality] : William Bretten say it is the fairest wool that he saw this year : and I packed 4 sarplers at Campden of the same bargain, where are 2 good, 2 middle. There will be in all, with blots, upon 27 or 28 sarplers whole." When the wool was packed long strings of pack-horses carried it by the ancient trackways across the Berkshire and Hampshire downs, and then through Surrey and Kent to the Medway ports, where the Celys had their vessels ready to convey it to the warehouses at Calais. Of the ruling prices in the Cotswold marts we do not hear much, but in the summer of 1481 " wool in Cotswold is at great price,

13s. 4d a tod, and great riding for wool in Cotswold as was any year this 7 year," and next year William Midwinter complains that he cannot buy under 14s. and 14s. 6d. a tod.[1] Whatever the cost price, however, the selling prices at Calais must always have allowed a fair profit—or the house of Cely would soon have gone bankrupt.

So much for the business, but there is one unromantic little episode in the private life of Richard the younger, of which Northleach was the scene, and which must therefore on no account be omitted. He confides it to his brother George in the course of the letter of May, 1482, already quoted, and he shall tell it in his own matter-of-fact style. "The same day that I come to Northleach on a Sunday before matins from Kurforde [Burford?] Wylliam Mydwyntter welcomed me, and in our communication he asked me if I were in any way of marriage. I told him nay, and he informed me that there was a young gentlewoman whose father his name is Lemryke, and her mother is dead, and she shall dispend by her mother £40 a year, as they say in that country, and her father is the greatest ruler as richest man in that country, and there have been great gentlemen to see her and would have her. And ere [hewyr in the original] matins were done Wylliam Mydwynter had moved this matter to the greatest man about the gentleman Lemeryke, and he said and informed the foresaid of all the matter and the young gentlewoman both. And the Saturday after Wylliam Mydwyntter went to London . . . When I had packed at Campden, and Wylliam Mydwyntter parted, I came to Northleach again to make an end of packing, and on Sunday next after, the same man that Wylliam Mydwyntter brake first to, came [to] me and told me that he had broken to his master according as Mydwyntter desired him, and he said his master was right well pleased therewith : and the same man said to me, if I would tarry May day I should have a sight

[1] In the same year fells, i.e. the skins with the wool on them, are £3 3s. 4d. to £3 the hundred.

of the young gentlewoman, and I said I would tarry with a good will.   And the same day her father should a' sitten at Northleach for the King, but he sent one of his clerks, and rode himself to Winchcombe.   And to matins the same day come the young gentlewoman and her mother-in-law [stepmother], and I and Wylliam Bretten were saying matins when they come into church.   And when matins was done, they went to a kinswoman of the young gentlewoman, and I sent to them a pottle of white romnay, and they took it thankfully, for they had come a mile afoot that morning.   And when mass was done, I come and welcomed them, and kissed them, and they thanked me for the wine, and prayed me to come to dinner with them ; and I excused me, and they made me promise to drink with them after dinner.   And I sent them to dinner a gallon wine, and they sent me a heronsew roast.   And after dinner I come and drank with them, and took Wylliam Bretten with me ; and we had right good communication, and the person pleased me well ; as by the first communication she is young, little and very well-favoured, and witty, and the country speaks much good by her.   Sir, all this matter abideth the coming of her father to London, that we may understand what sum he will depart with, and how he likes me ; he will be here within three weeks.   I pray send me a letter how ye think by this matter."

Of this very prosaic courtship, however—interesting as it is— we hear no more, and perhaps from the point of view of " the young gentlewoman " it is just as well that we do not, for only ten days later we find the honest suitor writing again to his brother (the reader shall this time have a taste of his orthography) : " Syr, Hary Bryan, the bryngar of thys, laburs me soor to goo and se Rawson[s] dowttyr ; I am behelding to hym for hys labur, for I know whell that he whowlde I dyd whell ; and I pray yow delyver hym som mony at thys tyme, and do whelby hym, for hyt ys seuyr I know, I hawhe many thyngs in my mynde, byt I hawhe ne laysar to whrytte, ze may wndyrstond partte be my letter that I sente yow before thys."[1]

In the time of the Celys, and much later, the affairs of the town were very strictly regulated by the local "Court"—or as we should now call it, the town council. The minute book of the Court, from the reign of Edward VI. to that of William III. is preserved, and is a mine of curious information. The town officers were a bailiff, who was attended by a sergeant-at-mace, six "arbitrators," honest, discreet burgesses, who were to attend the Court "apparelled in gowns or other decent upper garments," a town clerk,—"an honest inhabitant that can reasonably read and write," two wardsmen and two constables. No one could be admitted to the exercise of any trade within the town limits without the licence of the Court; thus in 1607, Symon Walbridge paid 12 pence to occupy the mystery of a barber, and three years later John Skilhorne 2s. 6d. to practise the science of a tailor. When the wool ceased to be purchased for export to Flanders, as was the case in the days of the Celys, more became available for the local manufactures, and we hear of such callings as a "narrow wayvar" a "brode wayvar" and a "huswyff's wayvar." A fatherly eye was kept upon the commissariat, and woe betide the Burford baker or the Bourton butcher who tried to palm off false weight or inferior quality upon the good citizens of Northleach. It is curious, by the way, and suggestive of a crowded urban population, that the local supplies had to be supplemented from such distant places—and even from Guiting and Winchcombe. The manners of the townsfolk, and especially those of the apprentices, were well looked after. A forfeit of twopence was imposed upon man or boy who ventured to attend church without wearing a knitted woollen cap "according to the statute"; and if, instead of going to church,

[1] The punctuation is mine: there are no stops in the original before the last period.

U

he was detected in the profane practices of card-playing or
"quoiting," the town exchequer took care to make a greater
profit out of him.   As for the unlucky apprentice who was
found out of his "master's or dame's" house after the ringing
of the Boothall (Townhall) bell, at 9 o'clock in winter or
10 o'clock in summer—it was nothing so easy as a gate bill
fine, or even a "draw" by the dean—the culprit was summarily conducted to the parish stocks and laid by the heels for
the rest of the night.   Provision was also made for contributing
to the defence of the nation and the Peace of the Crown.
About the beginning of the seventeenth century the quota to
be furnished by the town to the militia was only two men, but
each parish still had its "metae sagittales or butts," and on
stated occasions, after due notice had been published, the
inhabitants and their servants had to assemble there for practice
"with sufficient bows and arrows answering the laws in that
respect," under pain of forfeiting six pence to the Crown.

Between Northleach and Burford, and in fact all the way to
Witney, the main road keeps to the summit of the ridge,
which conveniently lies east and west ; but down below the
road on the left is a charming valley—the hiding place of many
a bright sunny village, each a cluster of well-stored farmsteads,
orchards and cottage gardens ; while here and there the spreading oaks and elms of a deer park indicate the dwelling of the
lord of the soil.   For the first three miles of its course this
valley is watered by a nameless stream, which joins the Windrush near the village of that name ; at this point this river,
which has hitherto taken a southerly course, turns abruptly to
east, and our valley is no longer nameless.   Up then over the
hill to Farmington and we soon descend again to the water-
side.   As for Farmington itself, it is a pleasant, well-to-do
village embosomed in trees, with a green, whereon three aged
sycamores shade the pretty thatched and gabled shed which
covers the village spring.   The church has suffered from
modern excrescences in the way of organ chambers and vestries,

and at some time the north wall appears to have been cut
through to form the present lean-to north aisle. As you stand
in the aisle and look upwards, you see the old external corbel
table above the arches.

Then a delightful lane by the brook side takes us to Sherborne, once a good rich manor of Winchcombe Abbey, and
now for ten generations the home of the Duttons. The old
church, alas! has been swept away, but at the last cottage on
the left as you leave the village, you will spy an exquisite
Norman arch, which now does duty as the cottage door : there
are the beak-heads on the jambs and the cross in the tympanum. No one seems to know its story or how it came
where it is ; but for my part I suspect it is all that is left of the
old church, and that it was rescued at the demolition by
some local virtuoso who reflected that it would "come in very
handy" for his cottage. That such things do happen we
saw at Bloxham, where an Early English doorway, probably a
part of the older church, now does duty at an inn.

The present church of Sherborne, a building of the
eighteenth century, need not detain us. It stands close to the
great house, which like so many of its compeers in the Cotswold, is a mansion "in the Italian style." It was built by
the present Lord Sherborne's grandfather about 1830, a period
when the rage for pulling down old houses and replacing them
"in the Italian style" was at its height. Those were the days
we know of long peace, high rents, and low death duties.
The old mansion then pulled down—and that with great
difficulty, so solid was its construction—consisted of two quadrangles, part of which dated from pre-Reformation times ; and
here the Abbot of Winchcombe on his periodical visits to
Sherborne, one of which was always the sheep-shearing festival,
took up his residence.

In connection with the pulling down of the old house, Lord
Sherborne once told the local antiquarian society a very interesting story. When the contents of the old house were being cleared

U 2

out preparatory to its demolition, it was decided to put the books and family papers into the very respectable keeping of the vicar of Windrush, an old gentleman who survived till about the year 1880, when he died at the ripe age of 96. As it turned out, however, the choice was a most unfortunate one. The books and papers were duly removed to the reverend gentleman's house, but so appallingly careless was he of his charge, that one of his servants managed to dispose both of books and papers to any one who would give a trifle for them, and thus many fine black-letter folios and ancient parchment deeds found their way to the shoemaker of the village, who cut them up into shapes for his boots and shoes. Nearly thirty years elapsed before the remnant that survived was rescued and restored to Sherborne House. The said vicar of Windrush seems to have been more conspicuous for piety than for scholarship ; for when he was making his round of the old house, attended by the housekeeper, previously to taking over his charge, he came upon an upper room, where a number of loose papers and parchments were lying uncared for. The worthy pair at once voted them mere rubbish and proceeded to burn them all, the vicar being the more determined upon this course, in that he observed that some of the parchments treated of sacred subjects, and he considered that the surest way to preserve them from profanation was to commit them to the flames. Such was the melancholy tale which Lord Sherborne had to tell the assembled antiquarians in 1888. There was, however, one crumb of consolation. By the fortunate accident of their absence from home two valuable volumes were saved from the clutches of the Windrush cobbler. These were cartularies of Winchcombe Abbey, dating from the thirteenth to the early fifteenth century, and therefore older than Abbot Kyderminster's version, which, as we saw above, perished in the great fire of London. These volumes being required for reference in some legal business happened to be in the custody of the family lawyer at the time when the other papers went to Windrush. After this their whereabouts was forgotten for a time, but some years ago they were discovered safe in the strong room of a firm of Cirencester solicitors. It is a very curious coincidence if, as seems highly probable, this was the second time that these cartularies had escaped destruction by being away from their proper place. It is most likely that at the dissolution they were away from the abbey, and at the Grange at Sherborne, where they remained to find a place in the Dutton library. Had they been at Winchcombe they would have gone the way of all the other monastic treasures.

The fine old park stretches up the hill from the house as far as the high-road, and a mile away on the other side of the road is another park, isolated and wild, with a Jacobean hunting lodge worth all the great houses near it thrown together—at least, so says Mr. Hutton [1]; I have not seen it.

At Windrush, where Isaac Williams was once curate, there is not much to detain us. The church has a good Norman south door ornamented with beak-heads, and in the church-yard are some examples of a peculiar form of tombstone much in favour in this district two hundred years ago. It would be interesting to trace the genesis of the idea, and perhaps one of my readers, more versed in the ornamentations of Jacobean architecture than I am myself, may be able to supply the key to its history. I will content myself with an attempt to give some notion of its appearance. On the top of a raised tomb, of the usual shape, lies a long convex object which resembles nothing so much as the half of a long barrel vertically bisected. It is often enriched with transverse crinkles and bands, and the two open ends are closed with a fan-shaped scallop shell of the Renaissance type. A number of these tombs crowded together in a churchyard have a weird effect, especially in the dusk of evening.

The two Barringtons lie opposite each other, on either side

[1] *By Thames and Cotswold*, p. 33.

of the Windrush, and are connected by a causeway erected by
Thomas Strong, of London, Freemason. At the southern, or
Little Barrington end, is the "Fox" Inn, where a cup of good
cider can be obtained and a comfortable lunch. While it is
getting ready we may visit the village of Little Barrington, the
houses of which are scattered in a rather haphazard fashion on
the banks of a deep green hollow, a swamp in winter, and
treacherous even in summer, while the church overlooks the
Windrush, some little distance on the left. It is a small, rather
dumpy edifice much disfigured by poor stained and painted
deal furniture in the most atrocious style. If the whole were
swept away, including pulpit and desk, and the ordinary
church chairs substituted, the interior would be as charming as
the exterior. You descend into the church by seven steps,
through a bold Norman doorway : opposite you, in the north
aisle, is a fine octagonal font with the carvings on one of its
facets hacked way. This north aisle seems to have been
originally merely a lean-to, but when the tower was built at its
western end, the walls were raised and it was promoted to a
regular roof of its own : its east window, with a transom,
is particularly pleasing. As I have just hinted, if proportion
is not to be insisted on, the general effect of the exterior
is good, and is enhanced by the proximity on the west,
of a delightful old gabled house, shrouded in creepers and
standing in a well-kept garden. As you walk round the
church, you come upon two pieces of sculpture wide as the
poles asunder in character and date. The first, on the north
wall, very much mutilated, is a Christ enthroned between two
angels, which may date back to Saxon times : the second, on
the east side of the south porch—an amazing piece of local
stone-cutting, done early in the eighteenth century, " in
memory of the late Family of the Taylers of this parish, by
order of William Mury, carpenter." Mr. "Mury" seems to
have commanded the counterfeit presentment of four members
of this family, two men and two women ; and one wonders if

the cloaks of awful length in which they are arrayed was a device adopted by the artist to conceal his inability to deal with the outlines of the human figure.

Since we last saw the Windrush at Bourton, it has become quite a considerable stream, and worthy to be the home of the large trout that are taken between this spot and Burford. It comes sweeping down through Barrington park to the bridge, at the further end of Thomas Strong's Causeway, and then onwards through the wide green meadows to join the Thames at Newbridge. The park at Great Barrington may rival its neighbour at Sherborne in beauty; the house which Ralph Bigland, Garter King-at-Arms, describes as "an elegant structure of the Doric order" was built by Charles Talbot, George II.'s Lord Chancellor. His youngest son was the divine we have already met at Temple Guiting, and his eldest son, who made the grand tour accompanied by James Thomson the poet, died before Barrington came into the possession of his family. The estate was therefore inherited by the second son, who was created Earl Talbot, and who married Mary, "daughter and heir," as her memorial tablet informs us, "to Adam de Cardonnel, Secretary at War during several campaigns in Flanders to John, Duke of Marlborough." Their only surviving child, Cecil Talbot, married into the Caermarthenshire family of Rice, and was raised to the peerage as Baroness Dynevor. The present Lord Dynevor is her descendant. As for the earldom of Talbot, it passed (by a fresh creation) to a nephew.

If we enter the church we shall find this tablet to the heiress of Cardonnel in the chancel: it contains a fine medallion portrait by Nollekens, which must claim our admiration. But the most beautiful monument in the church is at the west end of the north aisle, near the door. It is a pathetic memento of two children of the Brays who died of small-pox—a disease which seems from the inscription to have been a particularly fatal one in that family. The monument consists of an elaborate group in marble representing a guardian angel with the children, a girl and a boy, the two latter attired in the full dress of the days of Anne, the details of which—brocaded petticoat, laced coat, cravat and perruque—are finished with the most conscientious minuteness. "She died of the smallpox at her Aunt Catchmay's, in Gloucester, on Munday, the one and twentieth of May, 1711, in the eighth year of her age, much lamented; Her extreme Good Qualities having engaged the Affections of all who knew Her. He dyed of the Smallpox upon Christmas Day, 1720, at the Royal Academy of Angiers, in France, in the fifteenth year of his age, so much esteemed for his good sense and Fine Temper that every gentleman of the Academy (Foreigner as well as Briton) seemed to rival each other in paying just Honours to his memory; and the Beautys of His Person were equal to those of His Mind."

In the north aisle lies the mutilated effigy of Captain Edmund Bray, clad in Tudor ruff and armour, with his sword on his right side. Sir Robert Atkyns accounts for this peculiarity by a story that the captain, having unhappily killed a man, and having been pardoned by Queen Elizabeth at Tilbury Camp, in token of his contrition refused ever afterwards to use his right hand. If this is not a true story, and it certainly has an *ex post facto* air about it, one might be tempted to imagine that the tomb-maker had been guilty of an oversight, or that Captain Edmund, like Ehud, the son of Gera, the Benjamite, was a man left-handed.

When Lord Chancellor Talbot purchased the estate in 1734, the Brays had been in possession for two centuries. They were a branch of the family from which the present Lord Braye is descended, and, save in the troublous times of the Civil War, they seem to have lived the happy, uneventful life of the country squire. Little or nothing is recorded of them beyond what may be gathered from their monuments, but in good King Charles's golden days the peace of Barrington was

broken by an outrage which was long remembered as one of
the most disgraceful of the many escapades of its perpetrator.
Fifty miles away, at Wooburn House, in Buckinghamshire,
resided a veteran supporter of the Parliamentary cause, Philip,
the fourth Lord Wharton. A zealous Puritan himself, he had
brought up his sons in the strictest principles of Calvinism, and,
when the exiled monarch came to his own again, the eldest was a
promising boy of twelve. He had doubtless already rebelled
in secret against the stern parental discipline, and, after a few
years of intercourse with the fashionable world, he was able to
throw off the yoke. In the words of Macaulay, " he early acquired
and retained to the last the reputation of being the greatest rake
in England." The one tradition of his family to which he
remained firm was its politics : amid all his excesses he was
ever among the staunchest champions of his party. One of the
strongest opponents of King James, and one of the strongest
supporters of King William, and, above all, the writer of the
telling and popular song, " Lillibullero," " Honest Tom," as his
admirers styled him, became the hero of the Whigs, and finally,
by royal favour of the House of Hanover, Earl and Marquess of
Wharton. In the summer of 1682 the future marquess, now
plain Mr. Thomas Wharton, and one of his brothers were visiting Sir Edmund Bray, an old Cavalier, at Barrington Park. Sir
Edmund kept a hospitable table and a good cellar, and one
night, when the company had sat late over their bottle, and the
host and the more self-respecting guests had (as it is only
charitable to suppose) retired to bed, the drunken remnant
headed by the two brothers Wharton, sallied forth in quest of
adventures. The house was then close to the church, and the
roysterers forthwith broke open the door, rang the bells " back-
ward or confusedly," cut the ropes, tore the Bible, broke down
the pulpit, and "committed many [other] horrible acts there."
Having done with the church, they went on to make further
havoc in the village, but by this time the alarm had been raised,
and the inhabitants, roused from their beds, drove them back

to take refuge in the house.   The Bishop of Gloucester, at this
time the good Robert Frampton, was not the man to let a
scandal of these dimensions pass unnoticed.   Under threat
of excommunication he summoned the offenders to meet him
at Stow, where they made due submission and handed over "a
handsome fine," which was devoted to the work then in progress
at Stow Church.   Among the Carte Papers preserved in the
Bodleian is a touching letter from the Bishop to Thomas
Wharton, written in the following November, in which he
reminds him of the contrition he had expressed at Stow,
admonishes him of the evils which follow from the sin of
drunkenness, and expresses his earnest hope that his promises
of amendment will be fulfilled.   Readers of Macaulay are
aware that the good Bishop's aspirations were not destined
to be realised.

In Barrington Church everything is now decent and in order,
but, except for its sepulchral monuments and a large Norman
chancel arch, the building is not particularly interesting.   It is
with reluctance that we quit this peaceful valley in order to gain
the high-road that takes us back to Northleach and our inn at
Fossbridge.   We may either retrace our steps through Little
Barrington, and there ascend the southern slopes, or, if time
allows, we can ride round through Taynton and Burford.
Burford, of course, we shall see again, but we may not have
another opportunity of visiting Taynton—one of the most charming villages on this side of the Cotswold.   Soon after leaving
Great Barrington the road enters Oxfordshire, and presently the
picturesque roofs of Taynton are seen bosomed in umbrageous
elms and sycamores.   It is a place not wholly made of small
cottages and farmhouses.   The many pleasant dwellings which
lie somewhere indefinitely between these two classes, and the
well-kept gardens now bright with all the glories of September,
are suggestive of a village population of the good old catholic
sort, a place, in fact, that might catch the fancy of a Jane Austen,
and tempt her to make it the scene of some unambitious tale

of rural life.   With its famous building stone close at hand, no wonder that the houses of Taynton look strong and solid. Blenheim Palace was built of Taynton stone—and Blenheim looks as though it would last for ever—and so, says tradition, was old St. Paul's.   But it is a long and hilly road to the nearest railway station, and the quarries are no longer worked

CHAPTER XII

THE great highway which brought us home yesterday from the Windrush Valley is as fine a cycling road as any in England. The devious lane which takes us down the valley of the Coln this morning calls for wary steering and a moderate pace. This, however, need not be regretted, for this is not a journey to be taken by express. It is this solitary valley which has found its *vates sacer* in Arthur Gibbs, and my pen shall refrain from lingering over scenes which he has depicted with such intimate sympathy in the pleasant pages of *A Cotswold Village*. Following the windings of the stream through the sunny Arcadias of Coln St. Denis, Coln Rogers, and Winson, each a study for the painter or the poet, you come to Ablington and the Tudor manor-house which he loved so well, and where some of the happiest years of his too brief life were spent. He will tell you of the strange charm the place had for him at first sight; how he looked up and read, cut in stone over the porch :

```
PLEAD  ·  THO
V · MY · CAVSE
O · LORD · BY
IHON  ·  COX
WEL  ·  ANO
DOMENY
1590
```

and how another legend over the solid oak door

PORTA PATENS ESTO, NULLI CLAUDARIS HONESTO

encouraged him to enter; and then of the ancient furnishing
thereof, the grim portraits, the latticed windows of the old-
fashioned passage, and, above all, the terrace and the quaint old
garden. These I pass in silence and press onwards to the
"Swan" at Bibury, where, luncheon over, I may sit awhile in the
garden by the rippling Coln, and realise that I have reached
Bibury at last.

Ten years ago Bibury was a name unknown to the majority
of Oxford men, though the hero of the following tale, which I
quote from a local guide-book, hails from the university:

"An Oxford scholar, more full of fun than money, proposed to a Bibury
landlord to teach him, for a noble, how to draw mild ale and strong beer
from the same cask. The offer was accepted; and, proceeding to the
cellar, the scholar bored a hole in a full cask of ale and desired the landlord to stop it with his finger. Then boring another where the strong beer
was to run, the landlord was to stop that with his other hand. The wag
then left on pretence of fetching some pegs; and, mounting his horse, off
he went, leaving the landlord a prisoner in his own cellar. The joke was
certainly at the landlord's expense; but so many called to have the laugh,
that it turned at length in his favour by the increasing demand."

The "Oxford scholar" of our own day, if a fisherman, might
have driven over to Burford "when the May-fly is up"; but
that was the limit of his excursion. The ten lonely miles, still
ten of the most untrodden on any high-road in England, that
lay between him and Bibury were beyond his horizon: Bibury
was still unknown and untalked of. Yet already there was
one circle of friends to whom the whole land from Cotswold to
Thames had come to be a household word, and to whose hearts
the old villages by the Coln had not appealed in vain. In 1871
William Morris came to live at Kelmscott, some dozen miles
away, and he soon made the whole countryside his own—"his
daily walks and ancient neighbourhood." Among the many
villages to which he would take his friends, Bibury must surely have

been one of the first, for does not Mr. Mackail record that he described it "lying down in the winding valley beside the clear Colne" as "surely the most beautiful village in England"?[1] Then in 1898 came Mr. Gibbs, and in the same year Leslie's picture of Arlington Row at the Academy. Bibury was no longer unheard of: visitors to Fairford and Cirencester would drive over and lunch at the Swan, and the question "Have you been to Bibury?" began to be heard at Oxford when the talk was of the country and the roads. Eight and twenty miles out and eight and twenty miles home, however, needs a long summer's day and no lectures—and I suspect that many a hard worked lover of the open road has discovered that the little local line to Fairford simplifies matters considerably.

Here, in the garden of the Swan Inn, or further on down the village street which skirts the river, you may banish every doubt, if you still nourish any, that Bibury is the fisherman's paradise. You have but to look warily over the low wall to mark the big fish lying with their noses up stream on the watch for any delicate morsel that may come floating down, or the circling eddy which tells you that they are "on the rise." Hard by the garden is the bridge, a favourite lounge at all hours when fish are to be seen, and in the garden itself is the spring, said to supply at least two million gallons a day: this spring swells the current of the river, and makes it so cold that cattle, which formerly had to ford it, heated by long journeyings, were often chilled, until at length, though not till the middle of the eighteenth century, the ford gave place to the bridge.

Further down at the foot of a wooded cliff, where the Coln takes a sweep to the east, is Bibury Court, a splendid Jacobean house, built by one Sir Thomas Sackville in 1623.

[1] Morris was, however, not the first poet who had been struck with the beauty of Bibury. Pope had been there in company with Swift when on a visit to Lord Bathurst, and in August, 1726, he writes to the Dean: "I shall never more think of Lord Cobham's, the woods of Ciceter, or the pleasing prospect of Bibury, but your idea must be joined with them."

At the back of the Court, and separating it from the village, is the church—since the twelfth century a wide and spacious building, but in Norman times small and without aisles.   The interior has a surprise in store for us, for the walls have been stained a rich terra-cotta colour, a peculiarity which at any rate gives an idea of warmth and throws the stonework well into relief.   There are inscriptions commemorating members of the Sackville family, and one in Latin to the memory of the Rev. Benjamin Wynnington, M.A., vicar, who died in 1673.   In his time the pulpit was furnished with an hour glass, and tradition relates that after the sands of the first hour had run out he would turn it, assuring the congregation that he intended to preach only one hour longer. This was the signal for the Squire to rise and retire from the family pew to smoke a pipe of meditation, but he always made a point of returning to the church in time to receive the benediction.   Opposite the south door, where everyone might see it on entering the church, a colossal figure of St. Christopher was painted on the wall.   Underneath was the following distich, expressive of the popular superstition that anyone who had looked on the figure was for the rest of that day safe from sudden or accidental death :

> Χρόfori scī speciem quicunque tuetur
> Illo nanque die nullo langore gravetur.

Traces of figure and couplet perhaps remain underneath the colouring.

Below Bibury the road diverges from the river to join it again at Coln St. Aldwyns, where Keble's father was vicar for many years, and where the poet himself helped his father as curate.   Close to the church is the spacious manor-house which Sir Michael Hicks-Beach has restored for his own resi-dence.   Nearly opposite the gates a lonely road strikes across the hills in a direct line to the Windrush Valley at Sherborne. On a fine clear day (and woe betide the cyclist who attempts it

on a wet one) it is a delightful ride, commanding the downs for
many miles in every direction, and, except at Aldsworth, where
the Cirencester and Burford road is crossed, you pass but a
single house for the whole six miles. As we descend the village street of Coln St. Aldwyns, a comfortable-looking inn on the
left, bright with a blaze of autumn flowers, tempts us to stay the
drinking of a cup of tea; but our halt must be a short one, for
Fairford must be gained before dusk, and there we shall have
much to occupy us. So on we ride down to the Coln once more,
looking up as we cross the bridge to the towers of Hatherop,
once an Elizabethan manor-house, but rebuilt fifty years since
on a more ambitious scale, and now "the Castle." We
leave the river to flow beneath the castle walls, and, crossing
over the neck of the little peninsula, meet it again at Quenington. That tall and venerable building on the right close to
Quenington bridge, with its high-pitched roof, canopied niche,
and postern door, is the gate-house of a Preceptory of the
Knights of St. John. The community was a small one, two
Knights only and a Preceptor, as we learn from a report made to
the Grand Master of the Order in 1338 by Prior Philip of Thame.
Nothing else remains to mark their dwelling but a part of the
moat which formerly surrounded it, together with the adjacent
church. As for this church, it has suffered much and long, but
still retains two of the finest Norman doorways in Gloucestershire, and that is all that need be said of it. At the dissolution,
when the Hospitallers went the way of the other religious
orders, their estates were granted to Anthony Kingston, that
scourge of the king's enemies, whom we shall meet again in the
next chapter. Then up the hill and past the so-called obelisk,
a forlorn column of uncertain date stranded in the middle of a
wheatfield; then along the edge of Fairford park, through the
centre of which flows the now broad and placid Coln—and we
are in Fairford town.

We are no longer now in a place whose name is unknown to
the world. Fairford windows and Fairford trout have spread

abroad its fame wherever an antiquary or an angler is to be found. But to the passing stranger the windows are nowadays far better known than the fish. Time was when the wayfarer who took his ease at the "George" or the "Bull" would be but ill pleased if he could not breakfast off a dish of trout, plim and plump, and fresh from the Coln; but now unless he be himself an expert with the dry fly, and pay his half-crown a day for his sport, he must be content with humbler fare. These two inns, by the way, together form one of the most striking pictures in Fairford. Standing, as they do, side by side in one long line, they occupy one whole side of the main street just where it is at its widest. The "George" is undoubtedly the most picturesque of the two. It retains its high-pitched roof, covered with the tiles of local stone, its bay windows two stories high, and its gothic archway, over which, in Wood's time, was "the same effigies of a man cut in stone . . . as there is on the tower of the church—perhaps the effigies of one of the Tames." Even in Wood's time it seems that anything gothic about a building was supposed to imply ecclesiastical associations, for he notes that "some think that the George Inn in Fairford was a chauntry house for priests to celebrate for the soules of the Tames in the parish church." But Wood was too prudent an antiquary to give the weight of his own sanction to this theory, and I am inclined to believe that when the Tames came to Fairford they found the "George" much what it is now, and that the "effigies" over the door was none other than that of St. George himself. As for the "Bull," it has a pleasant hospitable look enough till you get to the roof, and that gives you a chill, for it is of blue slate, and blue slate is an intruder which should never have been permitted to invade this Cotswold country. When, as in this case, it exhibits itself in close connexion with the native grey tiles, the effect is worse than ever.

This same clean wide street of Fairford has all the air about it of aristocratic repose. No one is ever in a bustle : even the new motor omnibus to Cirencester seems conscious of the spell, and

rolls along at quite a dignified pace—till it is out of the town.
Sometimes there is hardly a creature to be seen; sometimes
a group stands here and there talking over the local news, or
watching the carriages that drive in from the many country
houses round.   It would be an evil day for Fairford if it lost
its country clients and its visitors.   Statistics show that the
population of the small town, like that of the village, is diminishing.   No one with any knowledge of our social and industrial
history—I may add, no reader of *Cranford*, or *The Mill on the
Floss*—can look forward to the concentration of every industry
but the agricultural in the great centres of population as anything but a national disaster.   The process of decline is unfortunately too familiar.   First, what has been the staple product
of the town for centuries is no longer manufactured there; then
the weekly market is closed, and the railway takes the country
produce to the great cities.   The neighbourhood begins to draw
its supplies from co-operative stores, and the once flourishing
town dwindles down to little more than a village.   But this is
not all; when population goes, money goes with it; and then
what is to become of the monuments of the past in which our
little county towns are so rich—market halls, guildhalls, almshouses, hospitals, bridges? Where are the funds to come from
necessary to keep them from perishing?

Far be it from me to number Fairford among our decaying
towns, but it may be safely affirmed that it is not the thriving
place it was when its splendid church was built.   I think it
may be taken for granted that if trade had not been flourishing,
and population had not been increasing, John Tame would
never have rebuilt the church on so ambitious a scale.   Unfortunately, in the utter absence of any detailed information on
the subject, we have to be content with such scraps as the following, which are copied eternally from one writer by another
with as much gusto as if they gave us any real information:
"'Fairford,' says Leland, 'never florished afore the cumming
of the Tames onto it.'"   Well, the Tames were as princes in

wool-land, Fairford was the home of their choice, the important market of Cirencester was within easy reach, and, as I said before, we will take it for granted that a great clothing industry did develop here under their auspices.

John Tame is the hero of Fairford, and what he undertook to do he did heroically. Among other good deeds, he undertook to rebuild the church, and it would be impossible to find a more perfect example of its period—the close of the fifteenth century. Look first at the wonderful way in which the massive central tower has been made to harmonise with the other parts of the church. For this tower, excepting its topmost story, is not the work of John Tame: it is a legacy which he accepted from the Decorated Church which he pulled down. Not a church on the same lines as his own, but a cruciform church of which a central tower was an essential feature. Had he sacrificed this tower, its successor would doubtless have stood at the west end, as in the great sister churches of Campden, Northleach, and Winchcombe. As it is, the church consists of nave, lantern space under the tower, chancel, and north and south aisles, which extend eastwards so as to embrace the tower between them. The famous glass fills the twenty-eight windows, including those of the clerestory, and the question has been asked—Was the church made for the glass or the glass for the church? The old story was that the gallant John Tame captured at sea a vessel bound from Flanders to Italy and laden with painted glass, and that he then built the church to hold it. But even if we could bring ourselves to believe that the worthy wool merchant was in the habit of amusing his leisure hours by playing the bold buccaneer, it must be counted as a singular piece of good fortune that the set of glass which happened to be captured required exactly the regular and uniform set of windows, which we now have, to contain it. No, it is clear that the glass was made to fit the windows, and that whoever the artists were, they worked up to John Tame's designs. That the glass actually came from Flanders, and was the work of Flemish artists, is

Fairford Church.

likely enough, especially when we recollect the active trade then carried on between England and the Flemish cities ; and it has recently been suggested that the ape in the west window of the

south aisle, and the monogram on the sword of the

executioner point to a Flemish artist named Aeps, who flourished 1480—1528, and that the monogram should be interpreted " T. Aeps, Vitrifex."

How the windows came to survive the two great iconoclastic storms which passed over the country in the century which followed the Reformation is another puzzle. As to the first, that which burst forth in the reign of Edward VI., popular tradition is silent : its deeds of violence came to be forgotten after the later atrocities of the Civil War ; but I think the preservation of the glass on this occasion can be explained. The Lady of the Manor was then Alice Verney, daughter of Sir Edmund Tame, the finisher of the church, and grand-daughter of John Tame, the founder. She would naturally use all her influence with her husband, Sir Thomas Verney, to ensure the protection of the church which her father and grand-father had built, and of the priceless artistic treasures in which they had taken such pride. With respect to the second occasion the constant tradition has been that the glass owed its escape to the care and foresight of the lay rector, William Oldisworth, Esq., who was a resident at Fairford. Apprehensive of the consequences that might follow from a visit to the town of Essex's dragoons or Ireton's troopers, he had all the glass taken down from the windows, and carefully concealed till the hour of danger had passed away. This account is corroborated by the fact that the original order of the figures on the quarries has in some instances been disturbed, and that until the recent re-leading many quarries were inside out or upside down, owing to the carelessness of the workmen who replaced them. That the glass had been put back into the windows by July, 1660, is clear

from Wood, who was at Fairford on the 20th of that month,
"where Mr. William Oldsworth, the impropriator, did with
great curtesie shew him the beautiful church there and the
most curious paynted windows set up in the raigne of
K. Hen. 7." Now if Mr. Oldisworth had waited till the
Restoration to have the glass put back, it could not long have
been in its place when Wood saw it, and it would have been
only natural that his guide should have recounted to him with
some self-satisfaction the story of its preservation. Wood,
however, is absolutely silent on this point, and he is not the
man to have lost the chance of a dig at the "rascally Roundheads." But we are not left to merely negative evidence : in a
collection of poetical pieces, "composed by the best wits that
were in both the Universities before their dissolution," published
in 1656 under the title "Parnassus Biceps," is a poem on *The
Fairford Windows*, written by some cavalier versifier, the
whole point of which is an attempt to account (sarcastically, of
course) for the preservation of the painted glass at Fairford,
when it had been destroyed everywhere else.

> " Tell me you anti-saints why glasse
> With you is longer lived than brasse,
> And why the Saints have scaped their falls
> Better from windowes than from walls.

[Is it, he continues, because you have an interest in the
glass trade, or because the figures are a mere painted show,
fair outside and foul within like yourselves ?]

> If it be so, then Faireford boast
> Thy Church hath kept what all have lost,
> And is preserved from the bane
> Of either war or Puritan."

How long before publication these verses were written is not
known, but the net result seems to be, that if the glass was ever
removed at all—and the removal if it was to have been of any
use must have taken place at the beginning of the war—it

must have been back in the windows again at least as early as
1656 ; perhaps we may say seven years before that date, for
the unglazed windows must have been highly inconvenient,
and it would be only natural that the inconvenience should be
rectified as soon as ever it could be done with safety.

For a detailed study of the windows the excellent local guide
book [1] will be found indispensable, but if your time is limited
the parish clerk, armed with his long wand, will explain them
to you. His predecessor of forty years ago was a well-known
character, and after his death some of his quaint descriptions
were printed. I need only add that the windows do not consist
of a collection of isolated subjects, one having no relation to
another, but of a connected series disposed in regular order.

The windows of the chancel and the chapels which form the
termination of the aisles depict the leading events of the gospel
history ; in those of the aisles are figured the prophets, apostles
and evangelists, typical of the history of the Christian faith ; in
the clerestory are the saints and persecutors of the Church,
while the three west windows are occupied by the great picture
of the *Last Judgment*, flanked by the Old Testament subjects
of the *Judgment of Justice* and the *Judgment of Truth*. I had
well-nigh forgotten to set down that these three western windows
suffered severely in the great storm of 1703 described by Defoe,
when the fury of the elements made havoc of what had twice
escaped the fury of man. This accounts for the upper part of
the great window being mainly modern restoration work.

If the traveller is by this time wearied for a while of the simple
byways and unfrequented tracks across the hills, his smoothest
and easiest route is by the high road into Cirencester, and
thence along Ermin-street to Birdlip, where I shall rejoin him.
But if he shares my propensity to deviate from the beaten
track, I shall conduct him back to the Fossbridge Inn for one
more night by ways seldom traversed by the stranger. The
pace will not be very fast, but that will give us leisure to notice

[1] Fairford Church, with its celebrated windows, by Henry W. Taunt.

some things that one is apt to miss when devouring the high road at the rate of some ten miles or more to the hour. Thus in the Cotswold you may still see a team of oxen at the plough —once a common sight throughout the country—but now surviving only in a few out-of-the-way districts. A team now consists of six animals yoked two abreast ; but in the eighteenth century, according to an agricultural writer of the time, it consisted of five, worked in a single file and not harnessed with the yoke, but with collar and harness like horses. The writers of this period strongly advocate their use as being much more economical than horses, and under favourable conditions capable of doing the same amount of work. The principal objection made to them then was that, particularly in heavy soils, they " poach " (tread) the land too heavily. Harnessed to the ox-cart, or " wain " as it was called, a light cart without side rails, oxen were also used for draught purposes ; and in Herefordshire down to about the year 1730 these wains were the only kind of cart known.

From Fairford we shall follow the Welsh Way as far as Barnsley. A mile to the left from the point where the road from Quenington crosses ours is a singular finger post. One arm of it has the sign of the cross and the words " Betty's Grave," and on looking down you are startled to see a grave mound standing there in solitude by the way side. When I asked for an explanation in the neighbourhood I was told two different stories ; first, that Betty laid a wager she would reap an acre of wheat with her own sickle within a certain limited time, that she accomplished her task, and then fell down dead, and was buried where she fell. The second account was that she poisoned herself at Poulton, the neighbouring village, and was buried at four cross roads as a suicide. The last is of course the true story : it was the common practice to bury suicides at cross-roads, and the memory of the fact is in some cases still preserved by the name ; the exceptional thing here is that the grave itself is still well preserved. Our road next crosses Akeman-street at a point where there is now a small plantation, but where formerly a single tall ash served as an easily recognised landmark or token to travellers across the open downs, and hence the place was called Ready Token, a name which it still retains.

So on to Barnsley, where the church, which keeps the small window from Daglingworth made out of a Roman altar, has been modernised out of all recognition. An old house, now an inn, is said to have been built by Sir Edmund Tame, who used it as a half-way house on his journeys between Fairford and Rendcombe. Here we quit the Welsh Road, and follow a wild track which, skirting Barnsley Park and the rough tract of undisturbed down known as Barnsley Wold, lands us in the Foss Way a mile from our destination.

CHAPTER XIII

I AM about to say farewell to the Fossbridge inn, but I do not pretend to have exhausted its attractions. For the visitor who comes to make a stay of some weeks' duration there is the old garden behind the house, with the stone steps descending thereunto, and the praeterlabent Coln, where, when the fancy takes him, he may

> " Bait the barb'd steel, and from the fishy flood
>   Appease th' afflictive fierce desire of food."

At the same time his desire of food must be of the fiercest if it is not appeased by the ample resources of the inn kitchen and the deft cookery of his hostess. Or if he be a follower of the chase, there is the long line of outbuildings where he may stable his hunters; or if he be a scorner of horses and horsemen and swear that petrol is your only going, his motor. But the globe-scouring motorist will, if he be wise, keep clear of the Cotswolds; the high roads are good, but the gradients are steep, and there is one on either side of the Fossbridge which will try his engines pretty severely. Besides, the Cotswolds after all are not so extensive as, let us say, the Great Sahara, and they are infinitely beneath the notice of the traveller whose only object in transporting himself from one point of the earth's surface to another is to do so in the shortest possible space of time. Moreover, one of the principal charms of this hill country lies in the difficulties of the way. and what real lover of highways and byways in a strange country would consent to forgo every chance of taking the wrong turning and losing his way? No, if space is to be annihilated, the joys of Cotswold wayfaring are gone for ever, and the only chance the motorist has of getting any profit out of it at all is to arrange for a good solid breakdown every six miles.

Then there are other devious and pleasant paths which the sojourner at Fossbridge may explore at his leisure, but these he must explore for himself. The zigzag excursions with which I threatened the reader when we first penetrated into this corner of the Cotswold have now been completed, and we have only now before us a plain straightforward journey round the circumference of our territory till we once more cross the county boundary and find ourselves in Oxfordshire again, at the frontier town of Burford.

We have half-a-dozen miles of cross-country roads through the Chedworth woods, from which the late September sun has scarcely yet dried away the morning mist, and Withington village up to the Gloucester road at the Garrick's Head—a local worthy, I am afraid, and no relation to little Davy—and hence for three miles more we follow our old route as far as the Seven Springs. Here instead of turning down the Churn valley we ride straight on past Ullenwood to the cross roads at the foot of Crickley Hill: and then dismount and climb the hill to Birdlip, an altitude of nearly 1,000 feet. Now the learned deny that this melodious name, so suggestive of vernal airs and tuneful groves, has any connexion with matters ornithological. Destitute alike of sentiment or remorse they fetch it from a certain Scandinavian Viking with the dread name of Bythar Lipr: this, say they, in the process of phonetic decay became "Butter Lip" and finally "Birdlip." Documentary evidence is no doubt forthcoming, but I have not had time to follow it up, and for the present I am content to believe that the grand old Viking sailed up the Severn in his galley, landed at Gloucester, pushed along the

Roman Road and up the hill to this place, raided the country round, and returned to his ships laden with spoils (et ferenda et agenda), and so departed by the way he had come, leaving the terror of his name behind him.

Birdlip is a famous holiday resort for Gloucester people; there are inns and lodging-houses in plenty, and so bracing and invigorating is the air that a thriving hospital for consumptives has been established in the woods a mile away. We left Fossbridge early and cannot do better than turn in to the "Royal George" for lunch, and then enjoy a quiet pipe in the spacious, well-ordered garden on the edge of the hill. The view from this garden or from the fields further to the right is magnificent. In the middle of the vale lies Gloucester, dominated by the stately tower of St. Peter's: beneath you, straight as an arrow's flight for the six miles that stretch from the city to the hills, is the thin white line of Ermin Street. Right and left, like sentries set to guard it, are the outlying knolls of Churchdown and Robin's Wood, while in the distance rises the dark blue mass of the billowy Malverns, which has ever been the limit of our outlook from these hills. Hill, vale, and forest,—such are the divisions of Gloucestershire as marked out by nature, and I suppose there is hardly another county in England which embraces three portions so essentially distinct. Anthropologists say that racial differences corresponding to these three divisions may still be traced, that in the hills the Teutonic type prevails, and that the further westward you go, the more marked the Celtic element becomes. Certain it is that the country west of the Severn contrasts strongly with the distinctively English features of that part of the county which lies to the east of the river. The accent, or rather the intonation, of the inhabitants, their houses scattered over the length and breadth of the parish instead of being concentrated in the village itself, quite apart from physical characteristics, point to their Silurian affinities. Indeed, had not history ordered otherwise, the forest peninsula would probably to this day form a part, not of England, but of Wales, from which it is only separated by the deep and narrow gorge of the Wye.

From Birdlip to Painswick there are two roads: one through the Cranham woods to Prinknash, formerly a country residence of the abbots of Gloucester, and then by the Cheltenham road which is cut along the eastern side of Painswick Hill. The other leaves the Stroud road three miles from Birdlip, descends to the very bottom of the deep Sheepscombe valley, and then climbs up a steep ascent into Painswick. Both have their points, but the former is the shadier, easier and shorter. Sheepscombe is one of those scattered hamlets which are so frequent in the numerous valleys of this corner of the Cotswold, and which are absent from the eastern parts. High on the opposite hillside as you descend the valley a severe gloomy looking mansion frowns upon you from the thick plantation that surrounds it. Had Ebworth House existed in those days, and it is like enough that its predecessor existed, it would have been a fit residence for Sir Anthony Kingston, that foe to all rebels, and stern instrument of the royal will. The son of Sir William Kingston, himself an accomplished courtier, and Constable of the Tower when Queen Anne Boleyn suffered, he was one of the most fortunate of Henry's favourites: in this county alone three manors, Miserden, Quenington and Flaxley —the two last, the spoils of the dissolution—had been heaped upon him, and he had besides inherited from his father the manor of Painswick. He had led a thousand men of Gloucestershire into the north to suppress the Pilgrimage of Grace, and had been knighted for his services, and when in the next reign the western peasants took up arms in defence of the priests and the old liturgy, he was dispatched into Cornwall as provost-marshal. Holinshed tells the following story of the way in which he executed his office:

It seems that the Mayor of Bodmin, one Boyer, had been "a busie fellow among the rebels." His friends did their best

Painswick Churchyard.

to exonerate him, and pleaded that he had acted only under compulsion, " but howsoever it was, Sir Anthonie Kingston that was provost-marshall in the kings armie under the lord privie seale wrote his letter unto the said maior signifieng to him that he and other with him would come and dine with him such a daie.   The maior seeming to be glad thereof, made the best purveiance he could to receive them, and at the time appointed Sir Anthonie Kingston came with his companie, and were right hartilie welcomed by the maior.   But before they sat downe to dinner, calling the maior aside, he told him that there must be execution doone in that towne, and therefore willed him that a paire of gallowes might be framed and set up with speed, so that they might be readie by that time that they should make an end of dinner.

" The maior with all diligence caused the same to be doone ; so that when dinner was ended, Sir Anthonie calling the maior to him, and asking whether the gallowes were set up accordinglie as he had willed, the maior answered that they were readie.   Wherewith Sir Anthonie taking the maior by the hand, desired him to bring him to the place where they stood, and comming thither and beholding them, he said to the maior ; Thinke you maister maior that they be strong inough ? Yea sir, quoth he, that they are.   Well then said Sir Anthonie, get you even up unto them, for they are provided for you. The maior greatlie abashed herewith, said ; I trust you meane no such thing to me.   Sir said he there is no remedie, ye have been a busie rebell, and therefore this is appointed for your reward : and so without respit or staie, there was the maior hanged."

After this we are not surprised to find that his zeal for the king's peace found a field for its exercise nearer home.   The Enclosures Commission issued in 1549 was unpopular with the lower orders whether Romanist or Protestant, and rioting broke out all over the country ; the newly erected fences were torn down, the ditches filled up, and the deer parks ravaged.   Sir

Anthony Kingston, says a Bodleian MS. quoted by Rudder, "being Lord of the manor of Painswick caused a gallows for the insurgents to be erected upon Sheepscombe Green in this parish; and made a prison in Painswick, to secure all sorts of offenders; and supposing they might be useful to posterity, he also gave three estates in his lordship, since called Gallows-lands; one always to maintain the gallows, a second to keep two ladders in readiness, and the third to provide halters : and that nothing in so necessary a business might be wanting, provided that the tithing-man of Sheepscombe should be hangman, and that he should enjoy an acre of land in that tithing for his service." "There are many people now living," adds Rudder, "who remember the gallows, and the tithing-man for the time being still enjoys a piece of ground there called Hangman's Acre, but in this respect his office is a sinecure." History does not record the number of victims offered up to justice on Sir Anthony's gallows tree, nor, however useful his legacy proved to be, does "posterity" appear to have held his name in grateful remembrance. On his death without lawful issue in 1556 Painswick passed into his sister's family, but his name lingered for a time at Miserden, where there is an altar tomb with the fine coloured effigy of William Kingston, Esq., sheriff of the county, who died in 1614.

Painswick is a clean, trim-looking place with a rather modern air about it which marks it off from the towns of the eastern side of the hills. Some of the larger houses seem to date from the prosperous days of the earlier part of the last century, when the Wiltshire and Gloucestershire clothing towns still held their own against the growing competition of the north. The houses which face the main street have sloping gardens behind, and on the level plateau in the grounds of the "Falcon" inn is a famous bowling green, on which some dozen games may be played at once. Bowls is a game much cultivated in these parts, the local club holds regular meetings on summer

Painswick. Vicarage Lane.

evenings, and the matches played against neighbouring towns such as Tewkesbury and Cheltenham are the great events of the season. The bowling green at "The Bell" at Tewkesbury, with its thick, well-kept yew hedges, is one of the oldest and finest in England.

Of the older houses the gem is the Court House, just behind the church, so called not as one would naturally expect, because the Courts of the Lord of the Manor were held in it (the Lord lived at Painswick Lodge close by Sheepscombe), but because King Charles slept here on his march to Gloucester in August 1643 and held his court in the large room which still exists. A royal proclamation is extant "given at our Court at Paynewicke" forbidding his soldiers to rob or molest any of the country people who should bring provisions for sale to the market which he was to establish in his camp before Gloucester. A month later, and the king, foiled in his attempt upon the city, was here again—Essex and his army of relief had been descried upon the hills to the north-east and on a wet gusty autumn afternoon the beleaguering forces marched southwards up the steep ascent to Kimsbury camp. Tradition has handed down from generation to generation the pathetic story how Charles, in deep dejection at the failure of an attempt which might have proved the turning-point of the war, was sitting on a stone near the camp, when one of the young princes, weary of their present life, asked his father when they should go home. "I have no home to go to, my son," was the disconsolate reply.

Kimsbury Camp is an ancient fortification a mile to the north of the town, 900 feet above the Severn. It forms a conspicuous landmark in the long line of the Cotswolds, when viewed from the opposite side of the river, and from its summit we shall get our last look at the great stretch of vale and hill, with which our wanderings along the western edge of Cotswold have made us so familiar. It is a view of which we can never tire ; true, the same objects may again and again

Painswich Beacon and Kimsbury Camp.

be seen, but their relative position varies with our own point of observation, and there is never any lack of novelty in the setting of the picture. Again the majestic tower of Gloucester rivets our gaze to the north, but its outline is now defined against the dark background of the Malvern Hills ; westwards the distant peaks of the Black Mountains lift themselves above the sombre summits of the Forest, and far away in the vale to the south, the rays of the declining sun light up the broad expanse of tidal water that lies between the red-marl cliffs of Sedbury and Aust.

On the slopes of the Painswick hills, and in the woods which diversify them, the lover of wild flowers will find many treasures. The rare *Cephalanthera rubra* is a prize only for the initiated, but the commoner Helleborine and a variety of orchises, bee, birds-nest, pyramidal, and musk are to be seen by all who care to track them to their native haunts, and in the shade of the beech-woods may be found the curious browny yellow *Monotropa* with its scale-like leaves.

But Painswick is chiefly remembered by the majority of its visitors for its singular churchyard planted with long rows of yews clipped into the same oval shape. The first set of these trees was planted about 200 years ago, and there is a legend to the effect that their number has always been ninety-nine, and that it is impossible to increase it ; but, as a matter of fact, the number at present is, I believe, 118. Painswick has always taken a pride in its churchyard avenues, and Rudder says that in his day they were "the place of resort for the ladies and polite inhabitants of the town in fair weather." In other words, the churchyard was then a fashionable lounge : the polite inhabitants now find relaxation in the more rational amusements of tennis and golf. The picturesque gate-house, which forms the main entrance to the churchyard, was built a few years since with the timbers of the old belfry. As for the church, it is another of those fine Perpendicular churches

built in the later fifteenth century, when the country had ceased
to be distracted with dynastic struggles, and the clothing
trade was now on its upward course. In one of the many
skirmishes, which took place in these parts after the raising of
the siege of Gloucester, a party of the Parliament's soldiers had
taken refuge in the church, and some damage was done to it
" by firing the doores and casting in hand-granadoes"; but a
more serious disaster happened more than two hundred years
after this, when the spire was struck by lightning, and all the
upper part came crashing down through the roof into the
church.

On our way down the valley to Stroud it may be worth
while to turn aside for a few minutes to see the pretty
village of Pitchcombe, which lies in a hollow close to the road,
but so effectually concealed from it that, were it not for the
finger-post, its existence would never be suspected. So on
past mills and orchards (for we have now reached the apple and
cider country) to Stroud, where we enter the valley of the
Frome or " Stroudwater," and follow the river through Brims-
combe, Chalford, and Frampton Mansell to Saperton. This
charming valley is well known to those who travel by rail
between Swindon and Gloucester. The railway makes its way
along the slope of the hill on the south side of the river,
and so steep is the gradient that an additional engine is
always on duty to help drag the trains up to the tunnel.
Here the passenger with a parting glimpse at the tempting
sylvan shades, which we cyclists and pedestrians are privileged to explore, bids farewell to the " Golden Valley " (such is
its pet name) not to see daylight again till he emerges amid
the Oakley Woods on the high tableland of the basin of the
upper Thames.

Thanks to the tunnel Saperton has escaped the railway, and
the upper reaches of the valley retain all their primitive
seclusion. The village is perched high up on the southern
slopes, and looks down upon Daneway bridge and Daneway

Pitchcombe.

House, which we shall visit directly, but the church claims our first attention. Though (with the exception of the tower) it dates only from the early eighteenth century, it is a building of exceptional interest. To enter is to be transported in a twinkling back to the days of good Queen Anne. Instinctively, you look around for the rector in gown and bands, the musicians with bass-viol and hautboy in the gallery, and Sir Robert in laced coat and flowing periwig seated at his ease in the Squire's pew. Sir Robert, do I say? The Gloucestershire man, versed in the history of the Atkyns family, will of course remind me that there were two Sir Roberts, father and son; and that as the son survived the father only a couple of years, the chances are that they frequented the family pew together. And well they may, for the father resided at the manor-house quite close to the church, the son at Pinbury only a mile higher up the valley. The Atkynses were a family of lawyers, and for generations there had always been a judge in the family. Sir Robert the elder was Lord Chief Baron of the Exchequer, and purchased Saperton at the Restoration from the Pooles, who had held it since the time of Henry VII. His son, the younger Sir Robert, represented Cirencester in the Oxford Parliament of 1681, and was the author of *The Ancient and Present State of Glocestershire*, to which we have referred more than once. He died in 1711, the year before his book was published, and is buried in the south transept of the church; there you may behold him in effigy reclining in a dignified manner on his elbow: " He left behind him," says his epitaph, " Louise Lady Atkyns daughter of Sir George Carteret of Hawns in Bedfordshire, his most dear and sorrowful widow, who erected this monument to his memory, though he left behind him one more durable, The ancient and present state of Glostershire." Another monument presents the figure of a youthful knight, the eldest son of Sir Henry Poole: " Sir Devereux Poole, being but of tender age, was for his worthynes and valoure knighted in France by Henry the 4, the French king, after his

Saperton.

owne order, and there ended his dayse and was there buried
1590."

The church abounds in Jacobean carving, which was
removed from the manor-house before it was pulled down in
1730 by Lord Bathurst, to whom Saperton was sold by the
heirs of the last Sir Robert Atkyns. All this carved oak gives
the church quite a character of its own, and harmonises
excellently with the style of architecture. At the same time there
is no mistaking its origin. The massive communion table, for
example, has a lower shelf irresistibly suggestive of a side-
board, while the classic termini which ornament the bench
ends and the front of the gallery were plainly designed for a
very different scene. But the whole effect is fraught with a
peculiar charm which is further enhanced by the strongly built
waggon roof of the nave, and the exquisite pale green transparent glass of the windows, which has only in one instance
been displaced to make room for the vulgar abomination known
as "cathedral glass."

Though the church has gained by its destruction, we cannot
but regret the loss of the manor-house. It has been mentioned
in a previous chapter that in July 1644 the king was at Sir
Ralph Dutton's at Coberley : the next night he was here as the
guest of the Pooles. It was then "a brave sweet seat," and no
doubt one of the finest Tudor houses in all the country round.
It must have been strongly built, for it furnished Lord
Bathurst with ample material for his favourite hobby. As late as
1736 he writes to Pope that he has brought "a great quantity of
good hewn stone from the old house at Saperton to the great
centre in Oakley Wood," and this was doubtless by no means
the first time that he had drawn upon it.

From the churchyard, which commands a lovely view down
the valley, we descend to Daneway. On our way we pass the
mouth of the tunnel that carries the Thames and Severn canal
through the watershed which separates the basins of the two
rivers. The tunnel is nearly two miles and a half in length, the

whole length of the canal from Stroud to Lechlade where it joins the Thames being over thirty miles. It was opened in 1792, and was then looked upon as a colossal undertaking and a tremendous triumph of engineering skill. The idea had been ventilated in the reign of Charles II., and it had afterwards been one of Lord Bathurst's visionary schemes. No one can visit Cirencester without becoming familiar with this enthusiastic and hospitable Lord, the creator of its famous Park, and the intimate friend and correspondent of Pope. I therefore make no apology for the following extract from a letter of the latter to Digby written in 1722 : "I am told . . . . that Mrs. Mary Digby talks . . . . of seeing my Lord Bathurst's wood . . . . How much I wish to be her guide through that enchanted forest is not to be expressed. I look upon myself as the magician appropriated to the place, without whom no mortal can penetrate into the recesses of those sacred shades. I could pass whole days in only describing to her the future, and as yet visionary beauties that are to rise in those scenes ; the palace that is to be built, the pavilions that are to glitter, the colonnades that are to adorn them. Nay, more, the meeting of the Thames and Severn, which (when the noble owner has finer dreams than ordinary) are to be led into each other's embraces through secret caverns of not above twelve or fifteen miles, till they rise and celebrate their marriage in the midst of an immense amphitheatre, which is to be the admiration of posterity a hundred years hence."

The admiration, and not only the admiration but the patronage of posterity was, however, diverted to the railway ; and the canal at last was so little used that the tunnel became ruinous, and all traffic had to be stopped. It is only in the course of the last year or two that it has been repaired, and that the idea has been entertained of bringing the waterway again into competition with the rail. Daneway House is a building of the greatest interest. The oldest part dates from the fourteenth century and the rest belongs to the time of Oliver Cromwell.

It is now the headquarters of Messrs. Barnsley and Gimson, a firm of architects who have devoted themselves to the construction of furniture which shall be at once beautiful, useful, and durable.   They have also built houses in the neighbourhood on the sound principles of the builders of two centuries ago, and if any of my readers wants to know how to build and how to furnish, I advise him to pay a visit to the Daneway.   As to the name, it may go back to the year 894, when the Danes made a

Daneway House.

dash up the Thames valley from their stations in East Anglia with the intention of seizing some haven in the Bristol Channel, and there meeting with their ships which were detained by Alfred on the coast of South Devon.   In their march from the Thames to the Severn, it is permissible to guess that, like the canal and railway in after generations, they made their way down this valley and left their name behind them.   Their fleet, however, they did not meet ; and after waiting in vain for some time, they were defeated at Buttington, a spot on that narrow neck of land between Wye and Severn, which seven centuries later again became the scene of fighting.

If the traveller has a fine afternoon at his disposal he should not fail to ride up the valley from Daneway bridge to Tunley. The steep bank on the right is bright with masses of yellow ragwort and golden rod, and among them are growing great bushes of deadly nightshade (*Atropa Belladonna*). The lurid purple flowers are now over, but the black cherry-like fruit is lurking in abundance beneath the broad handsome leaves. So tempting is its appearance that the plant has often been destroyed by the country people in places where their truant children might chance to fall a prey to it. At Tunley he may leave his cycle and make his way on foot up the narrow unfrequented dell to Througham, an ancient lonely farmstead of marvellous beauty.

We resume our journey at Saperton, whence a delightful walk up the glen takes us to Pinbury. The house, as I have already said, was the residence of the younger Sir Robert Atkyns, and therefore in all probability the place where his book was written: sober and quiet, with its gables and high pitched roof rising against a dark background of trees, we feel at once that it is an ideal retreat for a student, and that it must have made a congenial home for one who was devoting the labours of his best days to the antiquities of his native county. In the old days there had been a house of nuns here, and the magnificent yew avenue in the grounds, said to contain the tallest yews in England, still bears the appropriate name of the Nuns' Walk.

As for the name, Penda, King of Mercia, invaded Wessex about the year 628, and if, as is asserted, it was here that he pitched his most southern camp, the transition from Pendaburgh to Penbury or Pinbury is easy.

Our way to Cirencester, which I shall henceforth take leave to spell Ciceter, in accordance with the neglected but ancient

Calmsden.   The Village Cross.

and established pronunciation, takes us to Park Corner, where the inn once stood at which Wildgoose and Tugwell, on their tramp from Gloucester to Bath, fell in with Lord Bathurst's friendly and hospitable keeper. For their exploits on this occasion, their sojourn at "the old Gothic building" in the Park, which "his Lordship used to say he could have built as old again, if he had had a mind," and their encounter with the learned Virtuoso, together with the dissertation of the latter on the advantages of antiquarian pursuits, I must refer the curious reader to the Fourth Book of Mr. Graves's *Comic Romance*. There is no inn for us at Park Corner now, but another half dozen miles will bring us safely to our destination. The road traverses a delightful, heathy and woodland tract, and then drops down to Daglingworth, where we are on familiar ground once more. We soon join Ermin Street at the well-known corner, and now the beacon tower of Ciceter, looming large above the rising mists of the chill autumn evening, is our signal that one more day of our Cotswold pilgrimage has been brought to a successful conclusion.

St. John's Hospital, Cirencester.

CHAPTER XIV

ETER, before the rise of Cheltenham the third town in
unty, and from the historic point of view still entitled to
ank, has not without good reason been styled the "Capital
Cotswolds." True, it lies on the very edge of the hills,
here they begin to fade away into the great alluvial plain
tretches southwards to the chalk downs of Wessex, and
its name from the great Saxon emblem carved upon the
de of Uffington. But in spirit as well as in appearance,
wn belongs to the hills rather than to the plain. Let the
r who has followed us in our rambles from Stow (and by
ime the *genius loci* should be to him as a familiar friend)
his stand in the clean, wide market-place, and, as he looks
d him at the substantial stone-built houses, say whether
es not feel himself still to be in a Cotswold town. As for
ast here is the stately church to remind us once more of the
wool-staplers ; and, for the present, where will you find
samples of Cotswold wheat and Cotswold barley than in
er market on a Monday ? For, after all, as even Mr. Rider

Haggard admits, the agricultural outlook in Gloucestershire is not so bad as it is in many other counties : there are still great flock masters, and large corn growers, within a dozen miles of Ciceter, whose names are no secret throughout the markets of the whole district, and there are even signs that the Cotswold wool, long superseded by the finer foreign growths, may once more contribute to the clothing of mankind. Mr. Apperley, of Stroud, who is both sheep-farmer and mill-owner, has discovered a method of softening the native wool, and has succeeded in weaving from it a cloth which need not fear comparison with some of the finest fabrics of the Yorkshire looms. Altogether, there are few towns in England where farming, both in theory and practice, is so much in evidence as in Ciceter. And the future agriculturist is caught young : there is the ancient grammar school founded by John Chedworth, one of a Cotswold family with a Cotswold name, Bishop of Lincoln in 1460, and re-founded a few years ago on a new site, and with new buildings, as the County Technical School. Here, in addition to the ancient Trivia and Quadrivia, or its modern representatives, youth is taught the elements of all the sciences subservient to the tilling of the soil ; while for the more advanced student there is the Royal Agricultural College, founded in 1845 under the patronage of the Prince Consort, and famous throughout the most distant quarters of the globe. As everybody interested in farming knows, it has its own farm of four hundred acres, where all the details of farming operations on the most scientific principles may be studied in actual operation. No wonder then that—though the former industries of the place have declined, including the famous Curriers' knives, once almost a monopoly, and, like the old Toledo blades, in high repute from one end of Europe to the other—there is an under-current of innovation, and a sensitiveness to new ideas and new methods, manifest beneath the placid and dignified exterior of the aristocratic and conservative old country town.

Apart from farming, it is as a hunting centre that Ciceter is

best known to the world at large. To this attraction it owes
many of its permanent residents, and a fair sprinkling of
hunting men take up their temporary quarters here for the
winter. Long ago the dwellers in these hills hunted to live,
and if any of their descendants now live to hunt—well, they
might live for a far worse object. The man whose pocket and
stable are full, may, if he chooses, ride to hounds every day of
the week. In 1886 the famous old Vale of White Horse pack,
so dear to Tom Brown, was divided into two. Mr. Miller, of
Cricklade, hunts the eastern division of the old country, and
Lord Bathurst the part round Ciceter. On Tuesday and
Friday you may hunt with the home pack, and on Thursday and
Saturday with the Cricklade. On Monday the Badminton pack
are always on this side of their country, while on Wednesday
the Cotswold meet is sure not to be very far off. For "further
information" I must refer the courteous reader to Mr. Gibbs's
chapter in the book already quoted, where he will find the
whole subject elaborated by one who knew the country well,
and was a genuine lover of the sport.

In the annals of Ciceter it has been naturally the Roman
period which has proved most attractive to its historians. Yet
the history of that period has to be based entirely upon the
labours of the spade and pick-axe ; of documentary evidence
there is none, and so completely was the Romano-British town
destroyed by the Saxon conquerors after their victory at
Dyrham in 577, and so long did it lie waste after its
destruction, that the very streets are now laid down on quite
different lines. There is no proof that anything like a town
existed here before Roman times, and the excavations that
have been made here and there into the Roman city which
now underlies the modern Ciceter seem to indicate that, like
Bath and Silchester, it was not primarily a military station.
Like its successor it probably served both as a centre
of urban life and as a market town for the surrounding
population. Fortified, so far as circumvallation goes, of course

it was, and remains of the wall may still be seen on the east side of the town ; three hundred years ago these remains were more extensive, and when Leland visited Ciceter the abbot told him that he had found in them arched stones inscribed with large Roman letters. But all the excavations that have been made show that the town was wealthy and important—among them one of the most recent, which revealed the foundations of the basilica or town-hall, a large building, which consisted of a nave and aisles some 320 feet in length : its western extremity terminated in an apse, and its eastern in a large portico supported by columns with Corinthian capitals. A complete account of Roman Ciceter, embodying the results of modern researches, remains to be written. The reader interested in this subject should read the introductory chapter to Messrs. Buckman and Newmarch's handsome volume, which will tell him all that was to be told at the time of its publication (1850) ; later light he will have to seek in papers scattered through the Transactions of Antiquarian Societies. He will, of course, visit the Corinium Museum, the first indispensable requisite for a right understanding of the whole matter being time, the second, time, and the third also time. He will then search out the " Querns," an assemblage of grass mounds and hollows outside the ancient wall, and from remains discovered there, probably the Roman cemetery. Here, too, is the amphitheatre, with its openings east and west ; but if the stranger inquires his way hither from the casual passer-by, let him be sure to ask for the "bull ring," for to the multitude " amphitheatre " is a word in an unknown tongue.

Interesting as all this is, it is not in the midst of a thriving modern town that the actuality of Roman Britain is most easily recreated in the imagination. The impress of Roman greatness is more quickly recognised amid the comparative desolation of Silchester or Caerwent, or even amid the secluded ruins of Chedworth, than in the busy thoroughfares of Ciceter or Gloucester. But if the vestiges of the Corinium of the

first four centuries have almost completely disappeared the
monuments of the mediaeval town have by no means
escaped unscathed. On the morning of January 7, 1400, the
streets of Ciceter were the scene of unwonted turmoil and
excitement. At midnight a party of unwelcome guests had
entered the town, and had taken up their quarters in the
various inns. The townsfolk, armed with bills and bows, were
now battering at the doors and calling for the surrender of the
intruders. The latter, however, in whose veins ran some of
the bluest blood in the realm, were in no mind to submit
tamely to "a crew of patches, rude mechanicals," and a free fight
was maintained till three hours after mid-day. The nobles
were then overpowered and taken for safe custody to the
abbey. Their crime was rebellion against the new-crowned
monarch, and their object the restoration of the deposed Richard
to the throne ; but having failed to surprise the King at
Windsor, and fearing his vengeance, they had retreated westwards, and had got as far as Ciceter in safety. Here, however, they found they had reckoned without their hosts : the
traders of Gloucestershire had had enough of arbitrary
government, and were zealous supporters of the new regime.
Having secured the persons of the rebel lords, they would have
handed them over to the King, had not an event occurred
which determined them to execute justice summarily and upon
the spot. A certain priest, who filled the office of chaplain to
one of the captured nobles, took it into his head to set fire
to some of the houses in the town, thinking to cover the
escape of the prisoners in the confusion that ensued. The
men of Ciceter, however, were only the more incensed, and in
the twilight of the winter evening they dragged forth their
victims from the abbey, and struck off the heads of the two
most prominent among them, Holland, Earl of Kent, and
Montacute, Earl of Salisbury, there and then.

In less than a century and a half from this time every trace
of this great abbey, in which the last moments of these two

z 2

unhappy earls were spent, was swept away. When the Great Destroyer, of his royal pleasure, made a grant of the abbey of Ciceter to one Roger Basinge, he made it upon the express condition that the whole of the buildings should be pulled down and the materials carried away. Thus the splendid church, recorded by William of Worcester to have been 245 feet long and 72 feet wide, and all the conventual buildings were utterly demolished. What became of the said " Roger Basinge, Esq.," and what use he made of his acquisition, I do not know, but in a few years the site had again fallen into the hands of the Crown, and in 1564 was sold by Queen Elizabeth to her physician, Dr. Richard Master, the ancestor of its present owner. The abbey stood on the north side of the parish church, where the Abbey House and grounds preserve its memory. The stone and building materials were soon dispersed. Dr. Master used up what fragments he could find in the house which he built for himself on the site—a house which was replaced by the present one two centuries later, and St. Catherine's chapel, in the parish church, is roofed with some groined vaulting removed from some chapel of the abbey or from the cloisters. A twelfth-century gate-way in Grove Lane, now one of the entrances to the abbey grounds, and a fragment of walling in Gosditch Street is all that is still to be seen in its original position.

The abbey was a house of Augustinian canons, founded by Henry I., and was one of the wealthiest foundations in Gloucestershire. The abbot, as has been already mentioned, was raised to the rank of a spiritual peer, and down to the dissolution he was unquestionably the chief personage in Ciceter. His powers and pretensions did not fail to give rise to bickerings and jealousies from time to time on the part of the towns-folk, but he always came off triumphant. He and his house were lords of the manor and ever ready to challenge any infringement of their rights. They had also, in spite of protests on the part of the diocesan authorities, established their claim to the control of the parish church, which was always served by one of their own canons, no vicar being ever appointed. Even at the present day the living, though styled a vicarage under the Act of 1868, is really a perpetual curacy, the incumbent holding office by the bishop's license, without institution or induction.

The history of the parish church, the largest church in the county, abbey churches excepted, has been exhaustively worked out by the late Mr. E. A. Fuller, and the visitor who desires to study it in detail will, of course, procure his useful little book, but even the most hasty tourist must not fail to devote an hour to its inspection. The first of its wonders to claim his admiration will be the great three-storied porch that faces the market-place. This is the Church-house, or " Vice," as it was formerly called (a corruption of Parvise ?), and previously to the rebuilding of the upper part in 1831 it contained two rooms, one above the other, as from the two tiers of windows on the exterior appears to be still the case : there is, however, now only one lofty room, the floor dividing the two rooms having been removed. What the use of these rooms was is not known for certain, but there is no trace of any liturgical purpose, and it is conjectured that they served as a meeting-place for the trade guilds of the town. The guild feasts would be conveniently supplied by the Church-house Tavern, which before the re-building abutted on the eastern side of the " Vice," while the crypt beneath it probably served as its cellar. After the dissolution of the guilds the "Vice" was let for various secular purposes, and in 1672 was utilised as the Town-hall. In this last capacity it has, of course, been now superseded by the new municipal buildings in Castle Street.

The general impression which one gains, both from the exterior and interior of the church itself, is that of a vast Perpendicular edifice, and, in fact, it is to this period that the greater part of it belongs ; thus the tower was built early in the fifteenth, and the nave early in the sixteenth century, while the various chapels, as they now exist, were erected at intervals

Cirencester Church Porch.

between these two dates. The chancel, however, which by an enlargement on its south side is thrown completely out of centre with the nave, is earlier, and some remnants of the original Norman church may be traced in its construction.

The piety and affection with which the inhabitants of a mediæval town regarded their parish church is well illustrated by the numerous donations and legacies which poured in towards the making and furnishing thereof. Nor was their generosity any the less because the money was to be expended under the direction of my lord abbot, who would not forget to have his monogram carved on a boss, or his arms emblazoned in a window. Thus, in 1457, Henry Garstang "honoured" the Lady-chapel "with worshipfull Vestimentis, y^t is to saye, ii wh^t copeyes and chisypl, ii tuniclys with pertenances on sute." This was "ye best sewt of ye chapel." Robert Rycarde, a "cloth-man," who had been bailiff of the town, bequeathed his "scarlet and crimson gowne to be bestowed in vestures and ornaments to be used yerely at the feast [of St. Anthony] and other tymes to the lawde of God and hym." Hugh Norres, who died in 1535, made a laudable attempt to encourage others to imitate him in his benefactions : "Item, I gyve to the use of the Parish Churche of Circester a pall of velvett in condycon that the said pall shall be used and occupied at the desire of eny man and woman that is or hath be or shall be speciall benefactours to the seid parish and not to be used otherwise nor to no other persons. . . . Also, if it fortun that any honest men or women be departed if it please the executors or over-seers [trustees] to have the use of the seid pall at their berying the which hath not geve nayther bequethed nothing unto the welth of the church I am content if he or she be rych, he or she shall pay for the usyng of the said pall iiis. iiiid. and any other man or woman for the use of the seid pall xxd., and with the seid money geven y ordeyn that yt shall be kep to the maynteyning of the seid pall and vestiments and copes in the vestry to honor God therewith." The Norres family were

grocers in the town, and among the brasses, brought together
in the Lady-chapel from different parts of the church, is one to
the memory of another Hugh, with an inscription of which the
reader will not be sorry to have a copy :

> " Reyse gracious Jhu to endless lyfe,
>   at thy grete dome where all schall apere,
>   Hughe | Norys, groc' and Johan hys wyf
>   nowe dede in grave and beryed here,
>   yo' p'yers desyring | There soules for chere
>   the x day of July the yere
>   of our Lord God m.ccccxxix."

A few years more and the old order had given place to the
new ; we are not surprised, therefore, to find the true Puritan
ring about another brass in the Trinity chapel to one Philip
Marner, who died in 1587 :

> " In Lent by will a sermon he devised
>   And yerely preacher with a noble prised ;
>   Seuen nobles hee did geve y⁰ poore for to defend
>   And £80 to xvii men did lend
>   In Ciseter, Burford, Abingdon, and Tetburie
>   Ever to be to them a stocke yerely."

Thus sermons for the souls of the living took the place of
masses for the souls of the dead. One more epitaph and I
have done with them ; but having seen at Saperton the monument of Sir Robert Atkyns, we must not omit to read the
humbler memorial at Ciceter to his successor. It is a simple
tablet on the wall of the angle of the Lady-chapel, now used
as a vestry for the choir, and commemorates "Samuel Rudder
of this Town, Printer. . . He was born at Uley, in this county,
Dec. 24, 1726, and died Mar. 15, 1801, a man of the strictest
honor and most inflexible integrity. His History of Gloucestershire will establish his character as a writer." His bones, with
those of his wife and son, rest in the churchyard, not far from
the east end of the Lady-chapel.

In the middle of the seventeenth century the church, no

longer under the watchful eye of a mitred abbot, had become sadly out of repair, and in a petition addressed to Archbishop Laud in 1639 the cry is her own: "I am in comlyness not much inferior to the cathedral church of Bath, but for want of whitelyminge of marl look rustily. My windows are parti-coulured, white in one place and red in another, but I was founded with rich coulured glass, such as is in Fayreford Church neare me in the same dioces, which is kept decently to this day. The chancell, where is receaved the sacrament, is un-sealed like a barne, my pavement is worne out and very unhansome." In the next century came the usual invasion of high wainscotted pews and galleries, as well as "a Grecian panelled reredos" exhibiting two mitres, two candlesticks, the candles thereof with gilt flames, and two vases of flowers, all carved and painted upon it. All this was swept away at the restoration effected by Sir Gilbert Scott forty years ago. "Sufficient remains of the ancient [choir] stalls were discovered to allow of a correct reproduction, and the whole church was re-seated in oak, the bench ends being copied from one belonging to the old [pre-Reformation] black oak seats, which was happily discovered in the back of a pew, where it had been hidden under some green baize."

During the Civil War the church was twice made to serve the purpose of a prison. It was indeed a common practice with both parties to lock up a batch of prisoners in the nearest church, there being ordinarily no other building available of sufficient size and strength. At the opening of the war the townspeople of Ciceter, like their neighbours at Gloucester, were staunch supporters of the Parliament. The town was defended by a garrison under Colonel Fettiplace—a name well known in Gloucestershire and the surrounding counties—and, according to a contemporary Royalist writer, many of the country people had been pressed into their service: "Some of the prisoners confessed (and others have made it good) how that the gentlemen and clothiers threatned them they should have no work. Others that they should be plundred. Others were violently fetcht from their houses by dragooners and made to get up behind them. Others were dragg'd from their ploughs, and others comming into the towne about businesse, were there detained, and threatened to be shot, if they offered to get out." "This," adds the writer, with pardonable exultation over the Royalist capture of the town, "is the liberty of the subject."

Even before actual hostilities commenced, the reception given to Lord Chandos of Sudeley, when he came to execute the King's Commission of array, was a sufficient indication of the temper of the inhabitants. He entered the town in his coach with a retinue of about thirty men, and after dinner was sitting in conference with some of the local magistrates and other influential persons, when the excited populace burst into the room and compelled him to hand over his warrant, and sign a declaration that he would not attempt to put it in force, either in Ciceter or anywhere else in the county. Late at night they departed and left him to his repose, but their attitude boded so ill for the next morning, that it was judged safer for his lordship to get clear of the town as soon as possible. Accordingly Sir William Master (grandson of the Doctor) conveyed him secretly through his house, and let him out by a backway—perhaps the old gateway already mentioned. In the morning the mob, finding their enemy had escaped, proceeded to wreak their vengeance on his coach, which they incontinently drew into the market-place and tore to pieces.

The turn of affairs came on Candlemas Day, 1643, when a vigorous assault of Prince Rupert carried the fortifications and barricades, and left over a thousand prisoners in his hands. These were secured in the church for the best part of two days and nights—their friends being compelled to break the windows in order to pass in provisions to them—and were then tied together and marched through the snow and slush to Oxford. The route of this miserable procession was by Burford and Witney, where they were again secured in the church; and when their approach was announced at Oxford, crowds of people streamed along the road to witness their arrival. "About a mile from the city," wrote one of their number, "his Majestie, with the Prince and Duke of York, came thither to see us drove along more like dogs and horses than men, up to the knees in mire and dirt, and along the horseway, and abound-ance of the scollers much rejoicing at our misery, calling and abusing us by the names of rogues and traitors."

For the rest of the war Ciceter remained in the hands of the Royalists, but not without one successful raid on the part of the enemy. Early one morning in the following autumn, the garrison were surprised in their beds and compelled to call for quarter. The occasion was as follows: after his gallant relief of Gloucester, Essex was so beset by the King's army that he was compelled to fall back upon London as best he could. The ordinary roads to the capital were blocked, but by a night march across the downs he reached Ciceter, forced his way into the town, and took two hundred prisoners, besides, what was more important to him under the circumstances, forty cart-loads of provisions, which had been collected for the supply of the besieging forces before Gloucester. Essex locked up his prisoners in the church for the rest of the night, and then abandoning the town, carried them with him towards Cricklade and the Kennet valley.

At the Revolution there was once more fighting at Ciceter. The parish register of burials, under November, 1688, has the following entry: "Bulstrode Whitelocke, Esq., kild at the King's Head when my Lord Lovelace was taken." This was, I suppose, the fourth son of the author of the *Memorials*, who had joined his neighbour, Lord Lovelace, of Hurley, in his march westwards to join the Prince of Orange at Exeter. Lovelace at the head of seventy of his friends and tenants got as far as Ciceter unopposed, but here he was informed that he would not be suffered to proceed further. The Duke of Beau-fort had called out the militia for the King, and a strong party, under Captain Lorange, were posted in the town. Lovelace determined to cut his way through, and a conflict ensued. Lorange and his son were slain, but Lovelace was at last over-powered, and sent to Gloucester Castle. According to Wood, Lorange came into Lovelace's room at the inn, and asked him "what he made there with his men all armed": Lovelace re-plied that he was going to serve the Prince of Orange. There-upon Lorange and his son fired at Lovelace, but missed him; Lovelace fired in return and killed them both. But according to another account that reached Wood, it was Whitelocke who killed them, and was himself so dangerously wounded that he died a day or two afterwards, while "Lovelace, who stood shak-ing all the while, was took prisoner." The latter story would fit in well with the entry in the register.

Had all the discontented lieges of King James, who after weeks of waiting for the "Protestant wind" were now flocking to the west to join the standard of his rival, been stopped as easily as Lovelace, matters would have gone hard with the invader; but he soon found himself in a position to threaten to burn Badminton to the ground, if his eager partisan were not forthwith set at liberty; and Lovelace was soon again on his march through the Cotswold at the head of a larger following than before. On the fifth of December he entered Oxford in triumph.

As for the worthy townsfolk of Ciceter, they had had the terror of the Duke and his militia before their eyes, but I suspect that if they had had the courage of their opinions they would have risen in Lovelace's favour, and saved him his involuntary journey to Gloucester. The direction of their secret sympathies had probably little altered since they had felt the chastisement of Rupert and his cavaliers, but other days were now in store for them, and they were soon to fall under the aegis of a family that was to prove to them that Toryism and tyranny were by no means convertible terms.

The great house on the western extremity of the town had

been built by that Henry Danvers, Earl of Danby, whose name is associated with the Botanic Garden at Oxford. In 1695 it was purchased by Sir Benjamin Bathurst, the son of a Northamptonshire squire, who had lost six elder sons in the service of the King during the Civil War. When Sir Benjamin departed this life, in 1704, he was succeeded by his eldest son, the famous Lord Bathurst, whom we have already had occasion to mention.[1] In the course of a long life—he died in 1775, within a couple of months of his ninety-first birthday—this enterprising and energetic nobleman changed the whole face of the country. He enclosed, planted, transplanted, cut away a hill here and raised another there till he had turned into Oakley Park what was then open and uncultivated down. You may now walk, ride, drive,—anything but cycle, or motor,—for five miles on end through the centre of the Park from Ciceter to Saperton, or lose yourself amid innumerable glades, avenues, and by-paths which thread the woods in every direction.

To those who have never seen Ciceter and its Park, Lord Bathurst is best known as the friend of all the leading literary men of his day. A strong Tory, and interested in politics as in everything else, he never took a leading part in the affairs of State, but it is impossible to wade very far into the journals and correspondence of men of letters of the time without meeting with his name. He was on intimate terms with Congreve, Steel, Pope, Swift, Gay and Prior, and when all these had passed away he failed not to introduce himself to Sterne. "This nobleman," wrote the latter to a lady friend in 1767, "is a prodigy; for at eighty-five he has all the wit and promptness of a man of thirty; a disposition to be pleased, and a power to please others beyond whatever I knew; added to which a man of learning, courtesy and feeling." He lived to see his son made Lord Chancellor (a privilege which he is said to share only with the

---

[1] From a younger brother of Lord Bathurst is descended Bathurst of Lydney, another beautiful park in the Forest division of the same county.

father of Sir Thomas More), but the son was a man of a different mould. It is related that about two years before his death the old lord was sitting up late with a party of friends, whom he was entertaining round his hospitable table in the country. At length the Lord Chancellor, who had had enough of it, retired to bed with the remark that health and long life (he reached the age of eighty) were best secured by regularity. As he closed the door his father, whose convivial habits had certainly not brought him to an early tomb, turned to the company with a merry twinkle in his eye and said "Come, my good friends, since the old gentleman is gone to bed, I think we may venture to crack another bottle." [1]

Readers of Pope know that the poet was a frequent visitor at Oakley Park. His letters abound in allusions to his friend's plantings, buildings, and improvements; he had a retreat in the woods which he called his bower—rather a singular name if it is represented by the classic alcove now known as Pope's Seat. How he spent his time he tells his friends in a letter of October, 1718: "I am with Lord Bathurst, at my bower: in whose groves we had yesterday a dry walk of three hours. It is the place that of all others I fancy; and I am not yet out of humour with it, though I have had it some months: it does not cease to be agreeable to me so late in the season; the very dying of the leaves adds a variety of colours that is not unpleasant. . . . I write an hour or two every morning, then ride out a hunting upon the Downs, eat heartily, talk tender sentiments with Lord B., or draw plans for houses and gardens, open avenues, cut glades, plant firs, contrive waterworks, all very fine and beautiful in our own imagination. At night we play at commerce, and play pretty high; I do more, I bett too; for I am really rich, and must throw away my

---

[1] In Elwin and Courthope's Pope (vol. iii. p. 148) this story is fathered upon Sterne; but Sterne died in 1768, and had therefore been in his grave four or five years at the time when the incident is represented as taking place.

money if no deserving friend will use it." An extract from the letter of another visitor will help us to realise the curiosity which Lord Bathurst's hobby excited in his contemporaries. This time the writer is a lady, Mrs. Pendarves, better known by the name of her second husband as Mrs. Delany. "A few days before I had your last letter," she wrote to Swift, in 1733, "my sister and I made a visit to my lord and lady Bathurst at Cirencester. Oakly wood joins to his park; the grand avenue that goes from his house through his park and wood is five miles long; the whole contains five thousand acres. We staid there a day and a half; the wood is extremely improved since you saw it; when the whole design is executed, it will be one of the finest places in England. My lord Bathurst talked with great delight of the pleasure you once gave him by surprising him in his wood, and showed me the house where you lodged. It has been rebuilt; for the day you left it, it fell to the ground; conscious of the honour it had received by entertaining so illustrious a guest, it burst with pride. My lord Bathurst has greatly improved the wood house, which you may remember but a cottage, not a bit better than an Irish cabin. It is now a venerable castle and has been taken by an antiquarian [?] for one of King Arthur's, 'with thicket overgrown grotesque and wild.' I endeavoured to sketch it out for you; but I have not skill enough to do it justice. My lord Bathurst was in great spirits; and though surrounded by candidates and voters against next parliament, made himself agreeable in spite of their clamour."

I have chosen to linger over this most amiable man, as Burke calls him in a famous passage, not only because he is one of the most interesting figures among the lesser lights of his generation, but because his devotion to rural pursuits gives him an especial claim to the notice of readers of a series like the present. "A rich man, furnished with ability, living peaceably in his habitation," he was the first landowner in the hills to set the example of enclosures and the new system of agriculture, which his neighbours so tardily followed. Thus to his initiative may be

ultimately ascribed that great change in the whole face of the
Cotswold, to which I have more than once alluded—a change
which, though too often at the cost of sacrificing natural beauty,
contributed for at least a century to the increase of the national
wealth.   Agriculture, however, even in the Cotswold, is not
what it was; though the dismal picture set before us in
the second of the two passages, which may appropriately conclude this chapter, is, I am glad to say, still very far from being
realised.

The graceful compliment to Lord Bathurst in the first
passage receives a tinge of gloom it is true in the second ; but
here the argument is not original.   Pope is here the professed
imitator of the elder poet, and his business was to make the
most telling application he could of the sentiments prescribed
to him.

> " His father's acres who enjoys in peace,
> Or makes his neighbours glad, if he increase :
> Whose cheerful tenants bless their yearly toil,
> Yet to their lord owe more than to the soil ;
> Whose ample lawns are not ashamed to feed
> The milky heifer and deserving steed ;
> Whose rising forests, not for pride or show,
> But future buildings, future navies, grow ;
> Let his plantations stretch from down to down,
> First shade a country, and then raise a town."
>
> Moral Essays, Ep. iv. (1731).

> " All vast possessions (just the same the case
> Whether you call them villa, park, or chase)
> Alas, my Bathurst ! what will they avail ?
> Join Cotswold Hills to Saperton's fair dale,
> Let rising granaries and temples here,
> There mingled farms and pyramids appear,
> Link towns to towns with avenues of oak,
> Enclose whole downs in walls,—'tis all a joke !
> Inexorable Death shall level all,
> And trees, and stones, and farms, and farmer fall."
>
> Imitations of Horace Bk. ii. Ep. ii. (1737).

Shipton Court before the recent Restoration.

CHAPTER XV

SEVEN miles over the hills from Churn to Coln, and ten from
Coln to Windrush—such is the bracing ride before us this morning. After last night's frost the mid-October sun is already high
above the broad acres of stubble and dew-drenched down, as
we quit the capital of the Cotswold by the eastern gate, and set
our faces towards Bibury and Burford. The tall hedges are
festooned with silvery wreaths of Traveller's Joy, and trees and
hedgerow alike are fast assuming all the varied hues of autumn,
the pale yellow of the ash, the deeper yellow of the elm, the
rich brown of the oak, and the fiery red of the beech. Three
miles out we diverge from the line of Akeman Street which
we have hitherto followed, and passing through Barnsley cross
the Coln at Bibury bridge. As we ascend the hill beyond, we take
our last look at Bibury Court and church, and soon cross the
infant Leach, where it comes down from Northleach, and
Lord Sherborne's hunting Park, to find its way through the
Keble country to the Thames at Lechlade. A mile further the
lonely village of Aldsworth lies on the hillside to our left.
Aldsworth is certainly one of the places where farming still
flourishes ; I doubt if it contains a single inhabitant who is not
in some way connected with the rearing of sheep or the tillage

A A

of the soil.   Resident parson it has none, and has not had for
years : at present he comes from Fairford, six miles to the south,
and formerly he came from Turkdean, six miles away to the
north.   This was a perilous journey in those days, up hill and
down dale, and not one to be lightly undertaken in bad weather :
the oldest inhabitant will tell you how it was the custom to post
a sentinel at a window in the church tower with his eye fixed
upon the ridge that bounds the northern horizon.   If he
descried Turkdean parson's gig outlined upon the summit, he
gave the signal, and the bell was rung for service : if no gig
appeared, the villagers for that Sunday went without their service.
It is only fair to add that there is no danger of such a deficiency
in future, for a vicarage house is now being built, and Aldsworth
will soon have its vicar resident in its midst.

From a notice affixed to the church door it may be inferred
that with some of the inhabitants it is a custom to leave the
church before the conclusion of the service, to the disturbance
of the rest of the congregation.   Perhaps this is a survival from
the days when the services were so irregular ; but matters must
have been much worse in the seventeenth century, if anything
like the same state of things prevailed here as at Ciceter,
where it was found necessary to fence off the west end
of the church by closing the aisles with strong spiked gates,
which were opened only for the admission of the respectable
part of the community, while the space without was the
resort of idlers, dogs, and children.   It was the duty of one of
the officials to keep order among this unruly assemblage, but
he found the task a hard one, and in 1641 it was ordered that
in consequence of the continuance of "divers abuses in the
church by unruly boys and children making a noise in the
time of divine service and sermons, to the great disturbance of
the minister and congregation" the sexton should "henceforth
walk about in the church and see a reformacion therein, and if
he find them unruly shall pen them in the vestry or belfry
until sermon be ended, that they may have such correction

for their fault as shall be thought fit by some of the best of the inhabitants."

Aldsworth church occupies a commanding position at one extremity of the village, and three centuries of neglect and defacement have hardly succeeded in obliterating all its interesting features; witness the quaint grotesques on the north side of the body of the church, with the richly ornamented corner buttress, and the tower with its short broach spire, which some genius with a nautical turn of mind has attempted to set off with four stiff ugly pinnacles, for all the world like miniature lighthouses. The visitor had better not inspect the interior, unless he wishes to see what the churchwardens a few generations back could do.

Just below the church is a beautiful old house, surrounded by a pleasant garden. It looks as if it ought to be the parsonage, and perhaps it once was. At any rate it is here that we have borrowed the church key, and after calling to return it, we may regain the high road by the drive. On the south side of the road, at the fifth milestone from Burford, you will find "Bibury Race Course" with its "Grand Stand" marked in the old ordnance map. It has disappeared from the new survey, and few traces of it are now to be seen—yet here it was that the once famous Bibury Club held their race meetings down to the middle of the last century. This club seems to have been formed when the enclosures of 1775 put a stop to the races which had long been held on Upton Downs a few miles nearer Burford. The palmy days of the Bibury Club were those of a hundred years ago, when the races were patronised by the first gentleman in Europe. In Nimrod's *Life of a Sportsman* may be seen a coloured plate of the course, with his Royal Highness, mounted on his favourite crop-eared cob, receiving the salutes of the leading members of the club. The Prince himself stayed at Sherborne, but every spare bed in Bibury and Burford (the course is exactly half way between these two

A A 2

places) was occupied by the multitude of visitors who crowded
to the sports. The Oxford man would hire a tandem and drive
over for the day, and to ensure his getting back to College the
same night would send on a pair of fresh horses for the return
journey. If, like Nimrod's hero and his friend, he had sat
too long over the bottle at Burford the consequences were
apt to be disastrous.

As for the earlier Burford races, like Dover's meeting at
Campden, they appear to have grown out of the Whitsuntide
merrymaking. At least as early as 1676 they had become an
annual affair. Nor did they by any means stand alone ; the open
downs afforded many a good stretch of galloping ground, and
where this was within easy reach of a town, as at North Cerney
and Baunton near Ciceter, horse racing was sure to become
popular. Charles II. twice visited Burford. The second
occasion was in March, 1681, during the session of the Oxford Parliament, when the King found it convenient to have
the Newmarket Royal Plate run for at Burford, thus anticipating for once the date of the regular meeting. The account of his
Majesty's two days' jaunt, given by a contemporary print, is
particularly interesting as illustrating the sporting possibilities
of a county still unenclosed. At six o'clock on the morning of
the 17th the King left Oxford for Witney in his coach. There
he mounted a horse which was in readiness, and rode hawking
across the downs to Burford. Here he was met by the Corporation and presented with a rich silver-laced saddle with
holsters and bridle "worth about fifty guineas." Then after
dining with Squire Lenthall at the Priory, he attended the races,
and when they were over he proceeded to Cornbury Park,
where he spent the night as the guest of Lord Clarendon.
After dinner the next day, he took horse and hawked across
the country through Wychwood Forest to "Woodstock plain,"—
Campsfield that is, where his coach met him and brought him
back to Oxford. It had of old been a common practice to
carry a hawk on a long cross-country journey, which might

be flown at any chance game that the rider put up. Even
long business journeys were beguiled in this fashion; Richard
Cely, for instance, the wool merchant, would ride down to
Gloucestershire with his hawk on wrist, and if he could bring a
fairly furnished game bag to his inn, his victualler's bill would
be so much diminished.

It is just on the site of the old race-course that our road
enters Oxfordshire, and joins the road from Gloucester and
Cheltenham. If we keep to the left down the hill we shall
enter Burford in the centre of the town, but the more impressive entrance is accomplished by keeping to the main road for
another mile, and coming down upon the town from above.
The scene which then presents itself will be our reward.
The great wide street flanked by its line of houses on either
side, a line broken by every kind of irregularity, descends
sharply to the river.   Facing us at the bottom is a
picturesque gabled dwelling, towards which the lines of the
street seem to converge, while beyond the river the eye rests on
the green slopes and copses of Shipton Downs. Burford is
fortunate in having escaped the invasion of the railway. It is
still one of those places which cannot be reached without the
expenditure of some time and trouble, and there is therefore all
the more satisfaction in accomplishing the journey. It remains
exclusive, select, aristocratic; your visit is an honour—to yourself. It is a real pleasure to reflect upon the fate which this
venerable town has escaped. With the whistle of the steam
engine, with signal boxes, telegraph poles, and the inevitable
red-brick suburb that springs up around a railway station, all
the old-world charm of one of the most beautiful spots in the
pleasant windings of the Windrush would have been annihilated.
For it must be remembered that in this narrow valley, unlike
the low, flat plains through which the Witney line runs, there
is no room for a railway to be lost; its presence must always
be obtrusive, and impossible to ignore. As it is, the stranger
who lumbers over the rampart of the downs in the toiling

omnibus from the station, five or six miles away, may still feel something of the joy of the traveller of old, who, after a long and weary journey over the hills at last descended into the warm and hospitable town, a haven of refuge doubly welcome from the contrast it presented to the bleak, inhospitable wolds.

Little is to be gained by a comparison between the High Streets of Burford and Campden; each is perfect in its own way, and each deserves its tribute of admiration. Campden is reserved, sedate, uneccentric; Burford homely, insinuating, full of surprises. As we descend the hill we may turn our backs upon the "classic" Wesleyan Chapel and devote ourselves to buildings of various styles from the fifteenth century downwards—notably the Tolsey (decorated of late with two stone chimneys, tall, unhappy-looking, and ill-sorted), the "George," where King Charles slept on his return from the memorable dash from Oxford mentioned in an earlier chapter, and the "Old Bear."

Now turn to the left near the bottom of the street, pass through a clumsy door in a high wall, and we are confronted with a melancholy spectacle. This dilapidated structure, with its crumbling and ruinous façade, is all that is left of the once splendid Elizabethan mansion known to all the region round about as Burford Priory. Much of the old house was pulled down and the rest remodelled early in the last century, but its lease of prosperity in its altered shape was a short one: in 1829 it passed out of the hands of the family which had lived in it for two hundred years; and, dismantled and neglected by its new owner, it has ever since been falling gradually to decay. In fact, it would be hardly worth while our turning aside to visit it were it not for the fact that it is intimately associated with one of the most fascinating personalities of his day, for here "probably"—(I dare not express myself with more certainty on this point than Dr. Gardiner)—in 1610 was born Lucius Cary, afterwards second Viscount Falkland. At any rate, the Priory was at this time the property of his

maternal grandfather, Laurence Tanfield, who was Lord of the
Manor of Burford, and also of the manor of Great Tew, both
of which estates he bequeathed to his grandson. He was a
distinguished lawyer, and when he died in 1625 he had been
Lord Chief Baron of the Exchequer for nearly twenty years:
his widow, who had a life interest in the property, died
four years later, and thus before he came of age the young
Lucius Cary found himself .the master of two country
houses of the first rank not more than fifteen miles distant
from one another. It is, however, with Great Tew that
Clarendon's famous passage has associated him, and there we
shall return to him. Burford Priory, where much of his
childhood had been spent, he found it expedient to part with,
and in 1636 he sold it to William Lenthall, afterwards Speaker
of the Long Parliament, who had already purchased the manor
of Besselsleigh, on the Berkshire side of Oxford, where his
descendants still reside. It was he who built the Priory
chapel, "a most elegant piece," as Bishop Skinner, who
consecrated it after the Restoration, described it. When the
house passed out of the hands of the Lenthalls, in 1829, this
chapel had already been disused for many years. The family
reached their pew, which was situated over the entrance, by
passing over the leads of the cloister connecting the
chapel with the house, but the pew is now gone and the whole
chapel stands empty. The elaborate plaster ceiling has
disappeared, and the only ornamentation that remains is a curious
piece of carving representing the Burning Bush, flanked on
either side by an angel, immediately over the doorway. A few
years ago there was every probability that this interesting
example of seventeenth century Gothic would soon become a
heap of ruins, but measures have lately been taken to arrest
the progress of decay: the shrubs which had forced their
way up through the floor have been cleared away, the roof has
been made secure, and the windows, which remind one of
those in Wadham College hall, have been reglazed.

Burford Priory derives its name from a Hospital or Priory of
St. John the Evangelist, of the history of which nothing is
known, except that the appointment of the Master or Prior
was in the hands of the Corporation of the town. This
appears from a letter of Warwick, the Kingmaker, to the
Bailiffs and Burgesses, requesting that the post may be given
to one of his chaplains. Warwick, in right of his wife, was
Lord of the Manor of Burford, and among the Corporation
records is a deed containing one of the two autograph
signatures of his known to exist, in which he grants a piece of
land to the town for the erection of almshouses. These
almshouses still remain on the same site, but were rebuilt in
1828. The said Corporation or Guild was extinguished in
1862 ; it was one of the oldest in the kingdom, and consisted
of an alderman and ten burgesses, who annually elected two
bailiffs out of their own body. Readers of Mr. Hutton's
By Thames and Cotswold will remember some queer stories of
its later history.

Burford is not like a city set upon a hill ; it is not a place
that forces itself upon the traveller's notice. Here and there,
rising behind some projecting shoulder of the hills, he may
catch sight of a grey church spire, dimly outlined it may be in
the evening mists, and may say to himself "that is Burford,"
but there is nothing else to reveal the whereabouts of the
modest little town. And this far off glimpse will hardly
prepare him for the sight that awaits him when, after
threading his way past Simon Wisdom's Grammar School and
Warwick's Almshouses, he suddenly finds himself face to face
with the imposing south façade of one of the largest and most
splendid of the great churches of Oxfordshire. The massive
Norman central tower shows that it must have been a church
of more than ordinary rank from the first. Its architectural
history has never been written, but I suspect that it was
originally a plain cruciform building, which many subsequent
alterations and additions have transformed into the stately

Burford Church.

fabric which we now behold. Its details are too numerous and too interesting to be entered upon in such a discursive volume as this, but it may be permissible to express a wish that the hand of the restorer had been stayed for another score of years, for it is upon record that the alterations going on under the name of restoration, in 1876, roused the horror of William Morris, and constituted one of the displays of unwisdom which immediately led him to found the Society for the Protection of Ancient Buildings, or, in more familiar language, the "Anti-Scrape Society."

The most splendid sepulchral monument in the church is that of the Lord Chief Baron, whom, according to Dr. Robert Plot, the author of *The Natural History of Oxfordshire*, the citizens of Burford had no reason to love : it was through his agency, he says, that they lost most of the privileges which were theirs by Royal grant, and which made them the equals of the burgesses of the county town. We shall see presently that at his other manor of Great Tew, as well as here, my lord judge was not particularly popular, but there was no doubt another side to the story, in the absence of which we may be content to suspend our judgment. At any rate, as he lies here in his judicial ermine and collar of SS, serious, dignified, and composed, he may command a tribute of respect. His wife, who erected the tomb and provided funds to keep it in repair, lies by his side : at the head kneels their daughter, the accomplished and saintly Elizabeth, Viscountess Falkland, whose papistical tendencies (she ultimately declared her conversion to the Romish church) are said to have been looked upon with much disfavour by her father ; and at the foot, clad in armour, Lucius Cary, Elizabeth's illustrious son. An inscription beneath the kneeling figure of Lady Falkland seems to suggest that the Chief Baron's merits were such as to entitle him to a place of sepulture at Westminster :

> " Pitty his memory ingaged should stand
> Unto a private church, not to the land."

Posterity will judge otherwise, and will reflect that his memory has a far better chance of immortality in the quiet country church. A few years after the erection of the monument, Burford was visited by a tourist—the tourist in those days was a *rara avis*—who did not fail to inspect the church and its treasures. His attention was naturally attracted by the Tanfield monument, and he noted in his journal the names of the figures represented thereupon: he has also recorded that one of them was not seen by him in effigy only, for the Lord Viscount Falkland (as he then was) happened to be present in the church at the time "in his own proper personage" together with "his Lady." The tomb was at that time hung with heraldic banners, but, in June, 1644, when Essex halted for a day or two in the town, in the vain pursuit of the King, his soldiers tore them down and made them into scarfs.

We may now turn to a series of memorials of a very different order. Three arches in the south-western extremity of the church open into a building, which was formerly a chapel dedicated to our Lady. After the Reformation its liturgical use was discontinued, and it was appropriated as a place of sepulture by one of the leading mercantile families in the town, and since then it has been generally styled the Sylvester aisle.

The history of the Sylvesters is that of the typical English tradesman of the middle class. Unlike the Tanfields, whose glory shone upon the town for some fifty years, and was then extinguished for ever, they have been a familiar name in Burford for at least four centuries. As clothiers, mercers, vintners, tanners, and even as surgeons and apothecaries, they carried on a thriving business from generation to generation: they repeatedly filled the office of bailiff, and when the Civil War broke out, and the King had to appeal to the generosity of his loyal subjects of Burford, it was a Sylvester who contributed the largest amount.[1] The first mention of the name which I have noticed

[1] £77, equivalent to about £1,150 of our money.

is in a deed of 1512, when Agnes Stodham conveyed to four
burgesses of Burford a rent from her tenement in High Street,
"now inhabited by Robert Silvester," for the purpose of keeping an annual obit in the church on Trinity Monday. How
much earlier the family had been reckoned among the citizens
I cannot say, but it is only in this present year (1904) that it
has become extinct on the death of the last survivor, and the
estate sold.[1]

The monuments in the Sylvester aisle have no pretensions to
artistic beauty, but the series of six plain altar-tombs, with their
conventional ornaments and merchants' marks, bear witness to
the former prestige of the family. The earliest, dated 1568,
bears the woolman's mark, already so familiar to us from the
brasses at Campden and Northleach, while others display
the arms of the Vintners' Company, and those of the Barber
Surgeons. But even in so spacious a chapel as the Sylvester
aisle, the space available for altar-tombs is limited, and after
the middle of the seventeenth century their place is taken by
mural tablets, dating from 1659 to the present day. It is,
moreover, not difficult to guess that the family fortunes suffered
a severe blow from the Civil War, and there is little likelihood
that either Thomas Sylvester or his descendants ever saw again
a single penny of the large sum he had advanced to the support
of the Royal cause. There was therefore less money available
for pious uses, and the more costly monument had to give way
to the simpler tablet. In connection with these tablets, it
may be worth while to notice that they exemplify, what is so
often to be seen in churchyards, the deterioration of the style
of lettering after the middle of the eighteenth century ; let
the visitor compare the tablet of 1753 with that of 1782, and he
will appreciate the difference.

The Sylvester aisle is connected, as we shall see directly, with

---

[1] A branch which parted from the main stock in the seventeenth century
still flourishes in Wiltshire, and Joseph Hunter conjectured that the
Sylvesters, of Mansfield, in Nottinghamshire, were another offshoot.

one of the two events, separated by the long interval of nine
hundred years, which have given Burford a place in the history
of England. The first was the battle fought between the rival
kingdoms of Wessex and Mercia, and its traditional site is on
the ridge to the south-west of the town, now traversed by the
Cheltenham road. Here Cuthred, King of Wessex, carrying the
war into the enemy's territory, gave Ethelbald of Mercia the
defeat which brought his victorious career to a close. This was
in 752 : but more than a hundred years before this date the
Mercian frontier had been advanced to the Thames, a frontier
which was once more secured by the victory of Offa at Bensing-
ton twenty years after it. Still, for the moment, the pride of
Mercia was humbled, and for many centuries, as each Midsummer eve came round, the people of Burford were wont to carry
through the streets of their town the painted figure of a
dragon, commemorating the signal victory of the Golden Dragon
of Wessex.

It is a far cry from the struggles of Mercians and Saxons to
the May morning of the eventful year 1649, when four hundred
mutineers stood upon the leads of the Sylvester aisle to witness
the execution of their ringleaders in the churchyard below.
Dissatisfaction with the new regime had broken out in several
regiments. The monarchy was abolished, but a form of government no less tyrannical appeared to have taken its place :
King Log had only been exchanged for King Ox. John
Lilburne, the leader of the malcontents, was in prison, but his
democratic doctrines had spread far and wide, and among
others Colonel Adrian Scrope's regiment at Salisbury had raised
the standard of revolt. Hoping to effect a junction with other
discontented regiments, the mutineers marched northwards to
the Thames. Unable to cross at Newbridge, which they found
too securely guarded, they swam the stripling river a few miles
higher up, and marched through Bampton-in-the-Bush and
Norton Brize to Burford. Here they thought themselves
secure enough to make a halt, and accordingly they took up

their quarters for the night in the town and some of the neighbouring villages. But their slumbers were soon to be disturbed. When the news of the outbreak reached London, Lord General Fairfax and Lieutenant General Cromwell had already set out for Salisbury. At Andover they received intelligence of the northward movement of the rebels, and at once started in pursuit. By a rapid march through Theale and Abingdon they crossed the Thames at Newbridge and reached Burford at midnight. The mutineers, summoned to surrender, made but a brief resistance. A large number effected their escape, but about four hundred gave themselves up and were secured in the church. Next morning a court-martial dealt summary justice : a cornet and two corporals were placed against the churchyard wall and shot, while their comrades were placed on the roof of the Sylvester aisle to learn a salutary lesson from the spectacle. Then Cromwell called them down into the church, and told them that though they well deserved to be decimated, the Lord General in his mercy had pardoned them all. Such was the end of the Levellers and the Levelling movement. On the lead of the font, rudely cut with a dagger, you may still read the words " Anthony Sedley Prisner 1649."

We leave Burford by Witney Street, and declining the ascent to the Oxford road, keep to the by-road in the valley. Through the wide green meadow land, dotted here and there with elm and willow, the Windrush holds its devious course past three of the most primitive villages in Oxfordshire, Swinbrook, Asthall, and Minster Lovel ; and first for Swinbrook. Cross the old stone bridge by the mill, and you are soon in the midst of this old-world village. The church which stands upon the highest ground strikes you as remarkably tall for its length, but you soon realise that this effect is due to the clerestory, which has been carried up above the original Norman nave. The tower is small, and has been run up through the west end of the church, but there is a large transomed Perpendicular window which fills the whole of the east end. To the south and south-

west of the church you may see all that is left—a few remnants
of terraces, fish-ponds, and out-houses—of what was, only a
century ago, a manor-house of the first rank.   Here the Fettiplaces, a family of great wealth and great connections both in
Oxfordshire and Berkshire, reigned for three hundred years.
The house which they built when quiet times returned after
Bosworth Field, and when the star of their powerful neighbours
at Minster had already set, must have rivalled any mansion of
its date in the county, and its panelled hall, with its windows
filled with heraldic shields, was the pride of its owners and the
delight of the antiquary.   Now, alas! not one stone remains
upon another, and it has taken its place among those desolate
sites, of which I could count some half-dozen in Oxfordshire
alone, where nothing but grassy mounds and hollows, and perhaps a venerable length of mouldering garden-wall, remains to
tell the tale of its former greatness.   But though the Fettiplaces
and the house that they built have vanished for ever from mortal
ken, their memory is still fresh in Swinbrook.   First there are their
charities, for the good they did is *not* interred with their bones,
including a dole of bread to the poor, and seven green coats (at
least, this was so in Skelton's time, 1823) annually distributed to
seven poor men, not to mention the privilege of sending two
poor boys to Christ's Hospital—and secondly there are their
monuments.   Enter the church and walk straight up to the
chancel : first look at the brasses on the floor (you may as well
be chronological) and then face north and admire the
economy of monumental space.   No room in this modest
chancel for a series of altar tombs such as larger churches boast,
yet here no less than six Fettiplaces recline in effigy, by means
of the simple device of placing them on shelves one above the
other.   There are two alcoves, if I may so term them, placed
side by side, each containing three shelves.   Now it is obvious
that the ordinary supine position would be impossible in such
an arrangement ; the figures therefore recline on the right side,
and gaze placidly (for their eyes are open) into space.   The

three figures in the western alcove, Alexander, William, and Edmund I., are of Tudor date, and have the head supported by the right arm, the elbow resting on a cushion, and their whole pose is somewhat stiff and conventional; the three in the eastern alcove, on the other hand, John I., John II., and Edmund II., which belong to Stuart times, are represented in an easier attitude; the body is supported by the right fore-arm, the head is slightly raised and the left knee bent, as if they were ready to spring up into life at a moment's notice, and only waited for the signal.

To turn from the contemplation of these ingenious monuments to the bust on the opposite side of the chancel is to come back to the everyday world. This represents Sir George Fettiplace, who died in 1743, the last of the line in direct male descent. The estate then passed to the children of his sisters, who assumed the family name, and when Richard Fettiplace died in 1806 the property was divided among his sisters. About this time the manor-house was let to a "Mr. Freeman from London," of whom the writer of a pleasant paper on the Lower Windrush Valley, in a recent number of the *Oxford Magazine*, gives the following account: of Mr. Freeman "no one knew anything, but . . . . references were waived, in consideration of his pleasant habit of paying down unending guineas in advance when called upon for security. He came down with a train of servants, and made himself at home in the neighbourhood by his open-handed hospitality. Soon after his arrival the 'holding-up' of coaches, and more commonplace highway robberies, became frequent on the London-Gloucester, London-Banbury, and London-Worcester roads; they never took place within ten miles of Swinbrook, but always far afield, and were accomplished sometimes by a single rider, sometimes by a gang of four. For a year the countryside was terrorised, till a shot from a well-guarded coach killed one of the robbers, who was identified, to the general surprise, as the wealthy Mr. Freeman's butler. He and his household were then arrested, and found to be well-known highwaymen who had made the Home Counties too hot for them, and then had moved to the West."

Close behind the church to the north stands a delightful old rambling farm-house, with a long sloping roof of exquisite colour, and its front covered with a wealth of creepers. Past the side of this an old road, at one point always covered for some distance by a running brook, leads through some charming out-lying patches of Wychwood to the top of Shipton Down, whence you may, if you are disposed, soon descend to Shipton village; but this is not our way to-day. We recross the river at Swinbrook mill, and continuing our journey down the valley soon arrive at our second village, Asthall. Few are the houses of Asthall— the bulk of the population of the parish lives a couple of miles away at the hamlet of Asthall Leigh—but its fine Elizabethan manor-house, its interesting church, and its lovely situation on a hillock rising above the river, combine to make it one of those places that dwell in the memory.

The gabled front of the manor-house rises immediately on the west of the church, and the two together make a delightful picture. On entering the church one is shocked to find that the effect is spoilt by the detestable " cathedral glass," and one longs to throw every door wide open and break every window to get rid of the prison-like feeling that it causes. It would be unwise, however, to run the risk of a prosecution for sacri-lege, so we console ourselves with the beauty of the details, the fine Transition-Norman chancel-arch with its birdsbeak mouldings, the Early English windows with the sills formed into seats, and above all the splendid chapel on the north, the roof of which towers above nave and chancel, and has a most striking effect when viewed from outside. This chapel takes us back to the story of Hayles Abbey and the Holy Blood, for the manor of Asthall was once the possession of Edmund, Earl of Cornwall, the son of the King of the Romans. When Edmund died in 1300 without legitimate offspring, he be-queathed Asthall to his natural son Richard, who assumed the

B B

surname of Cornwall, and in his family it remained for several generations. The architectural style, which is that of the fourteenth century, suggests that it was this family which built the chapel; and under a rich crocketed canopy on its northern side lies a female effigy in the dress of that period, representing probably the wife of one of the Cornwalls of the day.

From Asthall, in a dry season, the pedestrian may make his way to Minster by the river side, but the cyclist must cross Asthall Bridge and ride up to Asthall Leigh, whence he will

Asthall.

descend to the village by a road which commands a charming view of the valley and crosses the stream at Minster Bridge to join the main highway. Below the bridge the Windrush flows past the church and the ruins of the manor-house, which together form a striking picture when viewed from the high road —a picture the beauty of which is vividly enhanced by its setting of lofty trees, green meadow, and sparkling river.

As for the ruins, they are infinitely more attractive from a distance than when you are standing in the midst of them. For the last hundred and fifty years or more they have been abandoned to the ravages of man and beast. What man

and beast have spared has been seized upon by vegetable
foes, nettles, brambles, elder and the all-mastering ivy—in fact,
but for the solid strength of the original masonry, the whole
must long ago have become a shapeless heap of stones.   The
place was built, they say, by William, eleventh Baron Lovel, who
had served in France, but died before the struggle between York
and Lancaster began.   His son John, who sleeps beneath the
church tower, cut in alabaster, deserted the failing cause of Lancaster to greet the rising sun, and dying at the early age of thirty-
two, his honours passed to his son Francis, thirteenth Baron and
first Viscount Lovel.   Francis, at any rate, was a consistent
Yorkist.   He fought on the losing side at Bosworth, fled to
Flanders, and returned to take part in the attempt of Lambert
Simnel ; he was last seen swimming his horse across the Trent
after the battle of Stoke, in 1487, so says one account ; others say
he was slain in the field.   The story that he made his way home
to Minster, and perished of starvation, imprisoned in a secret
chamber, owing to the death of the attendant who supplied him
with food, is not heard of till the middle of the eighteenth
century, and, on the face of things, is extremely improbable.   If
he really escaped alive from Stoke, his confiscated Oxfordshire
home is the last place he would have made for, even if the
ports were then so well watched that a second flight to the
Continent was impossible.   But the story is a good one none
the less, and some of us may remember being fascinated by it
when we first met with it years ago in *Mrs. Markham*, or *The
Student's Hume*.

It is with a feeling of relief that we quit these *loca senta
situ* for the beautiful and well-preserved church—its plan cruciform, and its peculiar feature a central tower much smaller than
the square formed by the junction of the transepts with the
body of the church.   Hence the tower is mainly supported by
four detached piers, each of which, with the corresponding
angle of the transept, forms a diagonal archway—an arrangement difficult to describe on paper, but which a glance at

B B 2

Skelton's engraving of the interior of the church will render intelligible. The church is wholly Perpendicular, and must have been built in the middle of the fifteenth century, about the same time as the manor-house. It probably occupies the site of an earlier church, of which no traces remain above ground, and of which no written record has been discovered. How the place got the name of Minster if the church of some monastic society did not exist here, it would be difficult to say; but if it did exist, nothing further is known of it. What is known is that in John's reign, by the gift of Maud, the wife of William Lovel, the church became a cell to the French abbey of Ivry, that the administration of the revenues of this cell were transferred by Edward III. from the abbey to nominees of his own, that when alien priories were dissolved by Henry V. these revenues became Crown property, and that finally they were granted by Henry VI. to Eton College, in whose hands the advowson has ever since remained.

We must by no means leave the church without examining the beautiful monument of John, twelfth Lord Lovel, already alluded to. Richard Symonds, who served in the royal army during a portion of the Civil War, and who kept a diary of its marches, printed long ago by the Camden Society, was a young man of antiquarian tastes. He seized every opportunity of visiting the churches he passed by, and studying their points of interest, notes of which he regularly set down in his journal. He seems to have been particularly struck by the Lovel monument, and writes under date, June 18, 1644: "After his Majestie had beene at church [at Burford] and heard the sermon and dyned [at the "George"] he marched five myles to Witney that night. Two myle short of Witney, on the left hand as wee come from Burford, stands Minster Lovel, an ancient howse of the Lord Lovel, worth seeing." He then goes on to describe the heraldic devices in the church, and especially the monument, with its armorial shields. Even then

Minster Lovel. Dovecot.

the latter were not all perfect, and as they now exist they are due to restoration. This restoration took place about forty years ago at the expense of the Earl of Egmont, a collateral descendant of the Lovels. Owing to the sinking of one end of the tomb the figure had been broken across, and the whole monument was sent up to London, its defects repaired and the shields re-tricked—not without leaving some ground for subsequent criticism. Another interesting monument is the brass in the north transept to John Vampage, attorney in the King's cases ; in 1466 John Carpenter, Bishop of Worcester, appears as one of the executors of his will, and he seems to have died at Minster when taking over the Lovel estates as King's Commissioner during the minority of Francis Lovel.

Our route now takes us northward to Wychwood, and in three miles we reach Leafield, a modern parish, formed out of Shipton when the forest was enclosed. The village lies high just outside the southern limits of the forest, and the spire of the modern church is a conspicuous landmark for many miles round ; but there is not much to detain us except an ancient cross on the green "restored by the inhabitants as a memorial of their deliverance from the scourge of small pox" in 1873. We therefore turn to the left soon after passing the church, and follow the road right through the centre of the ancient forest. But this deserves another chapter.

CHAPTER XVI

TIME was when Wychwood Forest was a favourite resort of "Oxford riders blythe." It was not near enough for an ordinary afternoon's exercise, and not too far for a long day's excursion in summer term. On a saint's day when there were no lectures—such was the pleasant privilege of those times—a party would hire horses at Symonds's, in Holywell, where it will be remembered that Mr. Charles Larkyns was accustomed to stable his hack, and sally forth either by way of Bablock Hythe or Swinford Bridge for Witney, and thence through Leafield to Wychwood. After exploring the recesses of the forest, with eye and ear alert for all the woodland sights and sounds, they would ride back to dine at Witney off eels fresh from the Windrush, with piles of strawberries and a bottle of passable port (for whiskies and sodas as yet were not) for dessert. Then, when the sun had dropped behind Wytham woods, and the voice of Tom came booming across Botley meadows, they would ride slowly home. But those days are gone. The Scholar-Gipsy, if he still haunts the warm green-muffled Cumner hills, will look in vain for them now. Oxford had not then, as a sportsman of the old school racily puts it, become a "Dame school."

Be it also said that Wychwood had not then shrunk to its present circumscribed proportions. The change began as long ago as 1853: in that year it changed its legal status of forest for that of ordinary land, and ten years later the enclosures began. The old assarts, or clearances, had been few and strictly limited : now hundreds of trees were felled, and hundreds of acres of heath and copse were grubbed up and brought under the plough. Perhaps the best way to get a general idea of the extent to which modern clearances have reached is to compare the old Ordnance Survey with the new. In the older map it will be seen that the forest extends in an unbroken line from Capp's Lodge, a mile north-east of Swinbrook, to Charlbury : in the later one, the edge of the woodland is not reached till you have passed Leafield. Under the old system Wychwood was a royal forest, and was managed by a ranger, who resided at the Ranger's Lodge, which we pass on the left shortly before we reach the Burford and Charlbury road. When Arthur Young made his tour through Oxfordshire early in the last century, he found " the vicinity filled with poachers, deer-stealers, thieves, and pilferers of every kind "; these offenders, he declares, were a terror to the whole country-side, and he strongly advocated enclosure and cultivation. He was further influenced by the consideration of the amount of wheat the forest land might be made to yield : the " general benefit " of rendering " a large tract of good land productive to the public " far outweighed, he thought, any advantages to be derived from " the mere pleasure of wandering." Well, those were the days of the French War, and the nation was almost wholly dependent upon home-grown supplies, so that Arthur Young's point of view can easily be understood. But in the twentieth century, when the greater part of our wheat comes from over the sea, the destruction of Wychwood can be regarded only as a national loss. Tracts of open unspoiled forest have now become so rare in England that, as in the case of Epping Forest, our instincts are to preserve rather than destroy. Nor have the results from the economic point of view by any means answered Arthur Young's expectations, and it is generally admitted that the land would be now far more remunerative if it had been left undisturbed in its original state.

It has been mentioned in a previous chapter that in early times Wychwood and Woodstock forests were practically one, and that an unbroken stretch of woodland extended from the Cotswold to the Glyme. Subsidiary to the manor-house of Woodstock the King had a hunting lodge at Langley, a mile or so to the west of Leafield. Hither, when the deer of Woodstock and Ditchley had been granted a well-deserved holiday, the Court were wont to remove to rouse the game on the western extremity of their preserves. A portion of this lodge still remains at the back of a very modern looking farm-house, and there are the initials "H" and "E" for Henry VII. and his Queen, Elizabeth of York, cut large upon the stone.

But the rule that the deer were royal game, and might be hunted only by kings and queens, or their deputies, admitted of one exception. Once a year, on Whitsunday, there was an open day, and the inhabitants of all the neighbouring towns and villages flocked in crowds to the forest to exercise their ancient privilege of hunting. No doubt the royal keepers were on the alert to see that the privilege was not abused, and that rules of venery were observed ; but we can easily imagine that differences of opinion between the gentlemen in Lincoln green and the sturdy " blanketers " from Witney, or burly saddlers from Burford, were not unknown. At any rate, an outbreak of the plague in 1593 gave the Crown an excuse for stopping the annual carnival in that year, under the plea that the assemblage of large crowds would only tend to spread the infection. What compensation the other towns received I have not discovered, but a letter from the Privy Council to the people of Burford still exists, promising that " order shalbe given to the keepers of the said forest to deliver unto you two buckes to be spent amongest you at your own disposicŏns ; besydes this your forbearinge for this tyme shall not be any prejudice to your said ancyent custome hereafter." Prejudice or no prejudice, however, the annual hunting was dropped, and another custom took its place. Every Whitsunday the townsfolk elected a boy and girl to be "Lord and Lady," and marched up in procession to Capp's Lodge, where the Lord and Lady demanded of the keepers a "brace of best bucks and a fawn, with their horns and hoofs, without fee or reward." These were duly sent to the town in the following August, and a great venison feast was held in the Town-hall to which all the townsfolk were admitted. The Whitsunday procession to Capp's Lodge died out in 1827, but the feast went on till Wychwood was disafforested and the deer killed off. The dole of venison was then compounded for by the donation of £150, which was devoted to one of the local charities.

Those who visit the distant Wychwood bowers in summer in search of the botanical treasures they contain, must consult Mr. Druce's *Flora of Oxfordshire;* I can only mention here the rare sage (*Salvia pratensis*), the bee orchis and the deadly nightshade, the bushes of which attain a huge size. On this October day we are too late for the flowers, but the many various hues of the autumn foliage, the bright scarlet of the berries, and the rich brown of the carpet of bracken are more than enough to make amends for their absence. Away through the glades to our right, forming the eastern portion of the existing forest, is Cornbury Park, with its fine seventeenth century mansion. "Procured of the King," as Wood phrases it, by the great Earl of Clarendon at the Restoration, it gave him his second title, and remained in his family till it was sold by his great-grandson to the third Duke of Marlborough in the middle of the eighteenth century. This was Pope's Lord Cornbury, long one of the members for Oxford University, and one of the leading spirits among the Jacobite party in the north of the county. On our left, situated at the very highest point of the forest, though, since the clearances, outside its actual boundary, and about a mile from Leafield, is the High Lodge,[1] now used as a farm-house. Here it was that, previous to the '45, the leading Jacobite gentry of the

---

[1] Not to be confused with the High Lodge in Blenheim Park.

neighbourhood, with Lord Cornbury at their head, used to hold their secret meetings, and usually in the night time. Such was the story that the keeper of the lodge told Dr. Brookes, who was Rector of Shipton from 1773 to 1813; and the Doctor himself, from his own recollections of this exciting time, used to declare that "so strong was the attachment of the great families about this part of Oxfordshire to the Stuart family, that if the Scotch had been able to push forward, and the French Court had sent an army as strong as that which accompanied King William, they would have thrown off the mask and taken up arms in their behalf." Another of his stories was that, on one of his secret visits to England between 1750 and 1760, the young Pretender came to stay with Lord Cornbury at the Park, and, owing to the extraordinary respect shown to him, and to a word incautiously let drop by Lord Cornbury, was recognised by a Charlbury barber, who had been called in to shave his Royal Highness and dress his wig. Mrs. Sturge Henderson, in her *Three Centuries in North Oxfordshire*, records that another Charlbury man, one Robert Spendlove, who died in 1822 at the age of 96, remembered carrying bread to the West of England insurgents, who were concealed for the night at Cornbury on their way home from the abortive march to Derby.

A couple of miles beyond the High Lodge we reach the Burford and Charlbury road, and, turning to the left, we have an easy run of four miles down to Shipton. At the "Crown" with its fine old archway and mullioned windows, the cyclist who has time to stay may find comfortable quarters, and there is much in Shipton to make it well worth his while; but I cannot tarry with him to-day, for I have six or seven miles of stiff up-hill work in order to gain Chipping Norton before nightfall. Again the high-road carries me along the ridge of the hills; on my left is the valley that parts me from Rollright and Chastleton; on my right the hollow beyond which rise the woods of Ditchley and of Heythrop.

Darkness is coming on apace as I enter the old hill-side town and take up my lodging for the night.

Chipping Norton, though holding the rank of the third town in the county, is little more than a name to the outside world. It lies on no great thoroughfare; it is true it has a railway station on the Banbury and Cheltenham line down at the bottom of the hill, but for every five hundred people who pass through the Junction, four miles away, I doubt if more than one passes through Chipping Norton itself. Formerly it was otherwise. The main road from London to Worcester runs through the town, and the main road from Oxford to Birmingham is only a mile to the north-east. The Birmingham coaches baited at Chapel House, of which we shall have more to say directly, but the Worcester coaches turned to the left a mile on the Oxford side of that famous hostelry, and finished their stage in Chipping Norton. Probably now, owing to the motor traffic, the old road is becoming rather more frequented, but half-a-dozen years back, if a man told you he had been to Chipping Norton, he was sure to have been a hunting man who had stayed there to hunt with the Heythrop.

Yet it is by no means a place without attractions of its own. It is a clean, comely, breezy place, with a long wide street carried along the slope of the hill, the result being that the houses on one side are at a much higher elevation than those on the other. Altogether it is quite the place to break the journey on a long cycling or driving tour, a place where there is not much to see, and consequently not much to distract you from the creature comforts of your inn. It is, too, quite an appropriate place for adventures, and if his stern sense of duty had ever taken Mr. Pickwick down to Worcester by the London mail, I am quite sure something very interesting would have happened at the inn at Chipping Norton.

I hope no patriotic citizen of Chipping Norton will look askance at me for saying that the visitor to the town will not be overwhelmed with sight-seeing. There is, of course, the cloth factory, and Chipping Norton tweeds have quite a local reputation; but to-day, when we have walked round the town and visited the church, we shall be ready to start on our return to Oxford. The church, which stands on the slope below the main street, is one of the finest in the county; but that has not saved it from a somewhat severe handling by the restorer. Its history, as far as it can be gathered from its present appearance, is not difficult to read. It appears to have been built in the Decorated style, and to have had its nave rebuilt and its splendid clerestory added in the fifteenth century. To show off this clerestory the roofs of the aisles and chancel appear to have been lowered, with the result that the beautiful geometrical east window of the south aisle breaks the line of the parapet. The large square windows of the clerestory on the north and south, together with its fine east window over the chancel arch, have a very imposing effect: they ensure abundance of light, while the piers of the nave, which are carried up between the windows to the roof, add the impression of height. The tower was built in 1823, the original tower, a very good one, to judge from Skelton's plate, having been taken down; why, one would be glad to discover. It might have been thought that, after what had taken place not so many years before at Banbury, the pullers down of ancient buildings might have had the fear of such evil-doing before their eyes. Since 1823 the church has twice passed through the restorer's fire. First, in 1841, when the rood screen was destroyed, and most of the brasses taken up, broken to pieces and put away in a chest! and secondly, in 1878, when the unfortunate brasses, which had been relaid, were again removed. They have now been arranged on oak slabs, on the north wall—the excuse for which must be that all the matrices but one had disappeared. Again, but it is for the last time, I cannot help adding a word of regret that so many of the windows of this grand church have been degraded with " cathedral glass ": let us hope that some

day the sentence will go forth, and the worshipper be once
more permitted to see the sun and the rain, and the green
boughs waving in the wind.

The direct road to Enstone and Oxford ascends to the right
at the northern extremity of the main street, but in order to
redeem a promise, made in an earlier chapter, to visit Great
Tew, we must go a few miles out of our way. Accordingly, we
keep straight on by the Banbury road, and at the first cross-
roads we pass, a few yards on our right, all that is left of the
once famous coaching inn at Chapel House. It had its
gardens and its bowling green, and was well known to all
frequenters of the road as one of the pleasantest houses
of entertainment in the Midlands. But in the 'forties, when the
coaches came to an end, Chapel House, like many another
cheerful wayside hostelry, found its occupation gone; what was
left standing of the house was turned into labourers' cottages, and
the extensive stabling devoted to farm purposes. Its isolated,
desolate situation must have made it doubly welcome to the
half-frozen outside passenger, whose twenty-mile drive over the
North Oxfordshire downs enabled him to regard the blazing
fire and good old English cheer which awaited him with
feelings which may well be envied by the modern occupant
of an artificially heated railway carriage. Here it was that,
on a fine day in the early spring of 1776, Johnson delivered his
famous panegyric on inns. He and Boswell were driving from
Oxford to Birmingham in a post-chaise, and stopped at
Chapel House to dine. Like most of the other visitors to the
house, the Doctor was delighted with his welcome, and
" expatiated on the felicity of England in its taverns and inns,
and triumphed over the French for not having in any perfection
the tavern life. ' There is no private house, (said he,) in which
people can enjoy themselves so well, as at a capital tavern. . .
you are sure you are welcome : and the more noise you make,
the more trouble you give, the more good things you call for,
the welcomer you are. . . No, Sir, ; there is nothing which has

yet been contrived by man, by which so much happiness is produced, as by a good tavern or inn.'"

As for the chapel, which gave the place its name, it belonged to the Priory of Cold Norton (the name is appropriate), and was intended for the use of the laity ; the site of the Priory is marked by the Priory Farm, half-a-mile to the east ; while a further relic of the foundation is to be found in the Priory mill, more than a mile to the north. This Priory of Augustinian canons was founded in the twelfth century by William Fitzalan, lord of Chipping Norton, "to the honour of God, St. Mary, St. John the Evangelist and St. Giles." After the death of the last Prior, in 1496, the foundation died out, and its estates were bestowed by Henry VII. on the Convent of St. Stephen, at Westminster. From this house they were soon after purchased by William Smyth, Bishop of Lincoln, and given by him to his new foundation of Brasenose College, in whose possession they still remain.

Crossing the Oxford and Birmingham road, we soon pass the entrance to Heythrop Park, and a mile further the by-road to the right brings us direct to Great Tew. Great Tew—"Great" to distinguish it from Little Tew and Duns Tew—has been called the prettiest village in Oxfordshire ; for myself, I am content to admire it without presuming to award the prize. This, however, I will say, that the stranger who approaches it from any side except the north is quite unprepared to come upon so picturesque a spot. After travelling for miles over high, open stretches of cultivated down, he suddenly enters a forest-like country, and in a few moments finds himself in the midst of a veritable sylvan Arcadia. We have now once more, and for the last time, entered the confines of the yellow stone region, with which we first made acquaintance at Deddington, but the warm, rich tints of the stone have never been seen to better effect than in the cottages of Great Tew. Here it sets off to perfection the tall, many-gabled roofs of thatch, the mullioned windows, the rustic porches festooned with honeysuckle, and

the trim, well-tended flower-beds.   At the back of these cottages
the greenest of meadows and orchards slope down to the tiny
brook, while a well-timbered park guards the village at either
extremity.

It is the park at the southern end that has made the name of
Great Tew known to thousands who would otherwise never have
heard of the remote Oxfordshire village, for this park was the
home of Falkland.   The house in which he lived has given
place to another, but the walled gardens, opening into each
other in an orderly series, remain, and close at hand is
the church in which he is buried.   Brought hither from Newbury Field, and interred in troublous times, no monument or
inscription marks the spot where he lies, and not till 1885 was
the tablet now to be seen on the chancel wall put up to his
memory.   What his life was at Great Tew is known to all
readers of Clarendon's famous character of his friend, but the
often-quoted words must be quoted once again :

" Having once resolved not to see London (which he loved above all
places) till he had perfectly learned the Greek tongue, he went to his own
house in the country, and pursued it with that indefatigable industry, that
it will not be believed in how short a time he was master of it, and
accurately read all the Greek historians.   In this time, his house being
within ten miles of Oxford, [nearly twenty of our miles], he contracted
familiarity and friendship with the most polite and accurate men of that
university ; who found such an immenseness of wit and such a solidity
of judgment in him, so infinite a fancy bound in by a most logical ratio-
cination, such a vast knowledge that he was not ignorant in anything, yet
such an excessive humility as if he had known nothing, that they frequently
resorted and dwelt with him, as in a college situated in a purer air ; so
that his house was a university bound in a lesser volume, whither they
came not so much for repose as study, and to examine and refine those
grosser propositions which laziness and consent made current in vulgar
conversation. "

And elsewhere he writes :

" The lord of the house did not even know of their coming and going,
nor who were in his house till he came to dinner, or supper, where all still
met : otherwise there was no troublesome ceremony or constraint to forbid

men to come to the house, or to make them weary of staying there : so that many came there to study in a better air, finding all the books they could desire in his library, and all the persons together whose company they could wish and find in no other society."

The present road between Woodstock and Chipping Norton is a comparatively modern one, and half a century ago men were still alive who could remember its construction. The road along which Lord Falkland's Oxford guests would ride to enjoy "a better air," and "to refine those grosser propositions which laziness and consent" had made too current, was probably the one which runs across what was then open down in almost a direct line from Wootton to Great Tew. But "when civil dudgeon first grew high," these enviable excursions were undertaken no more, and the hospitable mansion, with its well-stored library, was deserted. The estate passed out of the possession of the family at the end of the seventeenth century, and a hundred years later the house which had witnessed these days and nights of the gods was pulled down.

Among the villagers, though the Falkland Arms still keeps his name alive, all traditions of the man himself and of his famous visitors have long faded away. Scholarship and philosophy were not calculated to make much impression upon the simple rustics of Great Tew, but the proceedings of Falkland's grandfather and predecessor were of a sort to touch them more nearly. An ancient elm in the park is still haunted by the restless ghost of the "unjust judge," and at midnight he is wont to drive around it in a coach-and-six. It was about the year 1614 that Sir Lawrence Tanfield, the Lord Chief Baron, bought the estate, and in 1624 "the poor oppressed inhabitants of Great Tewe" presented a petition against him to the House of Commons. He had thrust them out, so they complained, from their right of Cowhill pasture, claiming it as his waste. He had enclosed seven parcels of the best feeding, and impounded cattle straying thereon. He had digged up mearstones and marks to enable him to get possession of lands on which their ancestors had lived for four hundred years. He refused to give them the timber due under their leases for repairing, and fined them for not doing so. He would not pay his church dues. His lady was worse than he was, and declared that they were more worthy to be ground to powder than to have any favour showed to them, and that she would play " the very devil " among them. He had reduced the plough teams in the village, through his high-handed conduct, from twenty-six to twelve. He had taken the lead from the chancel to make pipes and gutters for his own house : he had pulled down the churchyard wall, and thrown part of the churchyard into a pasture of his own. Finally, he would not give the allowance of straw for kneeling on in church, which they had had from the parsonage barn for many years.

This is a pretty severe indictment, but, of course, there was another side to the question. In his answer the Chief Baron admits that there had been disputes between him and his tenants, but affirms that they had all been settled long ago by law or arbitration. As to the Petition, it was a tissue of lies, and was, in fact, the work of one John Hiron, who had not dared to put his name to it. The said John Hiron " is a man very malicious, of a violent spirit and extremely audacious, daring to affirm things untrue for truth without fear of God." The judge's answer seems to have satisfied the House, for we hear no more of the matter. He died in the following year, and his wife (let us hope, without having carried out her tremendous threat) in 1629, when her grandson entered upon the possession of the estate. The church stands in the park, and is only separated from the house by the gardens. It is little altered since Falkland's days, and its fine fifteenth century bench-ends, its brasses, and the monuments in the north aisle were then already venerable. As we leave the church we may look for the Tew Tree, a silver fir 120 feet high, and the land-mark of all the country round ; and then we may shape our course southward to join the Oxford Road at Enstone.

Enstone is a large parish comprising several hamlets, the principal of which are Church Enstone and Neat Enstone, separated by the Glyme. The manor belonged to Winchcombe Abbey, and the church was therefore dedicated to St. Kenelm. At the dissolution it was granted to Sir Thomas Pope, from whom it has descended to its present possessor, Viscount Dillon. The church lies a little to the right of our road from Great Tew, and is well worth a visit. The stone altar in the south aisle, with its panelled reredos, and pedestals for six figures now destroyed, will be familiar to many, who would never otherwise have heard of Enstone, from the fact that it illustrates the article "Reredos" in Parker's *Glossary of Architecture.* In the same aisle are a few surviving volumes of a parish library of chained books, including, as is usual in such libraries, Foxe's *Book of Martyrs.* This church, though it has not suffered extreme things at the hands of the restorer, furnishes an example of a most effective way of obliterating historical records, which has probably been practised in many, if not most, of the churches we have already visited. When the church was repaired in 1856, it was thought desirable that it should be re-paved throughout. In this way a large number of flat tombstones containing monumental inscriptions were covered over; and, as if this was not enough, several mural tablets were illegally taken down and buried in the same manner. This is even a more ingenious way of getting these tablets out of sight than the usual one of crowding them together on the walls of the tower.

As we approach Neat Enstone, before crossing the Glyme, we may notice on our left a small rivulet and a pool. There is nothing at all remarkable about them now, and anyone who had never heard of Thomas Bushell would certainly pass them by without notice. Yet here is one of the wonders of Oxfordshire, which every traveller made a point of visiting, and which was long a fashionable resort for all the surrounding gentry. Thomas Bushell, the contriver of the wonderful Rock of Enstone, entered the household of Francis Bacon early in the

reign of James I., and derived from his master a knowledge of what was then called natural philosophy, and a
love of mechanical experiments. He devoted a long life to
engineering projects for the good of his country—projects which
too often landed him in financial difficulties. His principal
undertaking was the working of the lead mines in South Wales,
which contained a certain proportion of silver mixed with the
lead, and were therefore Crown property. Of these he obtained
a lease from Charles I., and, when the Civil War broke
out, he supplied the King with money coined in a privileged
mint of his own establishment. An interesting letter of Charles
to Bushell, enumerating his many services, has been preserved.
He lived till 1674, and the last project we hear of his being
engaged in, is one connected with the lead mines of the
Mendips.

About the year 1629 he came to live at Enstone, and one
day, when he was cleaning out a spring near his house, he was
struck with the idea that here was a capital field for the exercise
of his ingenuity. What he accomplished the reader will best
understand by a reference to the two fine plates in Plot's
Oxfordshire, in which all the details are minutely depicted. In
one of them he will behold the trim house built over the Rock,
" containing one fair room for banqueting, and several other
small closets for divers uses, beside rooms above ": in the
other he is taken down into the " grot " beneath the house, and
finds himself face to face with the Rock and all its marvels,
which consisted of fountains and spouts of water of various kinds,
including certain jets " often used by way of sport to wet
the visitants of the grot." This was a kind of practical joke
vastly popular in those days, and the chance of repeating
it was not to be lost. After the Civil War the Rock
and its waterworks, which had suffered from neglect,
passed into the possession of the Lees of Ditchley, and
Sir Edward Henry Lee, the first Earl of Lichfield, repaired it

and added the circular island, which will be seen in the
middle of the pool in front of the banqueting house. On this
island jets of water are turned on "which water the whole
island, and sportively wet any persons within it ; which most
people striving to avoid get behind the man that turns the
cocks, whom he wets with a spout of water that he lets fly over
his head, or else, if they endeavour to run out of the island over
the bridge, with two other spouts."   All these "spouts" are duly
represented in the first plate, as well as "the man that turns
the cocks," evidently gloating over his unholy devices, while a
gentleman in full dress, with sword and ruffles, and a walking
cane in his hand, is making a dignified retreat across the bridge,
pretending to be utterly unconscious of the two jets, one of
which strikes him full on "the reins of the back," and the other
on his legs.

But the great day in the history of the "Waterworks" was
August 23, 1636, when they were honoured by a visit from
the King and Queen, and the latter commanded the Rock to
be named Henrietta, after her royal self. It appears that
Charles had paid Mr. Bushell a surprise visit some time previously, and had been much pleased with his host's ingenious
contrivances ; but this time their Majesties, who came over
from Woodstock, were expected, and an *Entertainment* had
been provided in the orthodox fashion. As the royal party
entered the place "there arose a Hermite out of the ground
and entertained them with a speech, returning again in the close
down to his peaceful Urn. Then was the Rock presented in a
Song answer'd by an Echo, and after that a Banquet presented
also in a Sonnet, within the pillar of the table, with some other
songs." These speeches and songs were printed at Oxford by
Leonard Lichfield in a small quarto, now very rare.

During the whole of the eighteenth century the waterworks
seem to have enjoyed some sort of reputation, and at the
beginning of the nineteenth it was still the fashion for strangers

who passed through the village to devote a few minutes to their inspection. A tourist of 1806 describes them as "no bad specimen of the taste of the period when jets d'eau were in fashion." In the summer time the leading families of the neighbourhood would assemble there for dancing and social intercourse; the proceedings began about ten o'clock in the morning, and lasted till evening set in; as many as sixteen family coaches-and-four were remembered by an eye-witness to have attended on one of these occasions. At last, about the middle of the century, the banqueting house was pulled down, and the whole of the elaborate structures and devices fell into decay.

A short distance on our right as we leave the village is a dolmen, locally known as the "Hoar Stone." It consists of six stones, three standing and three prostrate, and may remind us of the Whispering Knights at Rollright. The name "Hoar Stone" is, of course, properly applied to a single stone, and these were once rather numerous in North Oxfordshire, but many of them have been destroyed. It is an easy run along a good road to Woodstock, and here the circuit of our wanderings is completed. The eight miles to Oxford which remain, we have already traversed on our outward journey, but as we reach the top of Wolvercot rise, we may pause for a moment and bid farewell to the pleasant uplands we have left behind us. To right and left of us are Isis[1] and Cherwell, whose upper reaches and tributaries we have been exploring, now drawing together to form the "silver-winding way" of Father Thames; the course of the Isis bringing down the sweet water of the Cotswold we can plainly trace as it sweeps round the bend of Wytham woods past the great meadow of the Freemen of Oxford; the Cherwell is hidden from our view, but is only a mile away. In front of us the distant spires beckon to refreshment and repose; and in the evening of this our last day we may

---

[1] The poetical appellation of the upper Thames.

once more stroll down under the elms of Christchurch meadow
to the spot where the two streams meet. This evening a
gentle silence, not unaptly suiting with our present mood,
broods over their union ; to-morrow they will re-echo with the
random shouts and jostling oars of the gallant company of
freshmen, in whom Oxford ever renews her youth at the close
of the Long Vacation.

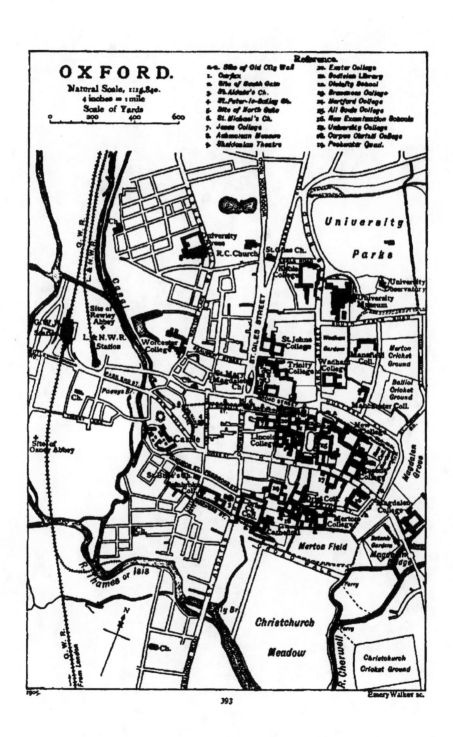

OXFORD.

Natural Scale, 1:14,840.

4 inches = 1 mile

Scale of Yards

0   200   400   600

Reference.

a-a. Site of Old City Wall
1. Carfax
2. Site of South Gate
3. St. Aldate's Ch.
4. St. Peter-le-Bailey Ch.
5. Site of North Gate
6. St. Michael's Ch.
7. Jesus College
8. Ashmolean Museum
9. Sheldonian Theatre

10. Exeter College
11. Bodleian Library
12. Divinity School
13. Brasenose College
14. Hertford College
15. All Souls College
16. New Examination Schools
17. University College
18. Corpus Christi College
19. Peckwater Quad.

Emery Walker sc.

1905.

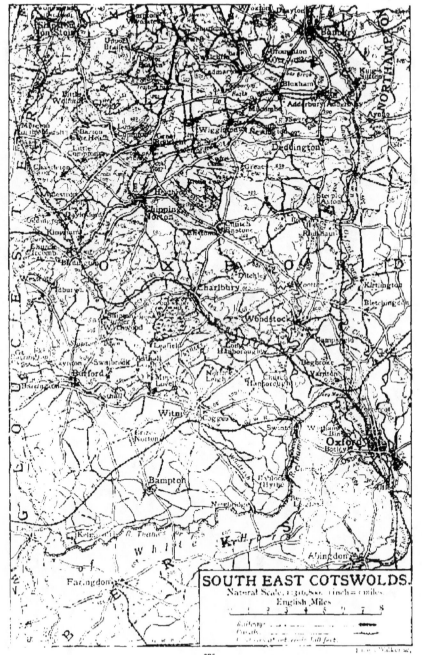

SOUTH EAST COTSWOLDS.

Natural Scale, 1:506,880. 1 inch = 8 miles.

English Miles

Railways
Canals
Contours at every 500 feet.

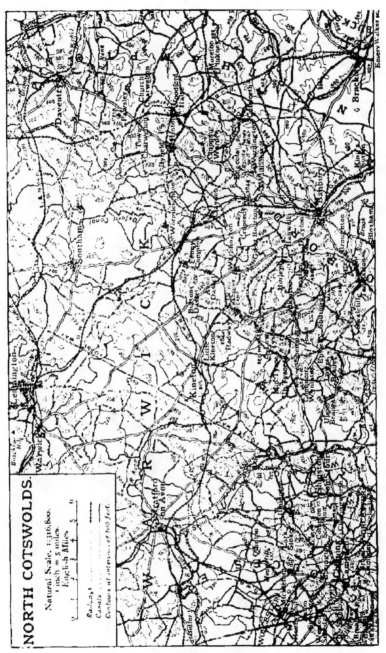

NORTH COTSWOLDS.

Natural Scale, 1:316,800.
1 inch = 5 miles.
English Miles.

Railways
Canals
Contours at intervals of 100 feet.

SOUTH WEST
COTSWOLDS.

INDEX

A

ABLINGTON, 300
Adderbury, 58–61
Akeman Street, 53, 258, 353
Aldsworth, 353–355
Alkerton, 82
Allen family, 179
Allestree (Richard), 94–95
Andoversford, 257–259
Andrew family, 112–113
Anne (Queen), 281
Apperley (C. J. "Nimrod"), 355
Apperley (Mr.), 336
Ashbee (C. R.), 187, 190, 191
Ashley (Prof. W. J.), 184
Asthall, 369
Astley (Jacob, Lord), 158
Aston-le-Walls, 108
Aston-sub-Edge, 219
Atkyns family, 327
Atkyns (Sir Robert), 159, 164, 263, 296,
    327, 332
Aubrey (John), 86
Aynho, 98

B

BALLARD (G.), 202
Banbury, 62–68
    Cakes, 64
    Castle, 64–66
    Church, 67–68
    Cross, 66
Bard (Sir Henry), 196
Barksdale (Clement), 174–175, 230, 255
Barnsley, 323, 353
Barnsley and Gimson (Messrs.), 331
Barrington (Great), 295–298
    (Little), 294
Barthurst (Allen, Earl), 329, 330, 349
    (Henry, Earl), 349
Barton, 277
Bassley (W.), quoted, 236

Beaufort (Henry Somerset, Duke of), 347
Beesley (Alfred), 62
Berkeley family, 260
Bibury, 165, 301–303, 353
    Racecourse, 355
Bigland (Ralph), quoted, 179, 295
Birdlip, 315–317
Blaket family, 171
Bledington, 169–171
Blenheim Palace, 41
    Park, 41–48
Blockley, 187
Bloxham, 68–69
Boswell (James), 42, 382
Boteler (Ralph, Lord), 251
Bourton Hill, 95
Bourton-on-the-Hill, 211
Bourton-on-the-Water, 167–168
Brailes, 131
Bray family, 295–298
Brent family, 211
Brimpsfield, 273–274
Broad Campden, 190
Broadway, 222
    Tower, 181
Brockhampton, 151, 256
Brookes (Dr.), 379
Broughton Castle, 74–78
Brown (Launcelot), 42, 141
Bruern Abbey, 175
Brydges family, 252–255
Buckingham (Humphrey Stafford, Duke
    of), 262
Buckland, 224
Buckle Street, 181
Burford, 355–366
    Battle, 365
    Church, 360–365
    Corporation, 360
    Priory, 358–360
    Races, 355–356
    Venison, 377
Burton Dassett, 114
Bushell (Thomas), 387–389

C

CAMPSFIELD, 40, 356
Canning family, 211
Cary (Mr.), 43
Cassey Compton, 279-280
Catherine Parr, 251
Cely family, 285-289, 357
Cerney (North), 265
Chandos (George Brydges, Lord), 253-255, 346
Chapel House, 382
Charles I., 39, 96, 118-121, 196, 260, 320, 329, 347, 358, 388, 389
Charles II., 226, 228, 261, 356
Charles Edward (Prince), 379
Charlton Abbots, 256
Charwelton (Church), 109, 112
  (Town), 109
Chastleton, 140-145
Chaucer (Thomas), 41
Channcy family, 102
Chedworth Villa, 277-278
Cherwell (The), 30, 31, 34, 51, 95, 98, 99, 102, 109-110
Chipping Campden, 182-206
  Almshouses, 194
  Battle Bridge, 208
  Church, 191-192
  Guild of Handicraft, 187-190
  House, 196-197
  Wonder, 197-201
Chipping Norton, 380-382
Chipping Warden, 107
Churn (The), 259-265
Cirencester, 335-352
  Abbey, 339-340
  Agricultural College, 336
  Church, 341-345, 355
  Hunting from, 337
  Park, 348-352
  Roman remains, 337-338
Clapton, 167
Clarendon (Edward Hyde, Earl of), 378; quoted, 384
Cleeve Cloud, 208, 230, 242
Cleveland (Thomas Wentworth, Earl of), 97
Clifford (Rosamund), 44-45
Coberley, 226, 259-261
Cold Norton, 383
Colesbourne, 262
Coln (The), 277, 278, 300-304, 353
Coln St. Aldwyns, 303
Compton (Sir William I.), 127-130
  (Sir William II.), 64, 130
Compton (Little), 137
Compton Scorpion, 211
Compton Wynyates, 125-131
Condicote, 162
Cope family, 91-94
Cornbury (Lord), 378
Cornbury Park, 378
Cornwall (Edmund, Earl of), 235, 369
  (Richard, Earl of), 235

Cotswolds (The), 146-149
Cowley, 261
Cromwell (O.), 366
Cropredy Bridge (battle of), 95-98
Crouch Hill, 78, 95
  Poet, 78, 89
Culworth Gang (The), 100
Cutsdean, 163

D

DAGLINGWORTH, 91, 265-268
Danby (Henry Danvers, Earl of), 349
Danesmoor, 101-106
Daneway House, 330-331
Daylesford, 149
Deddington, 54-57, 98
Delany (Mrs.), 351
Dent (Mrs.), 249
Ditchley, 46-50
Dobuni (The), 124, 168, 273
Dod (John), 92-93
Dover (Robert), 203-207
Dover's Hill, 203-207
Dowdeswell, 258
Drayton (Michael), 149, 205
Drayton, 89
Druce (G. C.), 378
Dugdale (Sir William), 128
Duntesbourne Abbots, 268
Duntesbourne Rous, 268-269
Dutton family, 260, 291

E

EBRINGTON, 208
Edgcote, 96, 102, 111
Edgcott (battle of), 94, 118-121
Edgehills (The), 109, 116, 121-123
Edward II., 273
Edward III., 186
Eldon (Earl of), 282
Elizabeth (Queen), 43, 252, 340
Elkstone, 270-273
Enstone, 387-390
Epwell, 125
Ermin Street, 258, 265, 270, 274, 316, 334, 118-121, 151, 322, 347, 363
Essex (Rober Devereux, Earl of), 39, 77, 118-121, 151, 322, 347, 363
Evans (Dr. A. J.), 124, 137-139
Evesham (Vale of), 208
Eyford, 151, 164

F

FAIRFORD, 304-311
Falkland (Lucius Cary, Viscount), 358, 362, 363, 384-386
Farmcote, 230
Farmington, 290

Fawsley, 77, 110
Fenny Compton, 114
Fettiplace family, 367-368
Fielding (Henry), 117
Fiennes family, 75-78
Fisher family, 215-216
Fitzhardinge (Lord), 256
Fletcher (Alderman), 38, 39
Ford, 179-180, 208
Fortescue (Sir John), 208
Fosbrooke (T. D.), 263
Fossbridge, 275, 311, 314
Foss Way (The), 153, 258, 275
Foxcote, 211
Fuller (E. A.), 341
Fuller (Thomas), 92

G

GAINSBOROUGH (EARL OF), 194
Gaveston (Piers), 56
George III., 41, 296
George IV., 355
Gibbs (Arthur), 300 ; quoted, 147, 168, 283
Giffard family, 273
Gill (Alexander), 194
Gloucester (Robert Frampton, Bishop of), 298
Glyme (The), 41, 51
Godstow, 44, 260
Grafton (W.), 224
Graves family, 216
Graves (Richard), 216-218
    Spiritual Quixote, 206, 210, 216, 334
Grevel (W.), 182-186
Grubham (Sir Richard), 280
Guilford (Lord), see North family
Guise family, 263
Guiting Power, 175-177, 230
Guiting (Temple), 177-179

H

HAGGARD (R.), 336
Haswell, 91-95
Harford Bridge, 173
Harris (Robert), 93
Hastings (Warren), 149
Hatherop, 304
Hawling, 230
Hayles, 232-237
Headlam (Cecil), 33
Hearne (Thomas), 202 ; quoted, 48, 216
Henderson (Mrs. M. Sturge), 379
Henrietta Maria (Queen), 389
Henry I., 45, 340
Henry II., 44
Hicks family, 192-197
Hicks (Baptist), 192-196
Hidcote House, 210
Hinchwick, 160-163
Holinshed (Raphael), quoted, 327
Howe family, 260-262

Hults (Jonathan), 201
Hutton (W. H.), 293, 360

I

ICOMB, 171
Idbury, 169
Ilmington, 211-212
Isbourne (The), 237, 252

J

JAGO (Richard), 117
James II., 348
Johnson (Samuel), 15, 42, 82, 382
Jones family, 142-145
Jonson (Ben), 62, 200

K

KALABERGO, 101
Kenelm, 238-241
Kenulf, 238
Keyte family, 252, 210
Kimsbury Camp, 322
Kingham, 171
Kingston (Sir Anthony), 317-320
Knightley family, 77, 110-112
Kyderminster (Richard), 241, 292

L

LANG (ANDREW), 200
Langley, 377
Latimer (W.), 220
Leach (The), 353
Leafield, 374
Lee (Sir Henry), 46
Leland (John), 306, 338
Lenthall family, 359
Lenthall (W.), 359
Lichfield (Edward Henry Lee, Earl of), 388
    (George Henry Lee, Earl of), 49
Lincoln (Hugh, Bishop of), 44-45
    (Robert Bloet, Bishop of), 45
    (Robert-Grosseteste, Bishop of), 235
    (John Chedworth, Bishop of), 336
    (William Smyth, Bishop of), 383
London (William Juxon, Bishop of), 137
Lovel family, 371-374
Lovelace (John, Lord), 347-348
Lydney House, 197, 349 note
Lydyat (Thomas), 82

M

MACAULAY (THOMAS BABINGTON, LORD), 164, 261

Marlborough (John Churchill, Duke of), 42
  (Sarah, Duchess of), 42
Massey (Col. Edward), 254
Master family, 340, 346
Mavor (W.), 41
Meon Hill, 203, 212, 215, 242
Merrymouth Inn (The), 169
Mickleton, 215-219
Milcombe, 69-71
Miller (Sanderson), 117
Mills (G. G.), 167
Minster Lovel, 370-374
Miserden, 274
More (Sir Thomas), 47
Morgan (Sir Thomas), 158
Morris (William), 301, 362
Morton (Sir William), 242, 254

N

NAUNTON, 151, 173-175
Newington (South), 71
Norres family, 343
North family, 84-89
Northampton (James Compton, Earl of),
  97-98
Northleach, 282-290

O

OAKLEY PARK, 349-352
Oddington, 190
Oldisworth (W.), 309
Oldys (W.), 60
Overbury (Sir Thomas), 211
Oxford, 1-33
  Boat Races, 29-30
  Bodleian Library, 8
  Botanic Garden, 31
  Castle, 12-14
  City Walls, 9-10
  Colleges:—
    All Souls, 26, 216, 220
    Balliol, 128-130
    Brasenose, 215, 383
    Christ Church, 20-23, 178
    Corpus Christi, 178, 270
    Magdalen, 26, 29, 214
    Merton, 23-28
    New College, 23-26
    Pembroke, 216
    Trinity, 84
    University, 265
    Wadham, 26, 29, 37, 359
    Worcester, 18, 241
  College Tenants, 83-84
  Examination Schools, 5
  Mesopotamia, 30-31
  Osney Abbey, 14-17
  Parks (The), 30-31
  Port Meadow, 40, 390
  Rewley Abbey, 17-18
  St. Frideswide's Priory, 19-20

P

PAGE (JUDGE), 53
Painswick, 317-325
Palmer family, 211
Parker (James), 19
Parnassus Biceps, 310
Pembroke (William Herbert, Earl of),
  105-107
Pepys (Samuel), quoted, 246, 255
Phillipps (Sir Thomas), 181
Pinbury, 332
Pitchcombe, 325
Plot (Robert), 57, 362, 388
Plowden (W.), 108
Poole family, 327
Pope (Alexander), 53, 58, 302 note, 330,
  350, 352
Pope (John), 86
  (Sir Thomas), 86, 387
  (Sir William), *see* Downe (Earl of)
Porter (Endymion), 203
Porter family, 219-220
Postlip, 243

Q

QUENINGTON, 304
Quinton, 212-215

R

RADWAY, 117
Red Horse (Vale of the), 122
Rendcombe, 262-265
Richard II., 339
Rochester (John Wilmot, Earl of), 50, 58
Roel, 175, 255, 256
Rogers family, 258
Rollright (Great), 136
Rollright Stones (The), 137-140
Rosamund, *see* Clifford (Rosamund)
Rousham, 58, 71
Rudder (Samuel), 173, 344, quoted 179,
  262, 282, 320
Rupert (Prince), 119, 151, 196, 346

S

SACKVILLE family, 309
Sainsbury, 220
Salisbury (Gilbert Burnet, Bishop of), 51
Sandys family, 274
Sandywell Park, 258
Saperton, 325-333
Scott (Sir Gilbert), 345
Scott (Sir Walter), 46
Sevenhampton, 257
Seven Springs, 259, 315
Seymour (Thomas, Lord), 233, 251
Sheepscombe, 317
Sheldon family, 132

Shenington, 81
Shenstone (W.), 217–218
Sherborne, 291–293
Sherborne (Lord), 291
Shipton, 379
Shrewsbury (Charles Talbot, Duke of), 164
Shutford, 81
Skelton (Joseph), 381
Slaughter (Lower), 165–167
   (Upper), 165–167
Smith (Utrecia), 217–218
Spencer family, 36–39, 210
Stainton (H. T.), 177
Stanton, 226
Stanway, 203, 207, 226–228
Steeple Aston, 54
Sterne (Laurence), 349
Stoke Lark, 211
Stour (The), 80, 136
Stow (Battle of), 158
Stow-on-the-Wold, 150–159
Stowell, 280
Stowell (William Scott, Lord), 282
Stroud Water (Valley of the), 186, 242, 325
Sturdy's Castle, 53
Sudeley Castle, 249–255
Swalcliffe, 80
Swell (Lower), 159–162, 164
   (Upper), 159–161
Swinbrook, 366–369
Sylvester family, 363–364
Symonds (Richard), 372

T

TADMARTON HEATH, 74
Talbot family, 99, 295
Tame family, 202, 263, 305–309
Tanfield (Sir Lawrence), 359, 362, 385–386
Taynton, 27, 298
Tew (Great), 383–386
Thames and Severn Canal, 329
Thorneycroft (Sir John), 69
Traitor's Ford, 124, 134

Tunley, 332
Tysoe (Middle), 125

V

VANBRUGH (SIR JOHN), 42

W

WALKER (JOHN), 60
Waller (Sir William), 39, 95–98
Wardington, 97, 101
Warmington, 114–116
Warton (Thomas), 15
Warwick (Richard Neville, Earl of), 104, 122, 360
Wells (J.), 15
Westcot, 169
Weston Park, 132
Weston-sub-Edge, 220
Wharton (Thomas, Marquess of), 297
Whittington (Richard), 260
Whittington, 259
Wigginton, 73
Willersey, 220
William III., 45, 164, 347
Willis (Browne), 238
Winchcombe, 196, 237–240, 292
Windrush, 203
Windrush (The), 168, 172–180, 295, 357, 366, 370
Wolford (Little), 134
Wood (Anthony), 26; quoted 15, 44, 77, 175, 201 note, 203–205, 210, 305, 310, 348, 378
Woodstock, 41–48, 390
Wordsworth (William), 107
Wroxton, 84–89
Wychwood, 48, 375–379
Wykeham family, 60, 76, 80

Y

YARNTON, 35–40
Young (Arthur), 376

THE END

CPSIA information can be obtained
at www.ICGtesting.com
Printed in the USA
BVHW010631061021
618252BV00027B/301